HOPE FOR THE FAMILY FARM

trust God and care for the land

Edited by
LaVonne Godwin Platt

Faith and Life Press
Newton, Kansas

Design by John Hiebert

Printing by
Mennonite Press, Inc.

CREDITS: Sources for theme quotes for each chapter: 1:
"The Earth Is the Lord's" by Wesley Granberg-Michaelson, in
Radix, Nov.-Dec. 1982, p. 3. 2: Jim Maurer, *Catholic Rural
Life*, June 1980, p. 7. 3: Wes Jackson, *New Roots for
Agriculture* (San Francisco: Friends of the Earth, 1980), p. 7.
4: "The Economic Structure of a Sustainable Agriculture" by
Marty Strange in *Meeting the Expectations of the Land*,
edited by Wes Jackson, Wendell Berry, and Bruce Colman
(San Francisco: North Point Press, 1984), p. 118. 5: *Catholic
Rural Life*, February 1985, p. 18. 6: Wendell Berry, *The Gift
of Good Land* (San Francisco: North Point Press, 1981), p.
144-45. 7: J. Tevere MacFayden, *Gaining Ground: The
Renewal of America's Small Farms* (New York: Ballantine,
1984), p. 146. 8: Joe Paddock, *The Things We Know Best*,
(Olivia, Minn., 1976), cited in *People, the Heart of Rural
America*, (Denver, Farmers Union, 1979), p. 10. 9: Parker J.
Palmer, *The Company of Strangers*, 1981. Quoted by John A.
Lapp in talk, "Toward an Ecopolitics," Symposium II,
Conservation / Ecology: A Mennonite Mandate, Laurelville,
Pa., December 1982. 10: Raymond Regier, "Peace and Justice
Issues in Food, Farming and Agriculture," unpublished
manuscript, 1985. 11: The Brandt Commission. *A Report of
the Independent Commission on International Development
Issues* (Cambridge, Mass.: MIT Press, 1980). 12: Frances
Moore Lappe, "The Family Farm: Caught in the
Contradictions of American Values" in Frances Moore Lappe
and C. Dean Freudenberger, *Food, Farming and Justice.*
Lutheran Church in America, lectures given at the Food,
Farming and Justice consultation, St. Olaf College,
Northfield, Minn. March 1-2, 1985, p. 5. 13: Wendell Berry,
The Unsettling of America: Culture and Agriculture (New
York: Avon Books, 1977), p. 58.

PHOTOS: Sources for chapter illustrations: 1: South Dakota
State University, Brookings, S.D.; 2: Farm Credit
Administration; 3: U.S. Department of Agriculture; 4 & 13:
Religious News Service; 5: U.S. Department of Interior; 6:
Paul Schrock, Scottdale, Pa.; 7 & 11: Bob Taylor, Cordell,
Okla.; 8: Willard Waltner, Freeman, S.D.; 9: United Nations;
10: Alfred Siemens; 12: Musée des Beaux-Arts, Lausanne.
Cover: Religious News Service.

Foreword

These are troubling times, manifested by a growing sense of disillusionment among our people. We uneasily witness evidence of policy disjointedness and confusion among our experts and national leaders alike.

It is clear that a serious erosion has occurred at the center of our national purpose. It is imperative that we begin to seriously rethink the purposes for which our public policy is intended.

Although a system of family farm agriculture has long been a hallmark of American agriculture, it is now threatened with extinction! Thomas Jefferson considered the widely dispersed ownership of land to be the keystone for the preservation of a viable democratic society, and he believed its best guarantor to be the family farmer. Accordingly, we need to address the possible implications that the elimination of family farm agriculture might have for such fundamental questions as the long-term survival of a functioning democratic society.

Nurturing and preserving our natural resources was once a central concern of farmers and politicians alike. Today, our soil, air, and water are jeopardized by an industrial-based agricultural system which treats our natural resources as simply another factor of production.

In recent years, there has been a thunderous silence in public policy toward the plight of farmers and the associated difficulties faced by the thousands of rural communities which depend upon farmers for survival. While the countryside suffers, and its people look elsewhere for a means of earning a livelihood, our national policymakers seem obsessed with a narrow agenda myopically focused upon ever larger military budgets. They continue to finance this steady expansion of our armed might by slashing spending for domestic needs and incurring mounting deficits.

Despite this grim setting, however, an impressive—and growing—number of Americans, dedicated to the more enduring goals of *sustainable agriculture* and *thriving rural communities*, have been asking some fundamental questions while seeking to understand the connecting interrelationships among the problems we face as a nation.

In so doing, they have rediscovered the existing linkages within our present system of agriculture which not only pollute our soil and water but are also hostile to the survival of family farms; between a structure of agriculture based upon the industrial model, wherein the ultimate values are "efficiency" and higher productivity, and its consequence of wreaking great damage to our natural and human resources alike.

They have also exhibited a new hunger for our spiritual roots which link each of us to other humans, as well as to those other life forms with whom we share this good earth.

Ultimately, this search has led to a renewed interest in theology, wherein our most basic hopes and values are revealed. We have learned anew, for example, that Hebrew and Christian Scriptures place human community in the *context* of the land, and that these texts' consistent call upon God's people to achieve *justice* cannot be understood outside the context of our interrelationships with each other. For the great prophets of the Hebrew Testament, justice does not exist in the abstract; we create it (or allow its absence) through the manner in which we handle our often competing demands for an equal share of the fruits of the Lord's good earth. Many are also coming to realize that justice also involves the nature of our relationship with the *rest* of creation, too. The National Catholic Rural Life Conference, recognizing the need to develop and articulate these concerns, recently began a series of national conferences to explore a theology of land and to formulate an initial statement of such a theology.

The essays in this book, compiled by LaVonne Platt, offer various dimensions to assist us in achieving an interconnected understanding of the serious moral crisis facing us. While each has its separate integrity, they together make up an interwoven whole. Their authors help us to understand the historical forces acting upon us in order that we might not placidly accept the argument that what we face is somehow inevitable; they give us a theological understanding of what it is to have a creation-centered consciousness; and they discuss in very human terms both the manifestations of the current crisis and some possible paths of hope to surmount it.

It is to be hoped that the readers of this book will also include those who shape and enact public policy. They—as we—need to understand that everything we do reflects our operative values, even if these values are seldom voiced.

The founders of this nation were very concerned with the health of the commonwealth, which represented the good of *all* of the people. This expression of the ancient concept of the common good supersedes the issue of individual monetary gain and provides the context wherein individual liberties can be attained and protected. In fact, without a healthy commonwealth, even individual liberty is ultimately at jeopardy. It is clear to me that in recent years this larger purpose of our national community has been largely ignored in the development of, and debate concerning, what is reputedly *public* policy. The furtherance of self-interest has come to supersede the good of all. Such a narrow and destructive focus must change!

If we are to become truly citizens of the good earth, cognizant of the needs of the land and of *all* of our fellow creatures of the land, we need to reform our thinking and to reexamine our values. Only in this way will we come to appreciate the responsibilities, and possibilities, inherent in the fact that we are all truly brothers and sisters. We must choose an ethic of *stewardship* which embraces our responsibility to live in harmony upon the land with each other, and with our fellow creatures with whom we share the planet.

Gregory D. Cusack
Executive Director,
National Catholic Rural Life Conference, 1981-87

Contents

Part IV. Family farms in the future

Introduction

This book is about rural people in relationship: in covenant with God, in caring for God's creation, and in community with other people. That covers a lot of territory, someone said, and it must. We should not consider ourselves as individuals in a particular place with boundaries that separate us and *our* land from other people and the rest of the created world. We must consider how we relate to the whole.

This concern is, of course, primary. It is the beginning of legends and the basis of myths by which people of all times have defined themselves. We of the Judeo-Christian heritage are no different from other peoples in this regard, as we know when we read the first two chapters of Genesis which, for us, establishes the terms of those relationships.

Early in this century, the agronomist L. H. Bailey expressed for his generation what we must consider today as well.

> Verily, then, the earth is divine, because man did not make it. We are here, part in the creation. We cannot escape. We are under obligation to take part and to do our best, living with each other and with all the creatures. We may not know the full plan, but that does not alter the relation. When once we set ourselves to the pleasure of our dominion, reverently and hopefully, and assume all its responsibilities, we shall have a new hold on life. . . . If God created the earth, so is the earth hallowed; and if it is hallowed, so must we deal with it devotedly and with care that we do not despoil it, and mindful of our relations to all beings that live on it.[1]

---

1. L. H. Bailey, *The Holy Earth* (Lebanon, Pa.: Sowers Printing Co., reprinted by Christian Rural Fellowship, 1943), p. 11.

The seeds that have developed into this book formed and ripened in discussions of faith and farming in the newsletter, *From Swords To Plowshares*, during the late 1970s and early 1980s. Questions about land stewardship and sustainability, how justice relates to land use, maintaining rural community values, land theology, and the rural heritage of Mennonites were among the issues raised in the newsletter.

Some of these concerns were raised again by North American Mennonites at the Laurelville (Pa.) Faith and Farming conferences in 1984 and 1985. They were discussed in numerous other meetings of rural people who were attempting to redefine their values and their practices in light of the economic and environmental uncertainty of the mid-1980s.

The need for greater dialogue on the applications of faith to rural issues became clear. It was also clear that there were articulate voices in rural communities across North America, people who could speak meaningfully and stimulate dialogue on pertinent issues. Some of these voices came from Mennonite and other peace church denominations, people with a heritage deeply rooted in the settling of rural North America. Could these voices add a useful dimension to the discussion already taking place by many others on the basic questions of land stewardship and sustainability, of community and economic justice? Answering that question has germinated the seed that has led to the growth of this book.

Most of the writers are family farmers or have come from a farm background. All have worked on rural concerns in their own communities. Nearly all have rural or small town addresses. Many of them wrote their chapters in late evenings after working days that included planting corn, tapping sugar maple trees, walking bean rows to pull weeds, canning grape juice, filling silos, cutting hay, marketing hogs, or harvesting wheat. Sometimes the writing was sandwiched between civic and church responsibilities. Some writers met with state legislators and voters to retain policies that favor the family farm structure of agriculture or testified in Congress on farm policy legislation. Some of them stood by relatives at a foreclosure sale, accompanied neighbors to meet with lenders to avoid bankruptcy, or helped reorganize a farm business when it was inevitable. They participated in support groups of farmers, organized community and church meetings to discuss rural concerns, or took part in organizations concerned with farm issues, peace, and international relations.

The book is divided into four parts. Part I introduces the overarching concepts of dominion and covenant theology and applies these concepts to sustainable agriculture in caring for the earth and sustainable social institutions in relating to one another within the structures of society. In the first chapter, Ron Guengerich describes *dominion* as "serving and guarding the earth and its people" in a shared responsibility that brings order out of chaos, highlights the responsibility of humanity to the rest of creation, and sees humankind as agents of equity and harmonious relationships in community. Roy Kaufman applies *covenant* theology to assert that "the land belongs to God, the land's bounty must be used for the welfare of all, and the land must be preserved and kept fruitful for all time." These theology chapters form a basis for the rest of the book— there is an undercurrent of the concepts of dominion and covenant throughout the book, although the words are only occasionally used by the other writers.

As the writers apply the concepts of dominion and covenant, the concept of *sustainability* is developed in succeeding chapters. Sustainability, as used here, is the property of natural or social systems that protects their future integrity, function, and productivity. Sustainable agriculture must protect those living and nonliving systems that supply resources (such as plant nutrients) and that provide services (such as pest population regulation) to the agricultural system and to all life on earth. Agriculture, to be sustainable, must be "ecologically sound, economically viable, socially just, and humane."[2] Art Meyer makes a case for sustainable agriculture, basing his discussion on the fundamental laws of nature that, as he shows, are "largely ignored in the practices of today's system of industrial agriculture." Don Reeves extends the discussion of sustainability to include "the social institutions by which farmers relate to the physical resources and to each other." Using land tenancy, taxation, credit, and markets as examples of social institutions, Don measures them against the criteria of renewability, impacts on community, and productivity.

Part II looks at the historical process that established the family farm and community structure of rural America. It illustrates models of farming and community that have grown out of that process or that are suggested by the values that would give greater sustainability and participation in the structures of rural community.

Margaret Hiebner and I look to the ideals of political democracy that gave shape and direction to America's national history, and suggest that, in our society, the *family farm* structure of agriculture is most conducive

2. Terry Gipps, quoted in Dana Jackson, "Sustainable Agriculture: A Concept Catching On," *The Land Report*, No. 26, (Spring 1986).

to care of the land and the relationships of people. Inherent in the discussion of family farming throughout the book is the definition of family farm as "an agricultural production unit in which the management, economic risk, and most of the labor—peak seasons excepted—are provided by a given family, and from which that family derives the bulk of its income." It is this structure of farming that "can best ensure dispersed access to land, stewardship of natural resources, and an equitable social structure in our rural communities."[3] This statement describing the role of the family farm in terms of its social, economic, and environmental functions in American society speaks clearly to the importance of family farms at a time when their continued existence is uncertain unless public policies are redirected to assure their survival.

Mark Epp calls on farmers to redefine standards of good farming to promote farming in a manner consistent with biblical principles. Focusing on the theological concepts of dominion and covenant, he describes an ethic of stewardship that can replace the ethic of profit taking and suggests characteristics of a good farmer who can help to build "a kind of agriculture and a lifestyle which models God's plan for his creation."

Community is an important concept throughout the book, the term being used to convey both the idea of a "sense of community" and the idea of "communities of people." Two chapters deal specifically with rural communities of people. In his chapter, Leon Neher shows how the social structure of a rural community is shaped by the type of farming that is characteristic of the surrounding area. The studies he cites indicate the benefits of family farms to rural communities.

Lois Janzen Preheim sketches four farm families in her profile of the Freeman, South Dakota, community. In the same chapter, Burton Buller describes alternative structures of community in the examples of the Amish and Hutterites, and Conrad Wetzel tells about rural communal living in the Plow Creek Fellowship where he and his family are members. Maynard Kaufman continues the discussion of alternative community structures by defining new homesteading, and Bill Minter proposes a Mennonite community land trust to offer another alternative that would retain important family farm values without the expense of land purchase for each new generation of farmers.

Part III centers on the relationship of family farmers to other people in the nation and the world. Jocele Thut Meyer and I look at family farmers'

---

3. "Family Farming and the Common Good," Interreligious Taskforce on U. S. Food Policy (now Interfaith Action for Economic Justice), February 1977.

connections to other rural people—the linking structures of their local communities and the natural, but often unrecognized, ties that bind them to rural people outside the mainstream of American society. Our chapter considers also the connections of rural people to urban residents, recognizing the inherent bonds of all people to the land and looking at ways we can identify with one another through our common search for a just and sustainable society in which we can all participate.

Public policy effects on family farms and rural communities is another topic which is considered in several chapters. Roger Claassen culminates the discussion in his chapter which shows the public policy ties to the search for economic justice in America. Public policy also plays a role in North American agriculture's links to the world community. Robert Epp and Gordon Hunsberger focus on this concern, among others, in a chapter showing the effects of militarism on agriculture in societies around the world and the relationship of international development to world agriculture and trade.

Part IV draws on the earlier discussions to envision a sustainable future. A major search in the 1980s has been to find appropriate responses to farm families facing economic crisis. In a three-part chapter, I suggest effective types of caring responses by individuals and groups, the Kansas Mennonite Farm Crisis Committee statement calls for involvement by the church, the state, and the federal government to bring about change, and Wilmer Heisey profiles members of the Mennonite Central Committee Farm Issues Task Force who help rural people work through situations of crisis on their farms.

In the final chapter, Robert Hull looks further at the concepts suggested in Part I to image a future where ecological and cultural sustainability interact to form community. Within the context of that discussion, he explores the idea of Mennonite community in the future of agriculture.

The book raises questions for dialogue: How does our faith in the Creator affect our relationship to the creation—the land, natural resources, non-human life, and humankind? How do we implement that faith on our farms, in our rural communities, and in the larger society to which we belong? This book seeks to stimulate discussion of these basic questions. Readers are invited to deal with this book as they would a growing plant—to prune it, to cultivate it, to give it further shapes. It is my hope that as the roots grow deeper the fruit will ripen and form new seeds for a future of hope and promise.

LaVonne Godwin Platt

"The Prairie Is My Garden," by Harvey Dunn

From the creation of the earth, pronounced as good, to the end of the age, when every living creature in heaven, on earth, under the earth, and beneath the sea blesses the Lord, the Bible tells us that this world is God's gracious gift to us. We are to hold its air, water, land, and all its life in trust for the Creator. Because we are created in God's image, we are to act toward the world and its gifts as God would, fulfilling God's intentions for creation.
—Wesley Granberg-Michaelson

1. Earth keepers in Eden

Ronald Guengerich

Most of us share similar assumptions about how the world is put together, how our communities should work, and how a well-behaved person should act. We share assumptions about the value of the natural world and about the way we should use its resources as well as the tools, gadgets, and machines of our culture. We share common ways of looking at the land and its use. These assumptions, which we often call common sense, are a major part of our worldview.

Our worldview has to do with the way we deal with the world around us. It allows us to make our way through the ordinary events and everyday encounters with each other. It helps us to know our place in our communities, our society, and our natural environment.

Some everyday ideas about land use

As we look at the way we treat the land, we can identify some assumptions about land and its use that seem to be a part of the usual North American worldview:

1. The land was created for us and given to us by God to control and use for our profit and pleasure.

2. The land is something which can be bought and sold like any other piece of goods.

3. The owner has the right to decide how to use the land (as long as that use is not determined to be illegal).

4. The owner can use any means to gain the largest immediate yield possible.

5. We judge the success of a person's land use in terms of the cash value of produce taken from the land each year.

6. We also judge the success of a person's land use in terms of the amount of produce harvested from the land each year.

7. Since the land can be bought and sold, a person who has more power—political or economic—can acquire land from those who have lost power. Reversely, a person who owns more land has more power.

These assumptions are so common in our society that many persons can barely imagine any other way of thinking about the land. We find it hard to come up with different assumptions because to do so we would need to rethink and rearrange many other parts of our worldview.

These powerful presuppositions about land use are supported by the rest of our worldview package, including our religious worldview. We have read and interpreted the Bible in a way which supports these assumptions and practices. From Genesis 1 and 2, we construct religious support for this view of the land.

Delight in our dominion over the land

When we talk about land in relation to the human race, we quickly discover that the word *dominion* takes on central importance. Genesis 1:26 and 28 lay the groundwork for our Western understanding of this word.

> Then God said, "Let us make [humanity] in our image, after our likeness; and let them *have dominion* over the fish of the sea, and over the birds of the air, and over the cattle, and *over all the earth*, and over every creeping thing that creeps upon the earth" (Gen. 1:26). (Italics added.)

> And God blessed them, and God said to them, "Be fruitful and multiply and fill the earth and *subdue it*; and *have dominion* over the fish of the sea and over the birds of the air and over every living thing that moves upon the earth" (1:28). (Italics added.)

Referring to the first two chapters of Genesis, Gerhard von Rad has written, "It is man's world, the world of his life (the sown, the garden, the animals, the woman), which God . . . establishes *around* man; and this forms the primary theme of the entire narrative. . . . In this world . . . man is the first creature." Quoting Benno Jacob, von Rad says, "In Chapter One man is the pinnacle of a pyramid, in Chapter Two the center of the circle."[1]

---

1. Gerhard von Rad, *Genesis: A Commentary*, tr. John H. Marks, Old Testament Library (Philadelphia: Westminster Press, 1961) (German, 1956), pp. 74-75.

This way of thinking undergirds what Frederick Elder has called the *exclusionist* view of man and nature. It sees man as standing above nature.[2] According to this widely-promoted perspective, time is the arena in which God, once and for all, created all forms of life, climaxing this work with the making of man. Man was given dominion and made unique so that "no item in the physical creation had any purpose save to serve man's purpose."[3] Man is superior to all of creation and he has been given the right to rule over it. The world, it is assumed, is given to man to use in whatever way he pleases.

The creation narratives are used as a full-bodied source of support for this human-centered, man-oriented position. According to this exclusionist view, the main theme of the creation accounts is, beyond all doubt, man. Looking at Genesis 2, these interpreters note that the order of creation is as follows: man, garden/vegetation, animals, and, finally, woman. Being first, man has first rights, as it were. Furthermore, man's superiority is highlighted by the fact that God brings all the animals to him to be named. Since, in Hebrew thought, naming is seen as an act of dominion, this proves man's power and authority over the rest of creation. As Gerhard von Rad says, "Name-giving . . . was primarily an exercise of sovereignty."[4] Thus, man (meaning *male*) stands over all creation. By this reading of the account, man is clearly dominant and central to the whole creation.

Even though the other creation account (Gen. 1:1–2:3) has both a different sequence and a different focus, the exclusionists—those who see man as apart from and the supreme authority over the rest of creation— interpret this passage as well to support man-centeredness. For example, Herbert Richardson says that Genesis 1 shows that

> *man* as the last creature formed by God is also the highest creature; to him is given the right of dominion over every other created thing. All other creatures are less than man from the point of what is technically called "dignity;" they are created for his sake and ordered to his good.[5] (Italics added.)

Dominion, then, from this point of view, is contrasted with powerlessness. In the exclusionist view, the agent of dominion is *man* and the subject of dominion is everything in the world with which man comes in

2. Frederick Elder, *Crisis in Eden* (Nashville: Abingdon Press, 1970), p. 13.
3. Lynn White, Jr., "The Historical Roots of Our Ecological Crisis," *Science* 155 (March 10, 1967), pp. 1203-07.
4. Von Rad, p. 81.
5. Herbert Richardson, *Toward an American Theology* (New York: Harper, 1967), p. 116.

contact. Dominion, hence, sets up a sharp vertical separation with man over the created world and everything in it.

This view infers that the land was given to us, without condition, for our benefit and pleasure. We can use it in any way that we want. As kings over creation, the world is our realm, and it will provide us with abundant benefits for a life of leisure, abundance, and power.

The Bible's other view of the land

Walter Brueggemann contrasts two perspectives,[6] which we see both in the Bible and in our present-day world. He calls one the royal conscious-ness and the other the prophetic. He notes the three components which define all human life and culture:

1) technology and economics, that is, our views about the material world and the way it works;

2) social structure and politics, that is, the way our world of human relationships is put together; and

3) ideology and religion, that is, our way of describing and thinking about values and authority.

The following chart lists assumptions of each of these three compo-nents from both the royal perspective and the prophetic perspective.

Royal perspective	Prophetic perspective
Economics of affluence	Economics of enough for all
Politics of power	Politics of justice and mutuality
Religion of God's accessibility	Religion of God's freedom

The royal stance we've taken for granted

In the royal view, material goods exist to be consumed. Prosperity and abundance are assumed to be the goals of every normal person. An abundance of consumer goods, it is assumed, will remove our anxiety about our survival. (But ironically, poverty and scarcity are the dark side of the royal system.)

In politics, the royal mind assumes that dominion and power are the basis of a successful society. The aim is to acquire as much power and control as possible (even if it means that the powerful take control over the weak).

All of this is supported by a religion which assumes that the power of those in control is God-given. God is always available and ready to help the

6. Walter Brueggemann, *The Prophetic Imagination* (Philadelphia: Fortress Press, 1978).

people in power because they reflect the will of God. God is the patron of the powerful and they are seen as the representatives of God.

Enough for all in the prophetic world

In the prophetic worldview, material goods and resources should benefit everyone. The goal is to have enough, *just enough*, for all. The model of this society is manna in the wilderness and daily bread, people comfortable under their own vines and fig trees. Abundance is no one being in a needy state. (See Exod. 16:18.)

The prophetic perspective sees social structure working so that all people receive justice, which means receiving what they need (rather than what they deserve). This creates harmony and right relationships, which produce a new community.

In this perspective, God is not identified as being on the side of the powerful and the power structures, but is *free* to do surprising and unexpected acts on behalf of God's people. God, not people, chooses when, where, and how God will be gracious and show mercy.

Seeing creation through prophetic eyes

In both the royal and prophetic systems, economics, politics, and religion fit together to form an interlocking worldview. It is easy to see that our modern Western, industrial, scientific worldview is firmly under the umbrella of the royal perspective. It has little sympathy for the challenge of the prophetic way.

Once our eyes are open to see another way, it strikes us that the Bible is pervaded with the prophetic outlook. Because of our easy acceptance of the royal view, we have interpreted the Bible to fit that mindset and have imposed that worldview on the Bible. Yet the prophetic outlook touches even those biblical passages which we most often choose to support the royal outlook.

If we read the creation accounts of Genesis 1 and 2 once more, looking for the prophetic note and letting go of our royalist ideas, what will we find? Watching carefully, we find the prophetic voice plainly present even in these supposedly royal passages.

1. In Genesis 1:26, dominion is given to both male and female. *Together* they exercise it. *Together* they are humanity (not "man"). Dominion is given to *all of humanity* at creation, not mandated to man to the exclusion of woman.

2. Shared dominion completely transforms the understanding of power. In the royal view, dominion means doing what *I* want, what benefits *me*, what is profitable *for me*; in the prophetic form, dominion means deciding

together what will be best for *us*, what will allow *all of us* to be productive, fruitful persons, together exercising power to bring harmony and health to every part of our world.

3. Dominion, therefore, no longer centers on the welfare of individuals seeking self-fulfillment through personal power, status, and riches. Instead, dominion becomes the shared pursuit of *shalom*. The Bible understands shalom as the healthy, holistic, harmonious state which results when *all* parts of the environment (God, people, and natural world) are in proper relationship.

The blessing by which God gives people their privileged mandate can be translated most accurately in the inclusive language of the American south:

Y'all be fruitful, and
Y'all multiply, and
Y'all fill the earth.
Y'all have dominion over it, and
Y'all subdue it.

4. The model for this type of dominion is clearly seen in the acts of God throughout the sequence of creation. God, through the powerful word, exercises dominion in several clearly described ways:

a. God *divides* and *separates*—light from darkness (1:4); waters from waters (1:6-7); land from sea (1:9). God thereby brings order out of chaos.

b. God *empowers creation* to be fruitful and productive—the earth *brings forth* plants (1:12); the water *brings forth* sea creatures (1:20); the earth *brings forth* living creatures (1:24). God enables his world to be productive.

c. God *fills* the environment which was created on the first three days. On day four, God fills the firmament of the heavens with sun, moon, and stars (1:14); on day five, God fills the air with birds and the waters with sea creatures (1:20); on day six, God fills the earth with living creatures (1:24); and then, in the final creative act, God fills the vegetative land with human beings (1:29-30).

d. God *establishes diversity*, boundaries, and groupings within the natural order—vegetation "according to their kind" (1:21, 24, 25); the heavenly lights to mark off days, years, and seasons, to be signs, and to separate light from darkness (1:14-18); and within humanity, God creates male and female (1:27).

e. God *names* the various parts which were created, thereby establishing mastery and order—Day and Night (1:5); Heaven (1:8); Earth and Seas (1:10).

f. God *blesses* various parts of creation, thereby empowering them to continue the creative activity which God began—sea and sky creatures are blessed with fruitfulness (1:22); people (male and female) are blessed with fruitfulness and dominion; and God provides resources to maintain fruitfulness for the use of all creatures (1:29-30).

g. God *evaluates* both the results of each creative act and the total overall result at the end of creating. After each, God sees that act as good; and the total created system, God sees as very good (1:31), which should be understood with the fuller meaning of being "pleasing, beautiful, satisfying, functioning smoothly."

h. God *rests* on the seventh day. Here, resting is also an act of dominion in that God has created a world which itself can exercise fruitfulness and dominion.

As God exercises it, dominion results in harmony: it empowers, sustains, and is rest-producing.

5. God created people saying, "Let *us* make [humanity] in *our* image and after *our* likeness." The creation of people happens as a *deliberative* decision. It is a *mutual* effort. It is a decision which reflects careful thought and grows out of some type of *relationship* in which God already exists. Creation needs to be seen as a relational action on God's part rather than the action of an isolated, independent tyrant exerting arbitrary power that has no need to be understood or justified.

6. People are created in the image of God. Since this is the case, we would expect that God intends humanity to exercise dominion in a way similar to God's use of dominion. If the description noted above gives us a clear insight into who God is, then this is also the image which God intends to be reflected in us. As God brings order out of chaos, so should we. As God recognizes the inherent value of the physical and animal world, so should we. As God operates and works in an orderly, earth- and life-enhancing way, so should we. As God extends blessing to the various parts of creation, so should we. As God rests, trusting creation to continue to be good, so should we. Exercising dominion, as a part of being made in God's image, is a work which, at best, brings order to all the world and, at the least, maintains that proper order.

7. Hence, the granting of dominion, when seen as the climax of the larger story, is in no way just the delivery of unrestricted power or a monopoly of force to man. Rather, it is the unique empowering of all people to carry on the purposeful ordering of the world as it was first done so beautifully by God.

8. While not in any way denying that humanity has dominion and a mandate to use the earth, we can see that the earth and its animal life

have meaning apart from humanity. (God called the earth good even before people were present.) And further, we can see that our use of the earth must be carefully guarded so that it does not become abuse.

Earth keepers of creation's garden

Within this prophetic account, humanity, even though it stands within creation, is its culmination. In this *inclusionist* view, humanity is "an inextricable part of nature."[7] Life (and the natural world) is viewed as a unity—all of which is good. To use a figure fitting for our age, we can view the earth as a self-contained biological spaceship that works properly only when its many complex and interrelated systems are in correct balance. For the ancient Hebrew, this balanced state was "righteousness" (i.e., having *shalom*). Though much importance rests on us, humanity is not considered in isolation.

While Genesis 2 does not use the word *dominion*, it suggests six thoughts about the place of land and humanity in creation:

a. The first human has the closest bond possible with the land or earth, the humus: God forms human *(adam)* from humus *(adamah)*. The human is truly an earth-creature. Here we see the making of a new form of life without losing its link with the material from which it was created.

b. The Lord makes every tree to grow out of the ground. The garden is related to and rooted in the ground. It is soil which produces trees which are "pleasant to the sight and good for food." We find an idyllic, peaceful scene in which the ground is the context from which humans and plants come.

c. The human is placed in Eden's garden with a specific role in relation to that environment. The human is "to till it and to keep it." This could also be translated "to serve it and to guard it," an interesting twist when placed beside "having dominion." Here the human is given the task of taking care of, protecting, maintaining, and preserving the garden. The garden is for the human's benefit, yet the primary work of the human is to be an *earth keeper.*

d. The single human is declared "not good; inadequate," (in sharp contrast to the evaluations of Genesis 1). A human being alone and isolated, guarding the earth, is not a pleasing model. Therefore, animals (also formed from the earth) are created and brought to the human to name and to care for. Yet, these other earth-creatures are not found to be a suitable complement for the lone human. Only with the creation of a

7. Elder, *Crisis in Eden*, p. 13.

second human, "bone of my bone, and flesh of my flesh," is a suitable companion found.

e. Even when the man and woman are driven from the garden, the role for which they were created continues. They are still to till the soil ("to serve the earth") from which they were taken.

f. The formation of another human is not the last creative act in Genesis 2. The last act, when "the two become one," is the culmination. Again the mutuality and harmony of all humans is highlighted.

Shalom-making dominion for the land

So, both creation accounts, when carefully read, give us a prophetic critique of the more common, self-serving, and distorted royal view. Dominion, within prophetic thought, is in no way a shameful word; it is a word applied carefully, but in sharp contrast to royal usage.

1. Dominion, defined by the manner in which God practices it, is not just an exercise of power. Rather, it is an act which brings about harmonious, healthy, holistic relationships. Dominion is not tyranny.

2. Dominion serves and guards the garden and those who live there. The relationship is marked by humanity being in control. But this control is not self-satisfying power, but a shared stewardship that enhances both people and the environment. Dominion is clearly a symbiotic relationship, not a parasitic one.

3. Dominion is further distinguished by being shared. Among humans no vertical dominion is intended (either in Genesis 1 or 2). Dominion, the empowered task of serving and guarding, is given equally to all humans. Dominion is, therefore, a horizontal relationship in which all humans are enabled to exercise their management powers.

4. Dominion describes the ordering, fruitful work of God as found in the creation accounts. God exercises dominion over the world, bringing order out of the chaos. Humanity exercises dominion as a manager responsible to God, with delegated power along the same lines as God exercised it in creation.

Therefore, dominion over the land, within the prophetic vision, highlights the responsibility of humanity toward the rest of creation. It sees humankind as the agents of equity, righteousness (right relationship), justice, and peace. Furthermore, dominion over the land is shown to be a shared, mutually beneficial activity.

Dominion, instead of being given to man, is given to humanity, and as such, the exercise of dominion must always be as concerned with humans relating to other humans in ways that strengthen each other as it is with humans relating to their physical environment. The land is one of the prime beneficiaries of humans, who serve as God's creative, shalom-making managers. Anything other than this type of dominion is a violation and despoilment of our earth.

For study and discussion

1. List the ideas which North Americans have about the land and its use. Where would the prophetic view suggest different ideas? What would these ideas be?

2. How does the prophetic view define dominion? Tell how this view would change our use of the land?

3. Since we have been created in the image of God, how does what we do and how we deal with the land fit in with what God did in creating the world, the earth, and everything in it?

Fairfield, Vermont

Human history itself begins with God entrusting his creation to humanity's care (Gen. 2:15). The land remains as a central focus of humanity's historical relationship with God. The earth upon which persons live connects them not only with one another but also with God. . . . God's entrusting all of creation to humankind established a permanent covenantal relationship among God, humankind, and the land.

—Jim Maurer

2. Trust God and care for the land

S. Roy Kaufman

Who controls the land and its resources? How shall the resources of the land be distributed and used? How shall the land itself, as the basic resource of human life, be managed?

These are land tenure questions—the most fundamental issues any human society has to face. Will the land be open to all or will only a few control it? Will its resources serve the needs of all, or will they be concentrated in the hands of a few? Will those who live on the land make these decisions or will these decisions be made by powerful people far removed from the land?

The world in which Israel lived

Very early, perhaps along with the rise of civilization itself, land tenure policies began to favor land monopolies. The land and its resources came under the control of a few people who held power. Once a society moved beyond a tribal way of life, the trend toward land monopolies grew dramatically.

In this setting in history, God called a people, Israel. God invited them to embody his vision of the way people, land, and faith should come together. The main direction for land tenure in Israel's world, as in ours, was toward land monopolization. But God called Israel to live out an alternative vision.

Israel against the nations

Old Testament scholar Walter Brueggemann says that the real faith question in the Old Testament is land tenure policy.[1] What is going on in the

1. Walter Brueggemann, "Theses on Land in the Bible," *Catholic Rural Life*, National Catholic Rural Life Conference, Vol. 34, No. 5 (Nov. 1984), p. 8.

Old Testament is that God is calling one particular people, the Israelites, to an alternative land tenure policy, an alternative vision for how life ought to be ordered in community on the land. "This alternative social experiment of Israel is an attempt to organize life outside of the land monopoly," says Brueggemann.[2]

It wasn't that God expected something more or something different from Israel than from the rest of humankind. But God prefers to have his will brought to life by a people who freely choose to obey God's will, rather than only to state it in abstract terms. (See Jer. 31:31-34.) Isn't that what the incarnation of Jesus Christ is about?

In the Mosaic covenant, God called Israel away from the notion that "the well-being of persons is a function of a social monopoly of force,"[3] represented by kings and armies who also monopolize the land, to the radical notion that God will serve as ruler. It wasn't that Israel was claiming land for itself, or claiming the position held by the Canaanite city-states and the empires all around. Instead, "the gift of the land meant merely that the old political regimes and their claim to ownership of all land was transferred to God Himself, and it was not given to Israel, for ancient Israel did not own it."[4]

Israel's struggle with the land in the Old Testament was both external and internal. The Mosaic covenant outlines the land tenure policy that God intends for human society. Israel's external struggle was to try to follow that alternative vision in the midst of a world in which Canaanites competed for the land and empires all around threatened them. But Israel also felt an inner struggle to remain true to God's vision. And along the way, the prophets spoke words of judgment and hope, holding up the vision like a beacon to light the people's way.

God's plan for living on the land

The laws of the Mosaic covenant which shaped Israel as a community of faith are complex. We can't just read through this legal material and find simple answers to our questions. We have to look behind the actions called for in the law—actions which no longer seem relevant to us—to understand the intent behind a specific law. Still, we can draw from the laws some principles which instructed the Israelites about their life together on the land.

2. Brueggemann, p. 8.
3. George E. Mendenhall, *The Tenth Generation: The Origins of the Biblical Tradition* (Baltimore: The Johns Hopkins University Press, 1973), p. 196.
4. Mendenhall, p. 225.

1. *The land belongs to God.* In contrast to the world around, neither the king nor the priests nor the state nor the people shall own the land, for it belongs to God. "No land shall be sold outright, because the land is mine, and you are coming into it as aliens and settlers," says God (Lev. 25:23, New English Bible). This principle is reaffirmed elsewhere as well: "The earth is the Lord's and all that is in it" (Ps. 24:1, NEB); "For the world and all that is in it are mine" (Ps. 50:12, NEB).

This principle means that God intends for the land itself to be shared justly and fairly among all persons in society. No one can claim a piece of land as his own, to do with as he pleases, for the land belongs to God. All persons are stewards of that which belongs to someone else, and not masters able to dispose of it as their own. *The proper role for humankind is to live in a relation of humility, trust, and obedience toward God.*

The plan to redistribute the land in the Jubilee Year (Lev. 25:8-34) was intended to remind the Israelites that the land belongs to God. The biblical vision removes the land from the sphere of human conflict in the sense that it declares God to be the owner and therefore the protector of the land, thus making the land itself the common inheritance of all persons in society.

The issue here does not have to do with whether Israel actually practiced the Jubilee, nor with the practicality of returning land to the original owners every fifty years, nor even with whether this text allows for private property. It is not a question of one economic system or another, of capitalism versus socialism. The issue is simply whether people who claim to know God acknowledge that the land belongs to God, that they are stewards of what is God's, and that therefore the land must be shared justly and fairly among all persons in society.

2. *The land's bounty must be used for the welfare of all.* The land's resources are not to be exploited for the benefit of those with power and wealth, but are to be used for the welfare of all persons in society. The Mosaic covenant shows a particular concern for those who are dependent—widows, orphans, and aliens. They are to be cared for by us from the bounty of the land. The commandments allowing the poor and the aliens to glean the edges of the fields (Lev. 19:9-10) and requiring a third-year tithe of produce for Levites, orphans, widows, and aliens (Deut. 14:28-29) are just two examples of this concern. The land must really be seen as a common inheritance, the source of life for the community as a whole.

This principle means that a society must be judged on how well it provides for the people who are powerless and dependent. *God intends for humankind to live in a relation of justice, peace, and love with one another.* No one has a right to the unrestrained accumulation of material possessions without regard for those who by nature or circumstance are disinherited and dependent. Again, it is clearly not just a question of tithing or expecting the poor to glean the fields. It is not a question of the merits of this or that welfare system. It is a question of whether those who claim to know God admit their responsibility for the welfare of all persons in society, and particularly for those who for whatever reason are marginal and disinherited.

3. *The land must be preserved and kept fruitful for all time.* The land should not be seen as a commodity that may be exploited for personal gain without regard for its long-term health and beauty. Instead, the land must be valued, both for its own sake and as the source of life for generations to come. Wendell Berry, the Kentucky poet, has written: "To live, we must daily break the body and shed the blood of Creation. When we do this knowingly, lovingly, skillfully, reverently, it is a sacrament. When we do it ignorantly, greedily, clumsily, destructively, it is a desecration."[5]

This same sense of the sacredness of creation lies behind the commands to grant the land a Sabbath rest (Exod. 23:10-11; Lev. 25:1-7). The whole sabbatical system, beginning with keeping the Sabbath as a day of rest, has the purpose of teaching us to trust God enough to respect the natural order.

This principle means that *the land must be used with reverence, care, and skill.* No one has the right to abuse the land. The issue is not whether it is good for the land to lie fallow every seventh year, as though it were some primitive method of land conservation. The issue is whether we trust God enough to do what the health of the land requires, whether we trust God enough to avoid abusing the land and ourselves and others in a frantic effort to provide for ourselves or to accumulate wealth. The problem is not a lack of knowledge or adequate technique, but a lack of trust in God. The abuse of the land through soil erosion or in countless other ways happens not because people do not know what is good for the land or how to conserve it. The land is abused simply because people become anxious and greedy when they no longer trust God. It is a question, finally, of whether those who claim to know God trust him enough to value and care for the land, both as the source of life for this and future generations and for its own life as the good creation of God.

Israel's struggle with the land

Within the biblical witness, Israel's struggle with the land came after the

5. Wendell Berry, *The Gift of Good Land: Further Essays Cultural and Agricultural* (San Francisco: North Point Press, 1981), p. 281.

people possessed the land, not before. Israel received the land not through strife, but as the gift of God. And as Deuteronomy 8 makes clear, Israel's primary struggle with the land was the inner struggle to be faithful to God after they possessed the land. On the eve of Israel's entry into the Promised Land, Moses warned the people, not about the rigors of the struggle against the Canaanites, but about the dangers of possessing the land.

It seems fairly clear that Israel did make a concerted effort to follow the alternative vision for land tenure we have been describing. Israel entered the Promised Land, and the land was divided among the people according to tribe and family. It was passed on from father to son as a family inheritance. The nation of Israel began as a tribal confederacy, communities of small landowners in a rural setting. But Israel always had to do battle both with the threat of external enemies and with the internal temptations of covetousness, greed, and lack of trust in God.

Eventually the people grew weary of the struggle. They decided that, if they were to have the land, they needed a king to help them manage and protect the land. This was, from the first, a fateful choice, as the story of the choosing of Saul (1 Sam. 8) shows, for it involved a subtle and yet direct abandonment of God's rule and God's vision for the land and its people.

With the change in Israel from a tribal confederacy to an empire under David and Solomon, we can also see the beginnings of a process of forming land monopolies. A king needs a capital, and so Israel developed an urban culture centered in Jerusalem. A king needs a standing army and a busy bureaucracy. So taxation and conscription increased, placing a burden on the landed farmers of Israel. Soon a commercial class of merchants appeared, closely tied to the royal court, to manage the trade of the empire. With these developments, the movement from self-sufficient, interdependent rural communities to a society in which common people have little control over their lives and their land had begun. In the prophetic writings (Mic. 2:1-2; Amos 8:4-8; Isa. 5:8), we have vivid descriptions of the way in which small farmers were cheated out of their livelihood and their land by greedy speculators.

The process of land monopolization picked up speed under Solomon and might have kept on going had it not been for the nonviolent revolt of the farmers in Israel against Rehoboam, Solomon's son. (See 1 Kings 12.) Their successful uprising broke the monopoly power of the Israelite empire. Divided, Israel and Judah were just two insignificant Palestinian states. But even then, the division of the kingdom only slowed the process of land monopolization.

In the story of King Ahab coveting the vineyard of Naboth (1 Kings 21), we see the process at work again in the ninth century B.C. Ahab reflected the worldly notion that land is a commodity to be bought and sold for personal gain and to be treated as one pleases. But in Naboth, God's vision of land tenure was still very much alive. For him, the land is an inheritance, "held in trust from generation to generation, beginning in gift and continuing so, and land management is concerned with preservation and enhancement of the gift for the coming generations. Naboth is responsible for the land, but is not in control over it. It is the case not that the land belongs to him, but that he belongs to the land. Naboth perceives himself and the land in a covenantal relation."[6]

Prophets kept the vision of a new order alive

While the kings of Israel and Judah monopolized and abused the land, the prophets of Israel held onto the alternative vision of life together on the land described in the Mosaic covenant. Their role is clearly seen in the story of Naboth and King Ahab, where Elijah the prophet appeared to denounce Ahab for his sins of greed and murder and to declare God's word of judgment. The prophets addressed their message both to people as individuals and to the nation as a whole.

The prophets' message was first of all a call to repentance. God was patient and had postponed the day of judgment. But when there was no repentance, the prophets announced judgment—the sure social and ecological consequences of a sinful way of life. In graphic detail, the prophets announced the ecological ruin which is the result of a life of injustice, greed, and selfishness (Isa. 24:1-6; Jer. 4:18-28; Hos. 4:1-3). As the Native American leader, Chief Seattle, said in the last century to the white conquerors who had seized the land as though it were their own, "Continue to contaminate your bed, and you will one night suffocate in your own waste."[7] The prophetic task, all too often, was to proclaim the end of the present order through invasion, war, exile, and the devastation of the earth.

Yet that was not all. From the first, even from the time of Moses, the prophets had indeed made clear that loss of the land and exile would be the result of unfaithfulness to God. (See Deut. 8:19-20; 11:16-17.) If people do not practice stewardship of the land and share it justly, if they do not use its bounty for the welfare of all, if they do not care for the land, then they will lose the land and their lives with it.

6. Walter Brueggemann, *The Land: Place as Gift, Promise, and Challenge in Biblical Faith* (Philadelphia: Fortress Press, 1977), p. 93.

7. Quoted in Wesley Granberg-Michaelson, *A Worldly Spirituality: The Call to Redeem Life on Earth* (San Francisco: Harper and Row, 1984), p. 30.

But the prophets also understood exile and loss of the land in a positive light. They harkened back to the time of Israel's origins in the desert and they saw in the Exile a new wilderness experience. In Hosea 2, God is portrayed as wooing the people in the wilderness, so that they may learn anew what it means to be faithful to God. The prophets saw exile, a sojourn in the wilderness, as a time for new beginnings when people learn again to trust in God and to depend upon God.

Finally, the prophetic message was a word of hope. Whether it was Jeremiah buying a field in the last days of the siege of Jerusalem (Jer. 32) or Ezekiel's vision from Exile of a new Eden in the desolate land (Ezek. 36), the prophets consistently announced not only judgment, but hope; not only exile, but restoration. Whether expressed in terms of a new beginning on the land after years of exile or as the future creation of a new heaven and a new earth, hope is rooted in God's action and purpose. The future belongs to God. And the future God envisions involves not only the coming of justice and peace in a new social order (Isa. 2:1-4), but also a new order of harmony and fruitfulness in nature and of humankind with nature (Isa. 11:1-9; 65:17-25).

The prophetic task, in short, was to keep alive the alternative vision of life on the land which had shaped the people of Israel in the first place and to do so both in prosperous times and in desperate times of loss and suffering. Their task was to help people see the certain social ruin and ecological devastation involved in abandoning the alternative vision of God. And it was to help people see that beyond the ruin and devastation involved in the collapse of the old order, God was still calling people to a new beginning, inviting them to incarnate once again his vision for what human life ought to be on the land. Warning about the consequences of life in the old order, and holding forth the vision of the new order—these are the prophetic tasks in the midst of the historical struggle of God's people with the land.

Caring for the land to please God

Our struggle, the Bible teaches, is not to be an external struggle for the land against other persons or nations. Instead, it is a struggle within ourselves in our relationship to the land, a struggle against greed and selfishness and pride, a struggle to trust God fully, to yield the ownership of our land and our lives to God, and to be content as stewards caring for the land and sharing its bounty for the welfare of all.

The gospel is all about self-denial and cross bearing, about letting ourselves be lost for Jesus' sake (Mark 8:34-38). And land, in the Bible, is only promised to those who are meek and humble, as in the third Beatitude (Matt. 5:5), or to those who have already yielded up all right to the land for the sake of Jesus Christ (Mark 10:29-30).

All of this doesn't nullify our struggle for the land, but it changes dramatically the terms and the nature of our striving. For now the struggle is not for our land, our rights, or our lives but instead an effort to see that the land is cared for and used in a way that pleases God, that serves the welfare of all persons, and that enhances the land itself.

Our model in this struggle, and the source of our ability to strive faithfully, is Jesus Christ, who "did not think to snatch at equality with God, but made himself nothing, assuming the nature of a slave" (Phil. 2:6-7, NEB).

For study and discussion

1. God wants us to live in humility, trust, and obedience toward him and in a relation of justice, peace, and love with our neighbors. In the biblical vision of land tenure, God also requires us to live in harmony, care, and reverence for the earth. Is it less sinful, or are the consequences less serious, when we break our relationship to the earth than when we break our relationship to others or toward God?

2. In the present farm crisis, we see a lot of struggle to keep the land. Is there a similar internal struggle with the land, to do what is best for the land, or does the external struggle to possess and to keep the land override consideration about what is best for the land? Does the farmers' struggle for the land reflect the vision of land tenure we find in Scripture?

3. What does the story of King Ahab and Naboth say about the current farm crisis? Are there similar dynamics at work in our day? Was Naboth's refusal to sell his vineyard to the king a selfish act, or did he refuse to sell because he felt responsible to God for the land and how it was cared for? What does the story tell us about the cost of doing what is best for the land?

4. More and more, we hear that farming is a business, and that the business of agriculture is the production of food. What does the biblical vision for life together on the land say about farming that makes profit and production the bottom line? What does the Bible see as the bottom line in our relation to the land?

5. How can we reconcile the kind of capitalist system in which we live with the biblical vision for land tenure? What are some ways we can own the land and still make it clear to ourselves and to others that the land belongs to God and that we are only stewards of it? Would another system like socialism make it easier? What would be the pitfalls in a socialist

system for living out the biblical vision of the land?

6. What parallels can be seen between Israel's experience with the land and the experience of today's Christians in relation to the land? Can North American Christians come to terms with landedness without becoming "like the nations," as Israel did, and resort to worldly means to own, manage, and protect their land?

7. Is the biblical vision for life together on the land only for farmers and rural people? What are some ways in which urban people—workers and managers, professionals and bureaucrats—can show their commitment to God's plan for the land? What happens when so few people, only 3 percent in our society, live close to the land? How can our society come to a new appreciation of the worth of the land, and of our dependence upon it and our connectedness to it?

Oklahoma

It seems that we have forever talked about land stewardship and the need for a land ethic, and all the while soil destruction continues, in many places at an accelerated pace. Is it possible that we simply lack enough stretch in our ethical potential to evolve a set of values capable of promoting a sustainable agriculture?
—Wes Jackson

3. Farming that renews land and people

Art Meyer

In the biblical account of creation, God gave humans a special responsibility for the land: "to till it and keep it." In the covenant with Moses, God called people to live together on the land in ways that would sustain both the land and the people. When we apply these biblical principles to farming, we call it sustainable agriculture.

Such a way of farming can endure over the long haul. Sustainable agriculture, says Dana Jackson, editor of *The Land Report* and co-director of the Land Institute at Salina, Kansas, "protects soil and water and promotes the health of people and rural communities."[1] It is farming that works in harmony with the ecology of the natural world. Wendell Berry, a Kentucky farmer-teacher-writer, says, "Sustainable agriculture does not deplete soils or people."[2]

Planet earth is one vast balanced natural system (ecosystem) into which energy from the sun is continually infused. But the earth's substances (such as water, oxygen, carbon, nitrogen, and phosphorus) are regularly recycled from the nonliving to the living environment.

Certain physical laws, called the laws of thermodynamics and the conservation of matter, set limits to this system. According to these laws, matter is recyclable; energy is not! That is the key concept for understanding sustainable agriculture. Modern agriculture has been able to circumvent the laws of thermodynamics for the time being, but only by exploiting stored energy in the form of fossil fuels and by exploiting the earth itself.

1. Dana Jackson, "Sustainable Agriculture: A Concept Catching On," *The Land Report*, No. 26 (Spring 1986), p. 8.
2. Wes Jackson, Wendell Berry, Bruce Colman, *Meeting the Expectations of the Land* (San Francisco: North Point Press, 1984), Preface, p. x.

We must conclude that, as John Carmody says, "any society expecting to survive on a finite planet must become a . . . sustainable society based on recycling—on reusing matter and reducing the use of energy." He says that the crisis of the land "comes down to simple blindness; we do not see how the world really works. Especially in the industrially advanced nations, we are living in blatant contradiction to the way the world really works, ignoring the basic laws of matter and energy."[3]

Wes Jackson, co-director of the Land Institute, Salina, Kansas, suggests that we should view agricultural problems differently than we often do. He says, "Most analyses of problems *in* agriculture do not deal with the problem *of* agriculture. Most talk is about problems with the way farming is done (problems in agriculture), not of the threat of agriculture to the biosphere itself."[4]

Agriculture has done its share to bring us closer to the great crisis looming over the world's environment. Note these alarming facts:

- "Since the dawn of civilization, one half of the earth's food-producing soil has disappeared. By the year 2000, one-third of the remaining soil will be lost."
- "By the end of the century, less than five percent of the earth's surface will be fit for farming. And at that time, our global population will exceed six billion."[5]

Farming's future at risk

In 1984, a group of farm, church, and rural life leaders saw agriculture's ability to produce in trouble. The supply of natural resources is running low. "The export boom of the 1970s, together with direct and indirect public policy incentives," they said, "spurred many farmers and investors to buy and plant as much as possible (including marginal, highly erodible land), and to remove conservation improvements." They noted that groundwater was being overdrafted and that pollution from chemical runoff and contaminated groundwater were serious problems in some areas.[6]

Soil erosion. Sustainable agriculture needs fertile soil. Lester Brown of Worldwatch Institute says, "Civilization can survive the exhaustion of oil

3. John Carmody, *Ecology and Religion* (Ramsey, N. J.: Paulist Press, 1983), p. 12.
4. Wes Jackson, *New Roots for Agriculture* (University of Nebraska Press, 1985), p. 1.
5. C. Dean Freudenberger, *Food for Tomorrow?* (Minneapolis: Augsburg Publishing House, 1984), pp. 15-16.
6. *Beyond Crisis: Farm and Food Policy for Tomorrow* (Washington, D.C.: Rural Coalition, 1984), p. 5.

reserves, but not the continuing wholesale loss of topsoil."[7]

Loss of soil by wind and water erosion is widespread. In 1977, Soil Conservation Service data showed 34 percent of United States cropland losing topsoil much faster than it can ever be replaced. Another inventory in 1982 put the figure at 44 percent.[8]

Soil erosion in the United States increases as crop rotation systems are abandoned. One study dramatically shows why this is so:[9]

Cropping system	Annual soil loss
Corn, wheat, clover rotation	2.7 tons per acre
Continuous wheat	10.1 tons per acre
Continuous corn	19.7 tons per acre

Cropland loss. The *Global 2000 Report* says that agricultural soils will deteriorate worldwide because of "erosion, loss of organic matter, desertification, salinization, alkalinization, and waterlogging."[10] Only half an acre of arable farmland will be available per capita by the year 2000, compared to one acre in 1970. At that time, according to the Food and Agriculture Organization, a 60 percent increase in food, fish, and forest production will be needed just to maintain current patterns of consumption.[11]

Loss of farmland may seem unimportant to North Americans. Don't we have too much land under cultivation? Isn't overproduction the real problem?

Without going into detail, let it be said clearly: there is no overproduction of food worldwide. Our present North American oversupply comes to us at tremendous cost to the environment. And it is hard to grasp the enormous growth in world population that is on its way. From 1975 to 1986, the population grew from four billion to an estimated five billion, and is expected to grow to six billion in only eleven years.[12] The time will come when every parcel of cropland will be needed, including that which is presently being degraded or lost.

7. "Where Have All the Farmlands Gone?" *National Agricultural Lands Study* (Washington, D.C.: U. S. Government Printing Office, 1981).

8. Lester R. Brown and Edward C. Wolf, "Soil Erosion: Quiet Crisis in the World Economy," *Worldwatch Paper No. 60* (Washington, D.C.: Worldwatch Institute, 1984), p. 6.

9. Brown and Wolf, p. 11.

10. *Global 2000 Report to the President: Entering the Twenty-first Century* (Washington, D.C.: U. S. Printing Office, 1980), Vol. 1, p. 1.

11. Erik P. Eckholm, *Down to Earth: Environment and Human Need* (New York: W. W. Norton Co., 1983), p. 136.

12. Elaine M. Murphy, *World Population: Toward the Next Century* (Washington, D. C.: Population Reference Bureau, May 1985), p. 2.

Water pollution. Modern farming adds greatly to the stress placed on water supplies. This pressure includes pollution from silt and chemicals such as pesticides and fertilizers, inappropriate irrigation practices, and overdrafting of groundwater aquifers.

"Agriculture is a major contributor [of silting], accounting for about three-fourths of this sediment [in the nation's water basins]."[13] Pollution of surface waters from farm runoff and wastes from animal feed lots is common. The overgrowth of aquatic plant life caused by too much nitrate and phosphate in lakes and streams leads to oxygen depletion when it decays, leaving us with lakes devoid of animal life.[14]

Larger amounts of nitrates are appearing in groundwater, due mainly to nitrogen-based fertilizer that leaches through the soil. Since 1950, the use of chemical fertilizers in the United States has increased more than 600 percent. According to the U. S. Department of Agriculture, plants can absorb little more than one-third of this fertilizer. The remainder either runs off into surface waters or filters down to the water table where it can enter drinking water supplies.[15]

Other chemical poisons used in farming are being found in our waters. According to the U.S. Environmental Protection Agency, pesticides have been found in groundwater in more than twenty states. The drinking water of millions is now tainted with these chemical poisons. A scientific advisory panel member says, "Groundwater contamination by pesticides or their residue is probably the biggest environmental issue of the next decade."[16]

Overdraft of water. Along with the larger harvests brought about by the worldwide increase of irrigation has come salt buildup and aquifer depletion. About half of the world's irrigated land has been damaged by waterlogging or has turned salty or alkaline.[17] Some 44 million acres of American cropland are irrigated—12 percent of the total. Each year irrigation adds 700 thousand tons of salt to the Colorado River alone. The resulting reduced crop yield and corroded equipment account for a loss of more than $50 million each year. This cost could double in the next twenty years.[18]

"In the Great Plains, 70 percent of the surface water is depleted rather than being diverted to the normal recharge of the aquifer," says C. Dean

13. Carmody, p. 14.
14. Carmody, p. 15.
15. Jonathan King, *Troubled Water* (Emmaus, Pa.: Rodale Press, 1985), p. 69.
16. King, p. 201.
17. *Global 2000 Report*, Vol. 2, pp. 151f.
18. W. Jackson (1985), p. 29.

Freudenberger. Strong evidence of the overuse of our water supply can be found in loss of artesian pressure, declining spring and stream flow, land subsidence, and saltwater intrusion. Vast underground resources of water that took thousands of years to collect have been seriously drained in a few decades. Between 1950 and 1980, the pumping of these water reserves has doubled. Daily, 21 billion gallons more water are used than recharged.[19]

A familiar example of overdrafting is the vast Ogallala aquifer that stretches from West Texas to northern Nebraska and beyond. At best, the Ogallala will support present pivot irrigation for only the next thirty-five to forty years. Some areas on the edges of the aquifer are already being returned to dry land farming.

Besides depleting the Ogallala, center pivot irrigation adds a chemical burden. The process of mixing pesticides and fertilizers with water in the pivot systems is contaminating the aquifer.

Fossil fuel depletion. The U. S. Department of Agriculture says that today one farmer can feed seventy-eight persons. What is less well known is that our overabundant agricultural production system is due to a temporary abundance of subsidized fuel. One report says that "without oil, our agriculture yields would be about one-fourth what they are today."[20]

While many observers have long felt that "highly mechanized, chemicalized, and capitalized farming cannot be sustained, cheap energy has so far enabled the agricultural sector to cover most of its shortcomings."[21]

Indeed, agriculture today is productive. Energy efficient it is not. It takes over two calories of energy for each calorie of food obtained for all agricultural production in North America. When energy costs for processing, distributing, and preparation are considered, the total cost is about 9.8 calories of energy per calorie of food consumed.[22] Third-World farmers, on the other hand, fertilizing with manure and cultivating by hand, produce five to twenty calories of food *for every calorie* they expend.[23]

The United States uses three times as much petroleum and natural gas per capita for food production as is used in the developing countries for *all* energy consuming activities (agriculture, industry, transportation).[24]

19. Freudenberger, p. 51.
20. Maryla Webb and Judith Jacobsen, *U. S. Carrying Capacity* (Washington, D.C.: Carrying Capacity, Inc., 1982), p. 28.
21. Jackson, Berry, Colman, p. 70.
22. Jackson, Berry, Colman, p. 68.
23. Colin Tudge, *The Famine Business* (New York: St. Martin's Press, 1975), p. 4.
24. Freudenberger, p. 64.

In light of Western farming's near total dependence upon oil, Freudenberger asks, "What about food prospects for tomorrow? What are our options when cheap, readily available fuel is gone, populations will be beyond six billion, soil fertility greatly diminished, and as yet no viable agricultural production and food alternatives are being developed on a widespread basis?"[25]

Genetic variability lost. During the past thirty years, scientists have developed plant varieties that are very responsive to chemicals and to an abundance of water. Seed companies largely control plant patent rights. They have become an integral part of our fossil fuel based agriculture in recent years, as more than 400 seed companies have been bought by large oil and chemical companies.[26]

Plant breeders have ignored many genes for disease, drought, and pest resistance, preferring those that give high yields in combination with abundant soil fertility and water. Thus, the genetic base of our crop plants has been seriously narrowed.[27] The so-called improved varieties of wheat and corn have replaced the older, locally adapted strains, sometimes causing their extinction. In some cases, the genetic resource base on which new high-yielding varieties were built has disappeared.

Efforts are being made worldwide to create seed banks to counter genetic losses. Louis Boss, of the Fort Collins National Seed Storage Facility, says, "The consequences of the loss of native seed germ plasm are staggering when one thinks that within one short generation human beings could throw away key evolutionary links in the food system, all in the name of progress."[28]

Wes Jackson comments on his concerns about the effects of agriculture on the environment. "Water mining, land salting, pesticide accumulation, fertilizer application, and genetic vulnerability," he says, "are of the same cloth. Any time short run 'efficiency,' affordable because of high energy injections, is the major consideration, the temptation to reduce biological variety is compelling."[29]

Put culture back into agriculture

How has North American agriculture become unsustainable? Is it not because agri*culture*—a way of living (culture)—has become agri*business*—

25. Freudenberger, p. 67.
26. International Coalition for Development Action, "World Food Security in the 80s—The Political Control of Seeds," *Seeds for Tomorrow* (United Nations ICDA Kit, 1983).
27. W. Jackson (1985), p. 30.
28. Freudenberger, p. 47.
29. W. Jackson (1985), p. 31.

a way to make a living (profit)? In making this shift, have we not changed from a food-growing service to a profit-making business?

For the last half century, government policies, agricultural colleges, farm machinery manufacturers, and oil companies have urged farmers to become more mechanized and industrially "efficient" to meet a worldwide increase in food needs. Sometimes this led to food surpluses. When prices for farm products fell, farmers decided (or were encouraged by financial advisers) to expand in order to survive economically.

Farm size grew, debt increased, and farming became more and more dependent on the "efficiency" of fossil fuel energy. Production costs rose along with fuel costs and interest rates, while land values decreased. Other countries (particularly in the Third World) could not afford to buy U.S. produce, one-third of which was now for export. Many farmers could not compete. They either went bankrupt or left farming. The pattern still continues.

Farming cannot escape the laws of ecology

By trying to make agriculture strictly a business, we run headlong into the constraints of nature. When we compare the basic laws of ecology with today's primary economic assumptions, it is easy to see why drastic changes are needed to achieve a sustainable agriculture.

The eminent biologist Barry Commoner suggests four basic laws of ecology in his book, *The Closing Circle*.[30] The following chart shows how today's ideas conflict with these laws:

Basic Laws of Ecology	Economic Assumptions
1. Everything is connected with everything else.	1. Our economic systems can operate independently of nature. Nature just gets in the way.
2. Everything must go somewhere.	2. Throw things away. The good life requires new things and the convenience of disposal. The more new things you have the happier you'll be.
3. Nature knows best.[31]	3. Nature is naive. It can be outmaneuvered, outsmarted. Science or technology will be

30. Barry Commoner, *The Closing Circle* (Beckman Publishers, 1973).
31. This means natural laws set the limits to human manipulation.

able to find a fix for any problem that nature gives us.

4. There is no such thing as a
free lunch.

4. You can have it all with little
effort. Energy and natural resources are unlimited. Economic growth is always necessary and possible. All that's
needed is good management.

Eventually agriculture—and all of society's systems, including business—must conform to these laws of ecology. By not conforming, we are
building up a vast environmental debt.

Sustainable food systems begin with earth stewardship

What can be done to reverse the course of the present agricultural system
which is not sustainable? To recover agri*culture*, we need to reaffirm the
biblical principles of earth stewardship. These universal stewardship
themes are clear and familiar. It is surprising that their application has
been so neglected.

The Bible gives us a mandate to care for the earth and *all* its creatures.
The call to stewardship begins with creation. It continues with the cove-
nant God made with Noah and his descendants and every living creature.
Just treatment of animals, crops, and the land was clearly an important
part of Mosaic law. The caretaker role of people is implied throughout the
Old Testament.

In the New Testament, Jesus illustrates humankind's role as stewards
in various parables (Luke 19; Matt. 25). The apostle Paul saw Christians
as "stewards of the mysteries of God" (1 Cor. 4:1) who fulfill God's ultimate
purpose to "redeem and restore the earth" (Rom. 8:19-21, paraphrased).
God's plan "is to bring all creation together, everything in heaven and on
earth with Christ as head" (Eph. 1:10, Today's English Version). "The
redemption of the world depends upon man's redemption," says Milo
Kauffman. "Christian stewards therefore must be concerned about the
welfare of the earth . . . and its creatures."[32]

A refreshing approach to the recovery of a theology of earth stewardship, called *eco-justice*, combines ecological living with economic justice.
William Gibson, coordinator of the Eco-Justice Project at Cornell University, calls for a rediscovery of eco-justice, which he describes as "the well-

32. Milo Kauffman, *Stewards of God* (Scottdale, Pa: Herald Press, 1975), p. 98.

being of humankind—all humankind—on a thriving earth." Eco-justice, according to Gibson,

> is the acceptance of the truth that only on a thriving earth is human well-being possible—an earth productive of sufficient food, with water fit for all to drink, air fit to breathe, forests kept replenished, renewable resources continuously renewed, nonrenewable resources used as sparingly as possible. . . . On a thriving earth, human well-being is nurtured not only by the provision of these material necessities, but also by a way of living within the natural order that is fitting: respectful of the integrity of natural systems and the worth of nonhuman creatures, appreciative of the beauty and the mystery of the world of nature.[33]

Eco-justice is concerned with solving the ecological crisis and, at the same time, securing justice for the poor. It focuses on responsible *earth* stewardship as well as responsible *person* stewardship. Eco-justice is what the Old Testament prophets were talking about. Eco-justice is what Jesus illustrated in his preaching and simple lifestyle. It is the fundamental concept behind a sustainable agriculture and a sustainable society, both of which are essential.

How we view the natural world and how we express our Christian faith will determine whether we can recover a sustainable agriculture. C. Dean Freudenberger stresses the importance of our task. "The outcome of the world food crisis, as well as the future course of American agriculture," he says, "depends on whether the constant resource abuse of the world can be stopped." But things will only be turned around when we begin to see the created world not as an object to be exploited but as a resource within God's order.[34]

Recognizing that biblical wisdom furnishes us with a foundation for building an ethic for a new agriculture, Freudenberger asks,

> Do our present technologies and attitudes about agriculture and its resource base reflect our sensitivity to the biblical understanding that all resources have meaning to God? Does our agriculture guarantee the interconnectedness of life forms and their patterns of existence, or does it go the other way? Do we relate to the miracle of life in covenant, or do we exploit it as we please? With a renewed spirit in Christ, are we committed to the renewal of agriculture so

33. Dieter T. Hessel, ed., *For Creation's Sake* (Philadelphia: Geneva Press, 1985), p. 25.
34. Freudenberger, p. 81.

that it reflects the great themes of biblical wisdom?[35]

People putting something back into the land

Models for a more sustainable agriculture are not widespread, but their number is increasing. Although agriculture colleges and extension services have focused on commercial agribusiness where financial profit is the primary goal, some of these institutions are beginning to recognize the problems of industrial agriculture. They are broadening their research and extension services to include a focus on sustainable agriculture.

But private groups are doing much of the research in sustainable agriculture. The nonprofit Land Institute at Salina, Kansas, is in the forefront of the search for sustainable agricultural alternatives. Researchers are working to develop a polyculture of perennials as an alternative to monoculture of annual crops that, in today's system of agriculture, is not sustainable over the long term.[36]

At the Rodale Research Center in Pennsylvania, a trained staff focuses on making a "transition from chemical-intensive to a purely organic or regenerative" agriculture. Their research team includes scientists who study soil fertility, horticulture, plant breeding, entomology, and aquaculture.[37]

J. Tevere MacFadyen traveled for three years studying America's small family farms. In his book, *Gaining Ground*, he describes self-reliant farmers who practice diversified agriculture in an attempt to move toward a system that is more sustainable than the large agribusinesses that are the most common features in our present system.[38]

Dick and Sharon Thompson are among the best known of the farmers who in recent years have changed to sustainable farming. Their careful records of production as they changed from chemical-based agriculture to a ridge-till system without chemicals illustrate the effectiveness of their practice. They rotate crops of corn and soybeans and raise beef cattle and hogs in a diversified operation on their 300-acre farm near Boone, Iowa.[39]

The Warren and Jennie Roberson farm near Lake City, Minnesota, is another model. Features of their system, for which they were named as

35. Freudenberger, p. 93.
36. D. Jackson, p. 8.
37. Richard R. Harwood, "Organic Farming Research at the Rodale Research Center," *Organic Farming: Current Technology and Its Role in a Sustainable Agriculture* (American Society of Agronomy, Special Publication 46, 1984), pp. 1-3.
38. J. Tevere MacFadyen, *Gaining Ground: the Renewal of America's Small Farms* (New York: Holt, Rinehart and Winston, 1984).
39. Information obtained while attending field trip at Thompson farm, 1985.

finalists in a contest of the National Endowment for Soil and Water Conservation, include:

- 1,200 acres, over half of it in forest, farmed with their son and his family;
- terracing, crop rotation, contour farming, limited use of chemicals, grass waterways, water diversions, twenty-seven erosion-control ponds;
- a sixty-two acre upland wildlife habitat;
- reforestation of 200 acres of marginal cropland;
- hilly land in pasture for beef cattle, the core of their operation.[40]

Amish farmers are often described as prime models in practicing sustainable farming. Most Amish farming is based on crop rotation, use of animal wastes for fertilizer, animal traction, contour farming, and good conservation practices.

Most Mennonite farmers have been no different from their neighbors in adopting industrialized agricultural practices. A few, however, have continued sustainable farming methods that they had begun years before. Walter Epp, Marion, South Dakota, says, "Spending most of our years on a small run-down hilly farm took a lot of hard work from the whole family to make it productive. This helped us develop an understanding of the importance of good stewardship and conservation practices. For myself, this has become an important aspect of applying my Christian faith."[41]

More recently other Mennonite farmers have adopted sustainable farming practices. Ben Brubaker, near Kutztown, Pennsylvania, changed to organic farming on his own land after successfully operating the experimental Rodale research farm for several years.[42]

The diversified livestock farm of Elmer Lapp, another Pennsylvania Mennonite farmer, is an example of sustainable farming. Guernsey dairy cows and Belgian mares provide most of the farm income, but Lapp also raises and sells guinea hens and collie pups. He raises a small number of beef cattle, hogs, and chickens for his household and that of his son who farms with him. The milk, eggs, and honey used on the farm are produced there, as are apples, peaches, and plums. Much of the feed for the livestock is grown on the farm, in a five-year rotation that includes corn,

40. Mary Turck, "Land Notes," (Minneapolis, Land Stewardship Project, undated).
41. Letter to LaVonne Platt, 1986.
42. Martin Culik and George DeVault, "Good Yields for 14% Less," *The New Farm* (Emmaus, Pa.: Regenerative Agriculture Association, Nov./Dec., 1983).

barley, and hay.[43]

Concerned about health problems associated with farming practices, Arlin and Margaret Hiebner, Henderson, Nebraska, are among the many farmers who have moved away from using anhydrous ammonia and other chemicals and are building up humus in the soil with natural fertilizer and crop rotation. Others have stopped the routine use of hormones and antibiotics with their animals and no longer apply herbicides to their crops.

Some Mennonite farmers are among those reclaiming land that has been degraded. Jacob and Marlene Tice from western Pennsylvania are restoring a farm that had been despoiled by surface mining for coal. After five years, they have been able to regenerate some of the land.

My family and I have been in the process of reclaiming about thirty-five acres of strip-mined coal land on an eighty-acre farm in east central Ohio for the past thirteen years. We successfully restored some of this land by planting a forest of over 11,000 trees.

These are just a few of many examples of people doing something to recover an alternative and sustainable system. It is refreshing to see growing enthusiasm for such an essential recovery. The benefits of alternative and sustainable agriculture are apparent. A recent article states them well:

> Alternative farming systems protect the environment and benefit wildlife. The extensive crop rotations . . . increase soil resistance to erosion and soil organic matter content, when compared with conventional intensive tillage, monoculture and row crop methods. Alternative farming practice, in most cases, will reduce soil loss. . . . The reduced or non-use of manufactured chemicals with these farming systems greatly decreases the environmental hazards and possible adverse effects on wildlife.[44]

What then are we to do?

Moving from today's unsustainable agriculture to an alternative sustainable model will be long and hard. For it to happen, several basic principles need to be understood.

43. Wendell Berry, *The Gift of Good Land* (San Francisco: North Point Press, 1981), pp. 216-26.

44. Robert I. Papendick, Lloyd F. Elliott, and Robert B. Dahlgren, "Environmental Consequences of Modern Production Agriculture: How Can Alternate Agriculture Address These Issues and Concerns?" *American Journal of Alternate Agriculture*, Vol. 1, No. 1 (Winter 1986).

1. Biblical ethics must be the foundation for all our agricultural practices. What happens to the land and all of its inhabitants must take priority.

2. Agriculture must become a way of life again, more a culture than a business. In a world of limited energy and natural resources, farming cannot be just a business following normal growth economics. It must incorporate a resource use system that is stable, steady-state, and compatible with nature.

3. Moderate-sized family farms should be advocated and protected. They are more likely to promote a sustainable agriculture. The loss of the family farm often leads to environmental degradation. A dramatic example is reported by the Land Stewardship Project, a Minnesota-based land ethics group. In 1958, Ed Hauck of Wabasha County, Minnesota, bought a dairy farm. He put in terraces, hay strips, waterways, and contours. By 1984, he had developed the farm into an award winning conservation showplace. Soil erosion had been cut to less than three tons per acre. In January 1985, Hauck became a victim of foreclosure. An insurance company took over the farm and rented it out to a cash grain farmer who plowed it up, removing all terraces, waterways, strips, and contours. Twenty-seven years of conservation went down the drain. The Soil Conservation Service now estimates an annual soil loss of thirty-five to forty tons per acre per year—a ten-fold increase.[45]

4. The 97.6 percent of the U.S. population not in actual farming must become informed advocates of an alternative food and farming system. They need to insist that state and federal governments provide incentives for people to practice sustainable farming. Their lifestyles should be just as ecologically oriented as those of farmers.

5. The church must become more involved in advocating a just and sustainable agriculture. Needed is a theology of ecology which will become the basis for this sustainable agriculture and for a sustainable society.

What the church can do

Many of the problems of agriculture, like most other human problems, are spiritual. Working for solutions is an important task for the churches. Although some denominations were involved in rural issues early in this century, interest waned in the 1960s and is only now, in the mid-80s, being revived. Some churches that were not a part of the earlier rural life

---

45. Steve O'Neil, "Will John Hancock Insure the Land for Our Children?" *The Land Stewardship Newsletter*, Vol. 3, No. 3 (Summer 1985), pp. 1-2.

movement have become involved in farm issues only recently.

Sustainable agriculture is a justice issue. Christians need to face this issue squarely, determine what the Scriptures say about it and act accordingly. All of us, not farmers alone, have a responsibility to help develop a food and agriculture system that nurtures both the land and its people. Only as we work together can the goals of a sustainable agriculture and society be reached. The love of Christ in our hearts should be motivation enough to move us toward those goals.

For study and discussion

1. How does the prophetic view of dominion (chapter one) and the covenant relationship of God's people on the land (chapter two) point us to the practice of sustainable agriculture—agriculture that follows the laws of nature?

2. Sustainability is an important concept to understand if we look at our relationships with the land and with other people in light of our covenant relationship with God. Look at the definitions and descriptions of sustainability and sustainable agriculture in this chapter and in the Introduction. Then suggest another way to state the idea of sustainability in your own words.

3. Consider how ignoring the laws of nature have led to problems in agriculture. How can the practice of sustainable agriculture help to overcome some of these problems?

4. What is the difference between farming as a way of living and farming as a way to make a living? Does changing the primary goal of farming from one of a food-growing service to one of a profit-making business affect our response to God's mandate to till and keep the earth? Does it affect our covenant relationship as stewards of the land for God?

Amish barn raising

Any social system must
allow for diversity among
its individual members.
What makes it a system
is the collective
expression of values, the
commonly held goals of
the participants, and the
central tendencies in
their behavior. To the
extent that most of the
individuals can realize
their goals, the system
may be said to work. To
the extent that only the
exceptional succeed, the
system fails. The glue
that holds the system
together is its consensus
about how things ought
to be, not necessarily
how they are.
—Marty Strange

4. Sustainable social institutions

Don Reeves

Sustainable agriculture refers to ways of farming that will still be viable for our grandchildren.

Most discussions of sustainable agriculture dwell on practices related to physical resources: care of soil and water, tillage, use of chemicals. I want to discuss the social institutions by which farmers relate to the physical resources and to each other. My examples are: land tenancy (including ownership), taxation, credit, and markets.

Some forms of these social institutions are sustainable, and will contribute to sustainable agriculture. Other forms are not sustainable. How will we know which forms will work? We test them by what they do: 1) to promote a sense of community and 2) to build communities of people.

These social arrangements might also be called social *inventions*. They are not natural phenomena. While many feel that humans have an inborn need to relate to the land, the concepts of owning and of leasing land had to be created. Not all people everywhere share such concepts as land holding. So far as I know, no Native American language can express the idea that a person could *own* a piece of the earth—that's simply unthinkable.

Because these institutions have been invented, they take a *variety of shapes*. And they are changed from time to time. Some changes are helpful. Others are not.

Describing these institutions or the process of change is complex. Personal, cultural, and spiritual values and behavior are intertwined. In the end, public policy decisions do the most to shape these institutions. Some shaping is intentional; some is unintended, as a result of seemingly unrelated decisions. We should learn from past efforts and be evermore conscious about the impact of public policies.

Whenever choices are made, the choices have *a value basis*. The values may not always be stated in words, or even thought about. But a basis always exists for judging whether a choice was good or bad, better or worse.

So, join me in thinking about some of the basic values on which viable rural communities and sustainable agriculture might be based. Following that, I will suggest ways we might apply these values to several of the social institutions by which we relate to the land and to each other.

Marks of sustainable social systems

My understanding of sustainable agriculture may be illustrated by looking at Moses' instructions for keeping the year of the Sabbath and the year of the Jubilee. While preparing the Israelite people for nationhood, Moses spoke about caring for their physical resources: "In the seventh year there shall be a sabbath of solemn rest for the land" (Lev. 25:4). Moses also spoke about what I'm calling social institutions: land ownership (Lev. 25:13-24); indebtedness (Deut. 15:1-6; 23:19-20); and bondservants (Lev. 25:39-55; Deut. 15:12-18).

These instructions may have grown out of the insight that if control over lives and basic resources gets concentrated into too few hands, the social order breaks down.

In each case, a crucial part of Moses' instructions deals with the need for renewal or built-in correction. Land is to be redistributed. Debts are to be forgiven. Bondservants are to be set free.

So, a first indicator of a sustainable system is endure-ability or *renewability*. If an institution yields good results, will it persist? Does it permit or encourage new entrants, particularly from a new generation? Does it promote proper care for the physical resources, so they will last indefinitely? If things get out of balance, is the system self-correcting?

A second and more basic sign of a sustainable system is whether, or in what ways, each social institution *impacts on community*, both on the *sense of community* in our relationships and the nature of *communities of people*.

How do each of these social institutions add to or diminish the sense of community?

In the Western world, we put much emphasis on each person. We tend to define human rights as individual rights as opposed to rights which come from being part of a community. Opportunity usually means individual opportunity, with less attention given to the economic and social order which enables a person to grow and succeed. Whole economic theories and systems assert that the greatest common good will flow from giving individuals as many opportunities as possible. Clearly, this emphasis has roots in our Christian experience, going back to the Reformation. It is also related to the rise of economics as a separate branch of social studies.

Luther and Calvin, in slightly different ways, emphasized individual work and vocation as part of religious duty. Each also put less stress on caring for the poor, once considered a moral duty of wealthy persons. These shifts set the stage for John Locke and others to assert that individuals were free to accumulate wealth for themselves as a result of their talents and work—the foundation of capitalist economies.[1]

I feel that this stress on individual accomplishment has served us poorly during the present farm crisis. If we think that the success of our farm or business is mainly our own doing, with little regard for its social or economic setting, then we can hardly escape feeling that its failure is also our own fault. In fact, for the most part, this is true neither for our successes nor our failures.

Many farms prospered, or appeared to prosper, during the 1960s and '70s because of a whole range of events beyond our control—general inflation and especially inflation of land values, a devalued dollar, a flood of oil money, optimism regarding development in poor nations, and an explosion of exports. We felt called to feed the world—at a profit!   In the same way, much of our current farm stress has been triggered by nonfarm public policy decisions—deficit federal spending, much of it for defense; large tax breaks; "dear" dollars; high interest rates; and curtailed exports.

It should be clear to Christians that the emphasis on individual opportunity, at least as it is expressed in our capitalist economy, is deficient. Some of these failings are recognized and offset by a variety of other social institutions, such as estate taxes. Others persist, as evidenced by the lack of access to basic necessities by many persons within our wealthy nation. Freedom, or even encouragement, for ever-larger farms means that many farm families are displaced. Whole rural communities are threatened. These results are not what we want. Yet we have not always related them to the emphasis on each individual's right to prosper, even at the expense of other persons or the community.

But justice and equity are also parts of community life which nearly everyone supports, although in varying degree. In each community, disadvantaged persons, such as the elderly or orphans, receive care. We have disdain for persons who exploit or take undue advantage of their wealth

---

1. See Prentiss L. Pemberton and Danel Rush Finn, *Toward a Christian Economic Ethic* (Minneapolis: Winston Press, 1985), chapters 3, 4.

or power. And nearly always, some attempt is made to provide equal opportunity, such as free basic education.

We also recognize the value of widespread participation, particularly in decision making. A sense of community usually grows as we work toward a common decision. The more persons taking part, the better the chance for a wise or just decision and the greater degree of ownership and cooperation in carrying it out.[2]

From the idea of a *sense of community*, let's turn to think about *communities of people*. The nature of social institutions determines the types of communities that evolve. Although we need to know more about the ties between social institutions and communities, the links seem clear: ownership of resources in the hands of a few (especially absentee owners), control over credit agencies or markets, and tax systems with preferences or loopholes destroy a sense of community and lead to declining communities.[3]

Another mark of a sustainable social system is *productivity*. We have often defined productivity narrowly and overstressed its importance. Nonetheless, making the land "yield its harvest" (Lev. 25:19) is good stewardship. It provides a richness of life not otherwise possible.

Social institutions play as large a role in productivity as farming know-how and cultural practices. So far as I know, people have never been well fed in a land where only a few people hold the basic resources of a community and make the decisions. On the other hand, the developing nations which have made progress against hunger in the past quarter century have, without exception, gone beyond questions of technology to give attention to such issues as access to land and fair markets.

Being secure on the land

We tend to think of land ownership as the basic social institution of agriculture. But even in the United States, half of the agricultural land is farmed by someone other than the owner. In many other societies, private ownership is not the norm.

As farmers relate to the land, the most important concern is security on the land. Can farmers plant a fruit tree, put in a terrace or a drain, or make other long-term improvements with confidence of being around to reap the benefits? Whether the farmer is owner or renter or has some

2. For a fuller discussion of a just, participatory, and sustainable society, see Tim Atwater, "Reagonomics and Beyond: A Working Paper," (Washington D.C.: Interreligious Taskforce on U. S. Food Policy, 1982), pp. 25-28.

3. *A Time to Choose* (Washington, D.C.: U. S. Department of Agriculture, 1981), pp. 141-52.

other form of use-right, is the tenancy of the farm family secure?

Ownership of land covers a wide spectrum. Private ownership, at one historical extreme, included the divine right of a king or a feudal lord to own not only the land but all the people living thereon. Other examples include the plantations and haciendas of our own history and some still existing in parts of Latin America. Current private industrial farms— where ownership, management, and labor are separated—are usually set up as corporations, another social invention. Our idea of the family farm usually includes at least partial ownership. Here and there, communities of persons, often with strong religious or social goals, are experimenting with other ways of land holding.

Public ownership of farmland (and other assets) runs a similar spectrum: the state-owned farms of eastern Europe; the community-owned collectives of China; the waning pattern of village ownership, with lifetime assignment of plots to families, in parts of Africa; the almost lost patterns of use rights, without any concept of ownership, which once prevailed among native peoples of both North and South America.

Wherever the notion of ownership exists, it is not a natural right, as some seem to feel. It had to be invented. Ownership is defined and defended by the state. With the exception of monarchies, ownership has never been absolute. At minimum, some part of the return from the land has been taxed, in one way or another, to help support the state or other common needs.

Land ownership nearly always carries with it other duties, which may or may not be written into law. Stewardship of the land has a strong base within the Judeo-Christian tradition. It also finds expression in our legal code, as, for example, in the sodbuster provisions of the 1985 farm bill. Several recent state laws make landowners responsible for erosion-induced damages to neighbors.

Where ownership and operatorship are separated, the rules and customs of other forms of tenancy determine the patterns of farming and the nature of rural communities. Serfs, peasants, sharecroppers, day laborers, and migrant and undocumented workers come to mind, and with them images of poor and miserable communities. At another extreme, land reform in Taiwan during the 1950s began with rent controls so stringent that land ownership was made unattractive.

Some of the harshest judgments in the Old Testament are toward those who abused their positions as landlords and hurt their tenants: "Because you levy taxes on the poor and exhort a tribute of grain from them, though you have built houses of hewn stone, you shall not live in them, though you have planted pleasant vineyards, you shall not drink wine from them"

(Amos 5:11, New English Bible).

We would do well to study ideas widely held among Native Americans: Mother Earth is sacred. She may not be owned. She must be cared for. All creatures are related, including humans. Earth's bounty is for the use of all creatures.

We may speculate what sort of nation the United States might have become had the Continental Congress permitted slavery in the New Territories of the Ohio and Mississippi river valleys. The decision to prohibit slavery (another social invention), supplemented by the Preemption Act of 1842 and the Homestead Act of 1862, helped assure that small farm agriculture would become the pattern across much of the United States.

It seems certain that our rural communities would have developed quite differently had different decisions been made. Persons who are used to running their own affairs are unlikely to let someone else run the affairs of the community.

I relate our whole system of political democracy to the results of these land-holding decisions. The network of volunteerism which so enriches our rural communities also rests largely on the small entrepreneurs in each community—family farmers and operators of small businesses.

A sense of community also seems easier to maintain in a place with some equality in control over lives and resources—where many persons are not dependent upon the decisions of a few.

Farm production is related to security of tenure. Longer term investments often are not made if farmers cannot see beyond the next harvest.

Short-term tenancy often contributes to exploitation of the land. In the United States, at least, owners as a group perform somewhat better than tenants in good soil and water conservation practices, but are still far from exemplary. The greatest differences between owners and tenants have to do with land structures, such as terraces, for which the productivity gains are long term.[4]

Socialist models of agriculture have consistently moved away from pure models toward patterns which provide more individual family security and incentive. Several socialist nations in Eastern Europe depend on small plots assigned to families on a lifetime basis for an undue share of fresh produce and certain livestock products. In the last decade, the Chinese have moved toward limited family-assigned plots and smaller work teams who have freedom to sell produce after meeting minimum quotas to the state. Recently, several African nations who had experi-

---

4. David E. Ervin, "Soil Erosion Control on Owner-operated and Rented Cropland," *Journal of Soil and Water Conservation* (Sept.-Oct., 1982), pp. 285-88.

mented with socialist models are making parallel shifts.

Whatever the patterns of tenancy, security seems a key to productivity.

With regard to privately owned farming ventures, the process of renewal needs immediate attention. Farmers are a rapidly aging group, both because of the loss of younger farm families and the lack of new entrants. If family farming is to remain the norm, more attention must be paid to the problems of entry for each new generation.

As each farm, or part of a farm, becomes available, who will take it over? As farmers exit or retire, will they be replaced by new operators or, as is often true now, will that farm be added to an existing unit?

Taxation shapes farming and rural communities

Taxes, as a social institution, affect the sustainability of agriculture in many ways. These impacts have received little attention until recently. Taxes, in general, and especially income tax rules, more than any other single factor, influence who will own and operate farms, what technologies will be adopted, how profitable farming will be, and ultimately, what will be the shape of our rural communities.

The first purpose of taxes is to raise revenue. Taxes can be drawn from three broad categories, or bases: *wealth*, *income*, and *consumption*. Within them are many options for raising needed revenues. As choices are made regarding what will be taxed, and at what rates, behavior will be influenced. Indeed, behavioral response is often a conscious second purpose of taxation; at other times, it is overlooked or misjudged.

Taxes on wealth are rather unevenly administered. In Nebraska, for example, we depend heavily on real estate (farms, houses) taxes to support schools and other units of local government. We do not, however, tax tangible personal property (cattle, tractors) or intangible property (bank accounts, stocks). Yet all of these are valued for estate tax purposes. By what logic?

Patterns of farm ownership and the nature of rural communities could be shaped by changes in real estate taxes. If widespread ownership were a goal, progressive rates might be adopted or homestead exemptions granted. If local ownership were preferred, there could be a surtax on absentee owners.

Consumption taxes are clearly intended to influence behavior. They are not always equally administered. Groceries, but not restaurant meals, are exempt from sales tax in Nebraska. Excise taxes are often heavier on items seen as luxuries or as sinful—entertainment, hotel rooms, alcohol, tobacco, gambling. Import fees are levied on goods deemed to be threats to domestic industries or jobs.

In recent years in the United States, certain income tax rules applied to farming have combined to make much of farming a tax shelter. Such shelters are most valuable to high-bracket taxpayers. The complex rules have fostered and subsidized expansion of farms and investment in farming by the most favored taxpayers: the wealthy. Concentration of farm ownership and investment by nonfarmers, in part a result of tax motivated decisions, have undercut the viability and sustainability of rural communities.

Tax motivated adoption of certain technologies has mixed results. In some instances, productivity has increased (genetic improvements). In other cases, productivity has actually declined (feed/gain ratio in hog production from keeping sows for only one litter). In still other cases, unsustainable practices have been encouraged (pivot irrigation of marginal land).

The 1986 tax bill eliminates the investment tax credit and capital gains benefits, but on balance probably makes little difference in the distortions arising from accounting rules. Farming will be somewhat less a tax shelter, but other shelters have also been reduced. The final net effect on patterns of farm ownership and sustainability of rural communities will probably not be known for years.[5]

Credit can aid renewal

Abuses by moneylenders are at least as old as the Bible. By historic standards, commercial credit institutions in the United States have performed reasonably well, at least during most of the past fifty years. Banking reforms of the 1930s and creation of cooperative credit unions have been helpful.

Within U.S. agriculture, the federal sponsored cooperative Farm Credit System and the federal Farmers Home Administration (FmHA) have helped "keep the industry honest." Subsidized FmHA lending, with some recent exceptions, has contributed to sustainability by targeting beginning farmers and those with limited resources. For the most part, FmHA lending has contributed to the process of renewal and to meeting the goal of dispersed ownership.

Both the Farm Credit System and the FmHA have been widely criticized, with some justification, during the present crisis for abandoning family farm goals.

5. Charles Davenport, Michael Boehlije, and David Marten, *The Effects of Tax Policy on American Agriculture* (Washington, D.C.: U.S. Department of Agriculture, 1982). Richard Dunford, *The Effects of Federal Income Tax Policy on U. S. Agriculture, Senate Print 98-273* (Washington, D.C.: Joint Economic Committee, U.S. Congress, 1984).

The current crisis is in large measure a credit crisis. Farmers are unable to service and repay debts, particularly those undertaken during the euphoria of the late 1970s. The crisis is real for many farmers. It probably arises less from the nature of the credit institutions, however, than from the interplay between credit and still other social institutions: fiscal and monetary policy, tax rules, and inflation.

Farm loans were tempting during the 1970s for farmers, investors, and lenders. Assets, particularly farmland, increased in value rapidly, in some years more than the nominal interest rate. Also, since interest paid on agricultural loans was deductible from taxable income, the after tax cost of borrowing money was further slashed—by more than one-half for high tax bracket borrowers. Credit, combined with the tax rules mentioned earlier, pushed consolidation and expansion.

Young farmers who wished to start farming had to compete with those who had both tax and credit advantages. Their parents often underwrote loans which later proved unmanageable.

The policy shift came in late 1979, when the Carter Administration and the Federal Reserve System undertook to slow inflation through monetary policy decisions. Credit and money supply were restricted; interest rates rose rapidly. The policy was made more difficult, and the interest effects more extreme, by increases in defense spending begun under Carter and accelerated by Reagan, and by the huge tax cuts of 1981.

Widespread realization of the new financial and credit era lagged by nearly two years. Farmland prices reached their peak in 1981.

As we work through this crisis, much farmland will be sold—more than one-third of the land in some communities within a five-year period. Terms of credit will help determine who the new owners will be. Currently, most purchases are for farm enlargement, or are made by nonfarm investors and are often then added by lease to already existing farms.

What steps can we take to strengthen the renewal process, to reinforce operator ownership, and to maintain opportunity for the maximum number of viable farms in each community?

A couple of modestly helpful things have happened. The 1985 farm bill reinforced parts of the family farm orientation of FmHA lending, a reversal of recent trends. The 1986 tax reform bill limits deduction of interest and deduction of artificial farm losses from nonfarm income for those not actively involved in the farm operation.

Other credit-related issues are unresolved. Both FmHA and the Federal Land Bank are amassing large inventories of land by default or foreclosure. We could insist that the rules for disposition of these farms include preferences for beginning, or restarting, or family farmers. Such rules are not yet in place.

Commodity price support loans may also be seen as a large source of subsidized credit to farmers. Recognizing possible trade-offs in operation of commodity programs, the subsidies in such loans could be limited to "family-sized" loans.

Finally, many conservation practices have a long pay-off period. Some will never pay off in a strict economic sense. Federal credit policies could reinforce such practices—through direct subsidized loans for conservation investments, or as a condition of eligibility for other farm-related loans.[6]

Markets and sustainability

Markets are my last example of a social invention or social institution to be judged by criteria of sustainability. Actually, markets are a complex of many such institutions, including: the pricing of farm produce and food, transportation and storage, terms of world trade, and farm commodity programs.

The most obvious sustainable markets are those in which all parties are treated justly. This statement of intent is easier than the practice, or even the definition of fairness.

Our market system is set up basically as a free market. Although we may argue that a free market will do most tasks of resource allocation as well as, or better than, an administered market, food and farm markets are not now free, nor are they likely to be in the foreseeable future.

In an increasingly interrelated world, nearly half the world's people live in socialist states where basic prices are set by decree. I noted earlier, however, that most of these nations have introduced some elements of incentive or market operations. On the other hand, nearly all the so-called market nations also have policies of protecting farm prices, subsidizing or taxing exports, restricting imports, keeping food prices low, or some mixture of these. As in the United States, such policies are often inconsistent with each other. The list of true free market nations probably includes only Hong Kong and Singapore.

Questions of market sustainability relate to the various ways markets are manipulated, by whom, and toward what goals.

In the United States, for more than fifty years, we have tried to keep farm prices stable by a series of land diversion plans and storage pro-

6. Roger Claassen, "Resolving the Farm Debt Crisis," *Economic Justice Prepare* (Washington, D.C.: Interfaith Action for Economic Justice, 1986).

grams. Sharp differences persist over what is a fair price level. Some, including myself, would target whatever price supports evolve toward family farmers, as opposed to investor-owners, and limit income support to each family's basic livelihood. However, past programs, combined with tax rules, credit programs, and inflation, have contributed to fewer and larger farms and to nonfarmer ownership.

Especially so long as we can grow more than we need, we should tie farm program benefits to good stewardship. The recent sodbuster law and conservation reserve are welcome steps.

In another departure from free markets, we have developed a whole family of domestic food distribution programs: food stamps, school lunches, meals for elderly, and supplemental food for women, infants, and children.

We and other nations give much food aid abroad. The sustainability of these programs is subject to political whim and to some extent the availability of foodstuffs. Jobs and assured income would be a more stable base for equitable access to food.

In cycles through our history, we have regulated, then deregulated, railroads. They and other shippers, often in collusion with major traders, have taken undue advantage of location, to farmers' and consumers' disadvantage.

The recent moves have been toward deregulation, resulting in lower rates where there is competition, higher rates where there is not, and abandonment of unprofitable service. In our area, several smaller cooperatives have been squeezed out, in part by unfair unit train freight rates. The next move will need to be back toward re-regulation, I hope, before too many essential services have been lost.

Vertical integration is another form of market manipulation. It involves growers and either suppliers of inputs or processors, or all three. Often such integration reaches across national boundaries, especially into the poorest nations.

In a battle for export markets, the United States, the European Economic Community, and other grain exporters are subsidizing grain exports, at great expense. The resulting very low prices undercut sustainable agricultural development in poor nations. Many of the poor nations must also try to compete in the same export market to service huge debts.

Import restrictions may be in the form of tariffs or import taxes. Increasingly, they have been quotas, or quality standards, or other nontariff measures, often to the disadvantage of the weaker trading partner. We seem poised on the edge of a trade war, with likely disastrous results for farmers everywhere.

In these and other ways, various market institutions will help determine the equity and sustainability of our agricultural systems. The form and effect of our markets are shaped by public policy decisions.

Translate the vision into policy

I have tried to outline the case that sustainable agriculture will depend in large measure on the nature of the social institutions by which we relate to the land and to each other.

The general character of these sustainable institutions is apparent. Much work remains to make clear the values on which these institutions must be based and to refine our collective vision, and then to translate our vision into acceptable practice and appropriate public policies.

Moses' instruction regarding the social institutions of his day came with God's promise: "Observe my statutes, keep my judgments . . . and you shall live in the land in security. The land shall yield its harvest; you shall eat your fill and live there secure" (Lev. 25:18-19, NEB).

It would be enough.

For study and discussion

1. Can you accept the idea that social institutions can be sustainable and that they can contribute to sustainable agriculture? Are the four institutions named in this chapter the same ones you would name as important?

2. What are the values by which you judge if a social institution is right or wrong, better or worse?

3. Name the marks of sustainable social institutions according to this chapter. Do you agree they are the right marks? What others would you add?

4. Can you cite some effects of a particular social institution on agriculture in your community—good or bad?

5. Do you agree that public policy should favor family farm agriculture? Which social institutions should be so tilted? How much? What are the trade-offs?

John Steuart Curry, 1897-1946

Family farming brings
with it certain
democratic and
community
values—widespread
ownership of economic
resources, equality of
opportunity, a belief in
the dignity of work and
the integrity of the
individual, and a concern
for the good of
community.
—Marty Strange

5. As family farms flower and fade

Margaret Epp Hiebner and LaVonne Godwin Platt

In the history of agriculture, the family farms of North America are relatively young. So, too, are the policies that have given them shape. Before European settlement, the land was cherished by native peoples who believed that no one could *own* the land they called Earth Mother. It belonged to all. Then came settlers who viewed the earth as property—to be owned by individuals, privately bought and sold, and left as inheritance to the next generation.

Land ownership shapes a new society

The English who settled in Virginia in 1607 were workers hired under a charter granted by the British Crown to the Virginia Company, a group of London merchants. The company wanted only to acquire products to sell to increase their wealth. But their workers found little to send to England. Being unfamiliar with the new land, they might not have survived the first years without the help of the native peoples who taught them how to work the soil and showed them what crops they could raise, including some marketable in England.[1]

Eventually, in order to keep the settlers in the New World, the Virginia Company allowed them some individual rights, including land ownership. When the royal colony of Virginia was formed to replace the London merchant group, they set up a system of English common law to govern the settlement. This made the settlers more dependent on each other and less dependent on the companies in England.[2]

1. John A. Garraty, *The American Nation: A History of the United States to 1877* (New York: Harper and Row, 1977), pp. 27, 28.
2. Garraty, pp. 29, 30.

Like Virginia, the other early colonies, settled by employees of English merchants, wanted to build trading posts. None of the first colonies permitted people to own land until communal ownership had failed.[3] The focus of the original colonists was trade rather than agriculture, but it was the coming of agriculture in a dispersed system of private ownership of land which allowed the colonies to flourish and which shaped the new society.

By 1682, when William Penn founded the Pennsylvania colony, the focus of colonization was on settlement rather than trade. Penn offered easy terms for land ownership, including "50-acre head rights," as earlier colonies had already done. He saw his colony as a "holy experiment" that was intended "to give liberty to any religion, and to many ways of life. . . . Penn believed in the essential goodness of human nature and framed laws with that principle in mind."[4]

Farmers form the framework of democracy

As the new nation emerged after the Declaration of Independence, land was an important issue to its leaders. Thomas Jefferson greatly influenced the new nation's land policy. He wanted the United States to be a country of small independent farmers.

Although he did not hold the view, widely accepted at the time, that private property was among the inherent rights of all citizens, Jefferson believed that government should make land available to as many people as possible. To him, agriculture was both the most fundamental and the noblest calling of humankind. He believed that "Cultivators of the earth are the most valuable citizens. They are the most vigorous, the most independent, the most virtuous, and they are tied to their country and wedded to its liberty and interests by the most lasting bonds."[5]

Jefferson's ideas set the tone for land policies during the settlement of the United States. Except for the plantations in the South and the hacienda system in the Southwest, the independent farmer became the norm for land ownership.[6] This pattern of dispersed ownership of land formed the framework for political democracy in the United States.

The pattern of widespread ownership of land was set in a series of decisions which implemented some of Jefferson's goals. The Northwest

3. Samuel Eliot Morison, *The Oxford History of the American People* (New York: Oxford University Press, 1965), pp. 48-53.
4. Morison, p. 129.
5. A. Whitney Griswold, "Jefferson's Agrarian Democracy," in Henry C. Dethloff, *Thomas Jefferson and American Democracy* (Lexington, Mass.: D. C. Heath and Co., 1971), p. 47.
6. Griswold, pp. 39-58.

Ordinance of 1785 made land available to farmers at low cost. It divided all land in the public domain into townships and ranges and provided for equal distribution of land by sections or parts of sections. The 1789 decision of the Continental Congress barred slavery from the new territories (the Ohio and part of the Mississippi river valleys), thus preventing the spread of the plantation system into the new areas.

A later series of Public Land Acts firmly established independent family farming in the West. The Preemption Acts in 1830 and 1832 gave squatters rights to land. The Homestead Act of 1862 opened the wide expanse of the Midwest and the Great Plains to settlement by family farmers. And the Reclamation Act of 1902 provided irrigation rights for small farms.

From the first, however, the policies designed to guarantee economic and political democracy in a rural society were never fully put into effect in the way that Jefferson had had in mind. The same laws that promoted family farms had loopholes that sometimes prevented the widespread distribution of land to the landless.

The Ordinance of 1785 had no acreage limits on purchases. Wealthy buyers often outbid the low-income settlers, purchasing more land and at higher prices than the settlers could afford.

The Preemption Acts improved on earlier attempts to provide widespread ownership of land by small farmers. These laws made it possible for the poor to settle the land while paying for it with the profits they earned from farming. But the Preemption Acts were also manipulated by speculators who made fraudulent claims on some land. They were avoided altogether by land companies who bought Indian lands from the federal government or Spanish and Mexican estates in new territories annexed to the United States.

Even the Homestead Act, which not only promoted western movement of American farmers but also encouraged immigration from Europe, was circumvented by land companies who acquired large holdings. Likewise, the Reclamation Act of 1902, aimed at opening new land for family farms in the West by providing irrigation rights for small farms, was from the beginning subverted by large absentee landholders.[7]

Despite these difficulties, the development of agriculture in the United States has upheld the family farm as a goal. Most farms throughout the nation's history have been family farms, where members of a family make the decisions, assume the risk, and provide most of the labor. The ways by which the nation has tried to attain the family farm ideal have often been

7. Ingolf Vogeler, *The Myth of the Family Farm* (Boulder, Colo.: Westview Press, 1981), pp. 37-66.

frustrated and only partly successful. Nonetheless, American citizens continue to recognize the close tie of widespread ownership of land to the exercise of economic and political democracy.

New machines remake the face of rural America

During the country's westward expansion, the industrial revolution was also underway. With new machines, farm production increased, and with expanding transportation, American producers began competing worldwide. Sigmund Diamond, in *Main Problems in American History*, writes of the industrialization of American society. "In the changes that transformed American society, nothing was left untouched," he says. "Land and people alike were being remade, as industrialization and urbanization changed the face of the landscape and forced millions of migrants from rural America and rural Europe to learn the techniques and disciplines of an industrial society.

"In 1870, mining and manufacturing together brought in only 14 percent of the nation's income, while farming earned 20 percent." By 1900, agriculture's share had fallen to 16 percent, exactly equal to the contribution of finance, while mining and manufacturing had each risen to 21 percent.[8]

Wheat gave value to the land

The grain trade, international in scope from its beginning, was important to farm survival. But the decisions that determined the market were largely outside farmers' control. Wheat was the main cash crop in the grain market (corn and oats were used mostly on the farms). Dan Morgan, in *Merchants of Grain*, describes the importance of the grain trade to the western movement of the frontier. "Like other aspects of the American dream," he says, "the wheat business often promoted progress and economic exploitation simultaneously. Wheat provided the economic incentive for the settling of the prairies; it gave value to the land homesteaded by landless immigrants; and it helped to finance the extension of the railroads across the continent."

Wheat also became the center of a fierce economic battle "played out according to the hard rules of nineteenth-century capitalism." From this early struggle among farmers, millers, traders, and exporters for their share of the world wheat markets, farmers soon found that the "advan-

8. Howard Quint, Milton Cantor, and Dean Albertson, eds., *Main Problems in American History* (Homewood, Ill.: Dorsey Press, 1972), Vol. 2, p. 27.

tage always went to those who controlled the storage and transportation of grain."[9]

Tied too tight by the railroad lines

Railroads held the key to agricultural expansion, attracting settlers to the West. Distances were shortened and it became cheaper to ship grain and goods than it had been when settlers had to take their products to a river town to be transported by barge.

Private and government financing of railroads gave the wealthy opportunity to increase their capital. Farmers, on the other hand, became dependent on the middlemen between them and the source of capital to keep their products moving and the market open. The farmers became less self-reliant, less in control.[10]

Farmers tended to blame their problems on railroads and high interest rates, among other things, and political parties were formed to address these grievances. As a result, lawmakers at both state and national levels drew up regulations to govern railroads.[11]

Farm activists enter politics

Together with other farmer groups, the populist movement[12] developed in the late nineteenth century. The influence of these grassroots efforts should not be underestimated. Winning local elections and carrying out a national program, the populists and other groups drew attention to agricultural disadvantages. They demanded immediate solutions to their problems.

The populists, according to Theodore Saloutos, "recognized that farmers were fighting with backs to the wall in an effort to preserve their way of life from forces that threatened to uproot it." The agricultural frontier was disappearing and the farm family was falling apart. Farmers were not making money. On the other hand, cities were growing. Business was good for large corporations. But at the same time, corrupt political machines were in control and more and more people were immigrating to the United States. "The America they knew or believed they knew," says Saloutos, "was being ground to bits by a new, foreign, and frightening America they did not understand."[13]

9. Dan Morgan, *Merchants of Grain* (New York: Penguin Books, 1980), pp. 76-78.

10. Quint, Cantor, and Albertson, pp. 411-14.

11. John H. Dicks, "Populist Party," *The Encyclopedia Americana* (New York: Americana Corp., 1973), Vol. 21, p. 559.

12. The Populist Party of the late 1800s should not be confused with the recently organized far right extremist group that uses the same name.

13. Quint, Cantor, and Albertson, p. 87.

Populists wanted the federal government to pump more money into circulation in order to raise farm prices and improve the agricultural economy. They also thought that the government should own the railroads, as well as the telephone and telegraph lines. They said that taxation should be less burdensome for the farmer and levied more on those with large incomes. The populists favored land ownership because humankind "was placed on earth by the laws of God and nature, not by those of any political or economic system." According to them, families were entitled to as much land as they needed to make a living. It was the government's duty to see to it that they got it.[14]

This movement brought people closer to their government. Populist leaders, such as William Jennings Bryan, had great influence. According to the historian Samuel Eliot Morison, the populists "registered a deep lying unrest that would presently break forth and carry William Jennings Bryan to prominence, Theodore Roosevelt to achievement, and Woodrow Wilson to the presidency."[15] The ideas of the movement became embedded in Midwest philosophy and practice so that even after the movement ended, the effects lingered on. Under both Theodore Roosevelt and Woodrow Wilson, many of their demands were met. President Wilson's New Freedom policy had its roots in an agrarian past and in populism. In the 1920s and '30s, these ideas appeared in the platforms of both parties.

Help from the New Deal and ruin

After World War I and the economic collapse of the late '20s and early '30s, pivotal decisions were made that changed the course of the nation's agriculture. Although President Hoover tried to address the problems of the time, creating the Federal Farm Board which marked the beginning of government involvement in farm pricing, he couldn't begin to stem the tide of economic decline. When Franklin Roosevelt became president, he limited the supply of farm commodities in order to increase prices. Early in his administration, Congress enacted a farm policy that in many respects still operates in the 1980s.

The farm policy of the 1930s helped the nation out of the depression. It also helped certain individual farmers, but it ruined others. The New Deal, as Roosevelt called his domestic policy programs, established a subsidy payment program for landowners who agreed to plant less, thereby raising prices for the commodities but requiring less labor to work the farms.

14. Quint, Cantor, and Albertson, p. 90.
15. Morison, p. 742.

It was intended that landlords would share the subsidy payments with their tenants. Many landlords abided by the law, but others did not. A common practice among Southern landlords, especially those who had hired black tenant farmers, was to keep the entire subsidy payments. Often the payments were used by owners to mechanize their farms, reducing the need for farm laborers even further. One of the main net effects of the policy was the concentration of land ownership in fewer and fewer hands.

FDR's Secretary of Agriculture, Henry A. Wallace, decried the plight of agriculture, calling it "a philanthropic enterprise" in which everyone profited except the working farmer. Wallace declared that if American farmers were to feed all the hungry people in the world, "hundreds of thousands of American farm families would be destroyed." He went on to say that "the condition of greater balance and justice we now seek ... can certainly not be obtained by arranging that everybody work under the profit system except the farmer."[16]

Wallace was speaking during a time when, more and more, the land was being cared for by tenants; ownership was in fewer and fewer hands. The native people who had cherished the land were on desolate reservations; the homesteaders and other landowners, having long experienced outside control by the railroad and large grain companies, were at that time faced with the economic depression of the 1930s. Many had lost their land to larger, wealthier nonresident owners. Farm policies that had upheld the ideals of Jefferson were changed to create a very different structure of farming. The family farm that had been the norm as a result of Jeffersonian policies faced an uncertain future.

Frederick H. Buttell, a sociologist, sees the decline of the family farm rooted in the growing use of tractors and chemicals, a trend that began in the late 1930s. Farm prices rose and farm incomes became steadier with the coming of commodity programs. But such progress did not always spell success. "Mechanical and biochemical technologies placed a premium on farmers' access to credit, which in turn benefited large farmers," says Buttell. "The overall result was a spectacular decline in the number of farms, especially small ones."[17]

Sending surplus crops overseas

Although government intervention in the farm economy has continued in the half-century since it was begun, these policies have changed through

16. Quint, Cantor, and Albertson, pp. 264-65.
17. Frederick H. Buttell, "Agricultural Land Reform in America," in Charles C. Geisler and Frank J. Popper, *Land Reform, American Style* (Bowman & Allanheld, 1984), p. 57.

the years to reflect changing economic, political, and social conditions worldwide. Right after World War II, food shipments from North America helped to prevent famine in the war-torn nations of Europe and Asia. From 1945 to 1949, the United States supplied half of the world wheat trade. By the late 1940s, the nation had a tremendous surplus and by 1950, the U.S. Department of Agriculture "had become a vast planning agency that reached into every rural county of America with credit, crop insurance, scientific advice, and farm programs that controlled how much farmers grew and how much they received for their grain."[18]

American grain exports were promoted by the U.S. government and the international grain companies. In 1954, Congress passed Public Law 480 to organize an ongoing system of food exports in a three-fold attempt to promote the foreign policy of the United States, combat hunger, and dispose of surpluses.

P.L. 480 gave foreign governments authority to purchase American farm commodities with American loans that they could pay back over a long term. This interaction of the U.S. export and import economy, as well as the role of agricultural products in political and military diplomacy between the United States and other nations, and the needs of developing nations dependent on food aid have affected the health of the American farm economy in the past three decades.[19]

In the early 1970s, several factors combined to make American products attractive overseas, thus greatly increasing grain sales. Responsible for this growth were the devaluation of the American dollar, low interest loans to U.S. corporations to start overseas processing plants for livestock feed, and easy loans to developing countries to expand imports. A decision by Russia to increase its livestock herds led to the single largest sale of grain by the U.S. All this was helped along by high oil prices that put money into circulation in the world banking system.

Early in the 1980s, the situation changed, influenced by the drop in oil prices. The dollar rose in value. Countries that had been importers of American farm products became self-sufficient in agriculture. Other countries increased their production to enter the export market, and American commodities lost their competitive price advantage. In 1982, the world market for agricultural raw materials fell all at once, in a depression brought about by the stronger U.S. dollar and higher interest rates being imposed on debtor nations. After a peak for U.S. exports in 1981, the value of American farm exports steadily dropped each year for the next five years.

18. Morgan, p. 143.
19. Morgan, pp. 146ff.

Laws and greed sap family farms

On the domestic scene, the farm economy of the '80s was in many ways a reversal of the conditions of the '70s. Through most of the '70s, farmland values were high, credit was easy, technological advancements were encouraged, and loans for expansion were readily given.

Those policies that favored expansion and high cost agriculture led a generation of American farmers into dire straits. In 1982, Marty Strange, co-director of the Center for Rural Affairs, said that "the 1970s are going to go down as the decade of unprecedented greed in American agriculture. People started buying more land and paying more than it was worth, more than they could afford to pay for it by farming it." He blamed the government for the deepening crisis. "They responded with more credit, more debt. They created a $10 billion Economic Emergency Loan Program (1978) to be run by the Farmers Home Administration. For the first time in history, federal farm credit [through FmHA] was provided to farms that were larger than the family farm and did not need to rely on farm income."[20]

When interest rates rose, beginning in 1979, and land values dropped in 1982, many people who had borrowed money against land in order to expand their farm operation couldn't meet their payments. Other farmers hit by drought in 1980 or 1983 also suffered.

A concern for efficiency has also affected family farming. After 1950, agricultural production increased sharply, but at an expense to the economy and the environment, costs often ignored by usual accounting procedures. Described as an efficient system because of its increase in production, the industrialization of American agriculture has had negative effects as well. Michael Perelman, in *Farming for Profit in a Hungry World*, says, "A realistic measure of the 'efficiency' of a system must be based on consideration of its over-all impact on the present quality of life as well as its potential for the future."[21]

Many of the changes in family farming in recent years have come about because of factors outside agriculture. Our federal tax system and farm credit policies have sometimes been major threats to family farms. In recent years, tax laws have encouraged growth and expansion, led to overproduction and lower prices, stimulated an increase in absentee ownership, favored certain kinds of farm assets over others, and given greater benefits to capital-intensive agricultural operations than to labor-inten-

20. Marty Strange, "Taking Back Control of American Agriculture," speech to the National Catholic Rural Life Conference, 1982, edited by Sandra Pollard.
21. Michael Perelman, *Farming for Profit in a Hungry World* (Montclair, N. J.: Allanheld, Osmun & Co., 1977), p. 3.

sive farmers. As a result, more and more farm assets are falling under the control of a shrinking number of high income owners.[22]

Without a doubt, government intervention is a permanent factor in the agriculture of the nation. The role of government can be either positive or negative in determining the future of agriculture. Family farmers who recognize that in our society individuals have a role in shaping policy will seek ways to promote the role of family farms as they relate to government policymakers.

Families and women facing changes

Throughout the history of the United States, family farming has been a way of life that has integrated values of caring for the land and for other people. The last one hundred years, however, have drastically altered the character of family farms. Today, 92 percent of American farm families have off-farm income. Because they have dual responsibilities of farm and off-farm work, the family structure and activity is changed. They tend to be less active in the communities where they live and work—there isn't enough time.[23]

In a Missouri study, Judith Heffernan found that one-fourth of the women contributed at least half of the family's total income from their nonfarm job. Women in her study suffered from stress and health-related problems such as depression, sleeping and eating disorders, and an increase in smoking and drinking. Due to lack of finances, their families cut back on medical insurance and other services. Their children showed evidence of increased anxieties and fears, demands for attention, crying, and rebelliousness. The children's school grades fell. The use of alcohol by teenagers in the families increased. In order to help the family budget, many of the teenagers did not buy needed shoes and clothing.[24]

Perhaps the most notable overall change in the farm family has come to the farm woman. In the past, a woman's routine was almost totally related to the farm and her family. She had to be involved in every aspect of the farm, from making meals and caring for the family to running errands for her husband, helping with the livestock and sometimes the field work. Her work was classified as supportive. Working almost always in the home setting, she often felt isolated. Her social life was the church, quilting bees, or school functions that involved other farm families.

22. "Economics, Statistics, and Cooperative Services," *Structure Issues in American Agriculture* (United States Department of Agriculture AER No. 438, November 1979), p. 152.
23. Judith Bortner Heffernan, Hearing Before the Committee on Agriculture, U.S. House of Representatives, May 6, 1985.
24. J. B. Heffernan.

Women in the past also contributed financially to the family income, selling their poultry and creamery produce in town. Often teenage daughters in farm families also contributed to the family income by working as hired girls on other farms.

With mechanization and specialization in agriculture, the farm woman's role continues to be vital. She often helps operate machinery, does the bookkeeping—which is now more complex, and still holds the family together. Often she also takes on employment off the farm. Neighbors now have less need of each other, so her social life is no longer necessarily only with other farm women.

Church has a stake in family farm health

Changes in agriculture have not only brought change to farm families, but also to the small communities and to the rural churches of which these families are members. Rural membership has dropped in Mennonite churches, as it has in the churches of other denominations.

From the beginning, Mennonites in North America were largely a rural people. In 1683, the first group of Mennonites and Quakers arrived in North America and settled at Germantown, Pennsylvania. Writing in *Land, Piety, Peoplehood*, Richard K. MacMaster says that in their quest for land, Mennonites were motivated by a strong concept of family and family bonds. "The family was the most basic of social units," he says of the eighteenth-century Mennonites and Amish in North America. As they moved from their first frontier settlements in eastern Pennsylvania, they did so partly in order to have enough acreage that they could provide viable farms for their sons and daughters when they divided their estates.[25]

For Mennonites, faith, land, and family were intertwined, and so they settled where the family farm was the norm. Later migrations of Mennonites, after the Homestead Act of 1862, did the same thing. For the most part, until perhaps the last generation, Mennonites were able to hold to their traditions and beliefs and continue their farming mode under a government policy that accommodated their style of living and farming. Then they, too, got caught up in the mechanization, the government policies, and other conditions that affected their way of life.

For Mennonites, as well as many other family farmers, farming has been seen as almost a sacred vocation. Theirs has been a close involvement with the land. Their commitment to stewardship has affected the

---

25. Richard K. MacMaster, *Land, Piety, and Peoplehood* (Scottdale, Pa.: Herald Press, 1985), p. 111.

way they used the soil. At the same time, they viewed it as their mission to feed America and the world. With all their good intentions and good motives, some misused and overused the land.

The family farm pattern in American agriculture, slowly declining for more than half a century, appears now to require a new sense of direction, or perhaps a sense of redirection, if it is to survive. Mennonites and other people who have been a part of the family farm structure are at a juncture in their history—indeed, in their way of life. Not only farmers and rural people, but urban people as well, have been shaped by family farm values and have depended on that pattern of life for a sense of direction. Now is a time when we must carefully consider our responses. Do we hang on tighter to old values or let go? Do we resist change or try to give it shape? If we want to affect our own future, what is the next step?

Restoring a right relationship with the land

Surely, now is the time to look again at the values and practices of family farming. Marty Strange has described family farms as:

> farms owned and operated by working farmers whose children learn responsibility by growing up in an environment where work and play go together, where taking care of the land is not just good economics but doing what's right, and where the loss of a neighbor is an occasion of sorrow more than of opportunity to enlarge the farm.[26]

Does this description of a family farm fit our view? If it does, can we build policies consistent with that perspective? Can we proceed on a course charted carefully and prayerfully in line with our Judeo-Christian faith and a land stewardship ethic that borrows from the native peoples who once cherished this land?

Doing so may help us restore our relationship to the land, remembering that from the beginning God gave humankind a duty to the land: "to till it and keep it" (Gen. 2:15b).

For study and discussion

1. Compare the current political structure of the New England states with the political structure of the southern states by looking at the type of agricultural system each region had in its years of development. Does the long tradition of town meetings in the New England states relate to their dispersed land ownership pattern of family farms?

26. Marty Strange, "Why Save the Family Farm?" *Catholic Rural Life* (Feb. 1985), p. 17.

2. In what ways does widespread ownership of land promote a strong economic and political democracy?

3. How might our methods of farming change if, in what we call our "sacred vocation," we understood "the world must be fed," rather than "we must feed the world?"

4. Do farmer-owned and operated cooperatives enable farmers to have more control over their markets and income than when they sell to and buy from industrial agriculture corporations?

5. Is there a difference in the stewardship of large agricultural units compared to smaller family-sized units, particularly in the use of chemicals and insecticides? What do we need to do to achieve a more responsible use of the earth that furnishes our food and fiber?

6. Within this chapter a number of questions are raised. Discuss these questions and consider how they relate to your view of the role of family farms in America.

It is the nature of any
organic pattern to be
contained within a larger
one. And so a good
solution in one pattern
preserves the integrity of
the pattern that contains
it. A good agricultural
solution, for example,
would not pollute or
erode a watershed. What
is good for the water is
good for the ground,
what is good for the
ground is good for
animals, what is good for
animals is good for
people, what is good for
people is good for the air,
what is good for the air
is good for the water. And
vice versa.
—Wendell Berry

6. Good farmers on family farms

Mark Epp

Who is a good farmer in today's world? What kind of farmer do others see as a model? How do farmers define success?

Is the way we identify a good farmer a sign of how we put our faith into our farming? On what do we base our answers: Christian principles or "the gospel according to *Successful Farming?*"

How farmers see themselves

Production is the most common measure farmers apply to each other's farming. Farmers always compare yields—bushels per acre, tons per acre, number of head of livestock marketed per year, and pounds of milk sold per cow. They watch these numbers closely. When a farmer hauls many bushels of grain off his farm at harvest, someone will say, "He's really a good farmer."

Any sign of prosperity is another gauge of the good farmer that some use. Many notice a neighbor's new equipment. A shiny, new tractor means that the farmer is doing all right. The newer the line of equipment, the greater the respect the farmer gets from others. Farmers with older equipment are thought of as poorer farmers.

Weed-free crops often measure the worth of a farmer. To some people, weedy fields mean that a farmer isn't doing a good job. Such a notion is widespread throughout the agribusiness community. "Your fields are a statement about the way you farm," says Ciba-Geigy in promoting its herbicides. "Two things are at stake when you put your corn or soybeans in each spring. Your livelihood. And your pride."[1] When farmers visit,

1. *Farmland News*, advertisement, Vol. 53, No. 2, p. 16.

weeds receive more attention than soil erosion or the waste of irrigation water. Hardly anyone talks about damage to the land that cannot be seen.

Among grain farmers, *the amount of land owned or farmed* is often considered to be an important ingredient of success. Big farms are admired. Neighbors point to them as examples of success, and many farmers aspire to that kind of reputation by expanding the size of their farms.

Still another measure of success is the *use of labor-saving technology*. Possession of equipment or technology is valued in and of itself, but the consequences—a farmer being able to spend more time away from the farm because of labor-saving technology—is also a sign of doing things right.

Choosing to be exploiters or stewards

These five measures that farmers use among themselves to test whether they are doing a good job gain support from the judgments of society in general. Today we live in a world in which the operative ethic is profit-taking—taking from the land as much as it can possibly bear. A student in the first day of class in Agronomy 101 learns that production is all that matters. Land and nature must be made to produce.

Today's agricultural ethic says that those who are productive and generate wealth are good farmers. Those who are not making a profit are poor farmers. Few people ever question the merits of a system that allows some to grow wealthy and leads others into bankruptcy. Yet thousands of decisions are made all the time as if the economic constraints were fixed and even right.

If a decision proves successful by the standards of today's society, it is deemed the right decision—even morally right. We use religious backing to support our notion that getting the most is good, whether it is in bushels or money. We say that responsible stewardship is using all the resources at our disposal. Anything less is seen as making unwise use of our God-given talents, even squandering our resources in a way that will impoverish the nation.

We have created an ethic of extraction rather than stewardship. In *The Unsettling of America*, the Kentucky farmer-poet Wendell Berry contrasts these points of view, using visual images of the exploiter and the nurturer.

> The standard of the exploiter is efficiency; the standard of the nurturer is care. The exploiter's goal is money, profit; the nurturer's goal is health—his land's health, his own, his family's, his commu-

nity's, his country's. Whereas the exploiter asks of a piece of land only how much and how quickly it can be made to produce, the nurturer asks a question that is much more complex and difficult: What is its carrying capacity? (That is: How much can be taken from it without diminishing it? What can it produce dependably for an indefinite time?) The exploiter wishes to earn as much as possible by as little work as possible; the nurturer expects, certainly, to have a decent living from his work, but his characteristic wish is to work as well as possible.[2]

At times, most farmers feel and act like the nurturer. Planting the crops, watching the young plants emerge, and carefully tending all phases of development are nurturing acts. Yet that is not the main reason we do it. An underlying motive involves material gain—we want to take from the land. That is more like the exploiter. At any rate, we must admit that we do not generally base our decisions on a piece of land's carrying capacity, the mark of the nurturer.

How do we relate these standards to our Christian faith? In today's prevailing mindset for profit-taking, greed is elevated to a virtue, and the standards of the exploiter are seen as good. This stands in sharp contrast to Christian teachings that greed is a vice, and stewardship, sharing, and nurturing are virtues. Because we want to serve both God and mammon, we have made our faith bend to include the qualities of both the nurturer and the exploiter. Thus we strive to be successful by society's standard of profit-seeking and also seek to do good work for the Lord.

If we are to be truthful, we need to face the fact that these are opposing positions. Does God see sharing as giving from an abundance derived through profit-taking and greed, or as joint ownership with God of property and resources? What does the Bible say about stewardship and our responsibility to God's creation? Can biblical principles guide Christian farmers to make wise choices as we decide what it means to be a good farmer?

Farming the land God owns

From Ron Guengerich's earlier discussion of Genesis 1 and 2, it is clear that we are not set apart from creation in the way that we sometimes think. Rather we are born of the soil—it sustains us and gives us life. It is impossible for human beings to maintain life apart from the soil or the rest of God's creation. Both the Old and New Testaments assume the

2. Wendell Berry, *The Unsettling of America: Culture and Agriculture* (San Francisco: Sierra Club, 1977), pp. 7-8.

unity of creation and emphasize the decisive role people play in the process of creation. According to the Bible, creation is all one piece.[3]

However, because we are created in the image of God, we have a special responsibility and relationship to creation. To be in the image of God means that we have a particular task to perform. God, the creator and owner, places humanity as trustee and steward. We are the custodians and conservers of the land for all creation, acting as God's caretakers on earth. To be a part of creation, yet created in God's image, places a tremendous responsibility on humankind. More than any other creature, we have the power to control the earth's destiny.

William Aiken, an environmental ethicist, poses the question of our struggle with the elements in dramatic terms. "Are we stewards of the good earth who should lovingly use our knowledge to enhance Nature's richness, stability and health, or are we rapacious conquerors of a clever, obstinate, wild and useless Enemy which we must enslave to serve our desires?"[4]

If our dominion over the earth is rightly understood as that of being God's representative here on earth, we will work to nurture and sustain all of creation and to maintain the earth's productivity forever. To have dominion over the earth is not to dominate it.

But some say that being God's steward means we are responsible to produce bumper yields at any cost in order to feed people. Some say that fallowing land is a sign of idleness and wastefulness. Some say that modern farming is a gift from God, and that God has given us rich agriculture as a blessing. Should we ever question the consequences of continuous cropping which pressures the land for every grain it can produce?

Through many examples of ruined agricultural land, history cries out to us to question our desire to produce without limit. God warned the Israelites about the ecological consequences of ignoring the sabbatical year and putting their trust elsewhere:

> So devastated will I leave the land that your very enemies who come to live there will stand aghast at the sight of it. You yourselves I will scatter among the nations at the point of my drawn sword, leaving your countryside desolate and your cities deserted. Then shall the land retrieve its lost sabbaths during all the time it lies waste, while

3. C. Dean Freudenberger, *Food for Tomorrow* (Minneapolis: Augsburg Publishing House, 1984), p. 82.

4. William Aiken, "Value Conflicts in Agriculture," *Agriculture and Human Values*, Vol. 1, No. 1 (Winter 1984), p. 26.

you are in the land of your enemies; then shall the land have rest and make up for its sabbaths during all the time that it lies desolate, enjoying the rest that you would not let it have on the sabbaths when you lived there (Lev. 26:32-35, New American Bible).

We have chosen to believe in technology and our own practices rather than to learn lessons from creation and to trust in God. Perhaps it is too early to see all the adverse effects of modern agriculture in North America. But with our increased dependence on fossil fuel and on mining the earth's resources for agricultural production, it will become clear in time that there are ecological consequences to that sin just as there were when Adam and Eve disobeyed God and ate the forbidden fruit.

While the sabbatical year was intended to keep the land from being misused by the people who occupied it, the Jubilee year was a provision that allowed people who had lost their land for one reason or another to return to it every fifty years.[5] As the rightful owner of the land, God was concerned that all people had access to the land for life and livelihood.

Consecrate the fiftieth year and proclaim liberty throughout the land to all its inhabitants. It shall be a jubilee for you; each one of you is to return to his family property and each to his own clan. The fiftieth year shall be a jubilee for you; do not sow and do not reap what grows of itself or harvest the untended vines. For it is a jubilee and is to be holy for you; eat only what is taken directly from the fields. In this Year of Jubilee everyone is to return to his own property (Lev. 25:10-13, New International Version).

The land is God's gift to us. But God is still the owner and has entrusted the land not only to us, but to all people. The land was not meant to be used by a few to make a profit at the expense of others. The notion that a good farmer is one who owns a large amount of land needs to be examined in light of the Jubilee concept. In the biblical context, good farmers are more concerned about involving larger numbers of people with the land than they are about accumulating as many acres as possible for themselves.

Similarly, we do not need to make high profits in order to be able to share. We may feel that we are doing God's work when we are able to share as a result of our abundant production, and in one sense that may be so. But the practice of gleaning as described in the Old Testament sheds important light on other ways to share.

5. John Hart, *The Spirit of the Earth* (New York: Paulist Press, 1984), p. 74.

When you reap the harvest of your land, you shall not be so thorough that you reap the field to its very edge, nor shall you glean the stray ears of grain. Likewise, you shall not pick your vineyard bare, nor gather up the grapes that have fallen. These things you shall leave for the poor and the alien. I, the Lord, am your God (Lev. 19:9-10, New American Bible).

Two points stand out: 1) the fruits of production (food) are meant for all people; and 2) the landowner (farmer) should not be overly concerned with getting the most from the fields, but rather with making sure people have access to life-giving resources. Notice that the writer says, "you shall not be so thorough that you reap to its very edge." Responsible stewardship does not mean that we squeeze every bushel of produce out of the land, but rather that we make sure that God's gifts to us are shared by all.

The image of gleaning was familiar to everyone during Old Testament times, but it carries little meaning in our society today. However, we can apply the concept to our lives. One example for today's farming would be to recognize our overuse of limited resources on our land to pressure production, when these resources could be shared more evenly to produce adequate food around the world. This means we should consider how our excessive demand for petroleum in North America tends to overprice it for use by the farmers of many developing nations. We need to think of a good farmer in our country as one who does not reap to the very edge of the field in order to have a surplus to sell but rather uses resources and land in such a way that all people, even those in other parts of the world, benefit.

Looking for the link between faith and farming

What are the lessons that can be learned from exploring these biblical teachings? Can we see a link between faith and farming?

We can contrast biblical principles with today's common view in three ways. The prevailing views today say that a good farmer:

- makes the land produce as much as possible year after year,
- acquires as many acres as possible, and
- shares with others from the abundance of the harvests.

The Old Testament writers would say that a good farmer:

- cares for and sustains the land, allowing it to rest,
- makes sure people have access to the land, and
- uses the land, productive resources, and fruits of the harvest in such a way that everyone benefits.

While not so explicit in the New Testament, land themes of the Old Testament are the basis for many of the teachings and parables of Jesus. His teachings about wealth and riches, in particular, dealt with responsibility both to the land and to the society that went along with ownership of land. As we see the Jubilee concept spelled out in the rules of society for land use in the Old Testament, we see it fulfilled in the incarnation of Jesus in the New Testament.

In 1982, Mennonite farmers in Ontario were surveyed to discover their land use practices, their attitudes toward trends in agriculture, and the principles by which they make decisions about land use. A majority—86 percent—said that their faith affects the way they farm and 80 percent believed that the Bible has a good deal to say about the use of resources. However, a majority also said that the church should *not* become more involved nor give more leadership in farm-related issues. They preferred to look elsewhere for help in making decisions about land use.[6]

Why would we prefer to look elsewhere? Could it be that by examining Scripture we will be confronted with principles we are not following? We are frightened at the prospect of discovering that what is the most profitable may not be morally right. Certainly, modern agriculture as we know it in North America, coupled with our sense of mission to "feed the world," has become quite profitable for some.

At the moment, however, modern agriculture isn't enjoying the best of times and many farmers are struggling financially. Perhaps now is the time to reexamine principles of faith and relate them directly to our farming operations.

Good farmers apply biblical principles

It is clear that the standards farmers use to evaluate themselves and each other are not always consistent with biblical principles. We need to replace the present standards with measurements that more closely reflect the will of God. When we hear farmers described as good farmers because they produced high yielding crops or bought another quarter section, can we introduce another list of criteria into the conversation—a list that is based on lessons learned from biblical teaching?

The following discussion outlines five principles of good farming for today based on biblical precepts. These five principles fit together like a puzzle; doing one will make it possible to act on the others as well. At the same time, it will help us build a kind of agriculture and a lifestyle which models God's plan for creation.

6. Gordon Hunsberger, "Farming by Faith," *Seeds*, Vol. 3, No. 1 (Sept. 1983), p. 16.

What are the marks of a good farmer who applies biblical principles?

1. A good farmer *involves the entire family in the farming operation in meaningful ways*. Some farm work should allow all members of the family to take part. Such activities could include harvesting strawberries, picking cherries, butchering chickens, irrigating, gardening, and choring livestock. The farm should also include activities for which separate members of the family are given full responsibility. Such a farm operation is designed to promote values of family togetherness and at the same time to develop and strengthen individual responsibility and self-worth. Each member will feel closely tied to the ongoing functions of the farm and will contribute according to his or her abilities.

Farms based on biblical principles may be contrasted with farms that are organized primarily to convert agricultural products into cash. On these specialized farms, one person usually does the bulk of the planning and work, while other members of the family fill secondary or supportive roles. Such farms may be more efficient in narrow economic terms, but they have important social and environmental shortcomings.

A diversified farm, however, not merely benefits the family and its members, but rather it also makes good agricultural and environmental sense. Good farmers treat the farm not only as a business but also as a home. At the same time, good farmers do not view the family farm as an end in itself. Instead, good farming helps the family to see itself as a springboard, a place to learn and practice the kind of relationships that can then be extended to other people, both on the farm through shared work experiences and in the world community with those whose lives interact with ours.

2. A good farmer *creates jobs on the farm rather than replacing jobs through mechanization*. When farm jobs are replaced, it is primarily done by additions of horsepower or chemicals. Both depend totally on limited resources and damage the soil and the environment in a variety of ways. But just as important are the human and social costs of these job replacements. Often the first jobs eliminated are those of family members. When a wife or children take an off-farm job, they may become partially removed from the farm. Neighbors become more scattered when, because of mechanization, one farmer can now farm more acres. In short, more and more people are separated from the land—the source of life and livelihood. As we see in the call for a year of Jubilee, the Bible pointed out God's concern when people became separated from the land. It should be our concern as well.

Farmers can start at home by involving family members and local workers. Before buying the new bale loader/stacker, for example, the farmer might consider what jobs could be provided instead for local young people. Instead of applying herbicide on the bean field, the farmer could hire workers to walk the field to weed it. Nearby urban people could be hired to do some kinds of jobs in the farm operation. Here again, a farm operation can be designed to provide both environmental and social benefits. A good farmer is measured not by how much time is spent away from the farm because of using large, shiny new equipment, but by the number of people actively and meaningfully at work on the farm.

3. A good farmer *produces high quality food, feed, and/or fiber rather than merely a commodity to be traded for cash.* Unfortunately, in most cases, our market economy is incapable of recognizing quality differences. So, it only rewards the producer for volume. In selling a bushel of grain, no price distinctions are made for protein content, pesticide residues, or other unseen quality factors. But as good farmers, we should visualize our products being used by our families and neighbors. Even if it means less cash in our pockets, we should stop being producers only for the unseen and impersonal marketplace.

4. A good farmer *is more concerned about the long-term health of the land than about maximizing production and profit.* Too many farmers have believed that healthy land and high profits can be achieved at the same time. We must recognize clearly that saturating the land with fossil fuel-based products in order to bolster production is not healthy. High yields in the short run are not necessarily a sign of healthy agriculture in the long run. We must come to understand good farming in terms of its ability to sustain itself over time. In the sabbatical tradition, a good farmer allows land to rest periodically and rotates cash and grain crops with noncash legumes and pasture. Applying the biblical concept of gleaning, a good farmer does not "reap to the very edge of the field," but uses shelter belts, grass waterways, terraces, and wide fencerows to maintain the land and the environment.

5. A good farmer *uses the land and other productive resources in a way that benefits all of society and future generations.* In the same way that a farmer has a responsibility first to the land and environment, a farmer also has a primary responsibility to take care of the public good, now and in the future. It is dangerous to assume that what is good for the individual farmer is good for everyone. We all know that individuals don't necessarily make decisions that are in the public interest. We also know from the Bible that God deeply desires access to and benefit from the land for all people. We should not think that we have fulfilled our responsibility to others by giving to charity out of our abundance.

It is important that we implement the biblical concepts and practices of gleaning and Jubilee in our farming operations. Can we explore ways that good farmers might seek to involve street people, the unemployed, refugees, and other landless peoples in meaningful work together with them on their farms?

Good farmers don't care to farm more acres, but rather see their neighbor as much more important to them than their neighbor's land. And, finally, good farmers do not overuse or abuse limited productive resources (water, oil, air, and minerals). Rather, they create an operation that can be sustainable for future generations.

These principles are already being practiced on some of our North American farms and could be applied in ever more creative ways. These practices should be encouraged, and we should meet together to rediscover the principles outlined for us in the biblical record. By doing so, we can begin to use our faith to guide our decisions and replace the ethic of profit-taking with an ethic of true stewardship.

I am convinced that we must do this in community. We cannot practice good farming and true stewardship by ourselves on "our" farms without engaging our neighbors, our community, and our congregation in the process. These principles have great merit in themselves if practiced on our individual farms, but they can only reach their full potential or accomplish God's purposes when a group of people covenant to put their faith into action.

For study and discussion

1. What are common ways of judging good farmers in your community? Are they more in line with biblical principles or with principles from the "gospel according to *Successful Farming*"?

2. Is it possible to be faithful to biblical teachings, while at the same time practicing modern farming as we know it?

3. Do you think the Bible has useful guidelines for making decisions about the way in which we farm? If so, list several guidelines that you are following or have followed. What other areas of your farming could be changed to be more consistent?

4. The Bible points out that we are to be God's caretakers here on earth. If we fail or refuse to do that in the manner described, can that be called a *sin?* (Is modern farming a sin?)

5. Do you think that being faithful to God may sometimes mean that we will make agricultural decisions that will not be the most productive in the short run? Why?

Fewer farms mean fewer farm service jobs and more people wanting them. Fewer jobs mean less money spent, so nonfarm business suffers as well. And as families leave to look for work elsewhere, they leave behind schools without students, churches without congregations and towns without citizens. Ten 3,000-acre farms may produce the same amount of food as one hundred 300-acre farms, but one hundred 300-acre farms will keep a community the size of Walthill [Nebraska, population 900] happy and healthy.

—J. Tevere MacFadyen

7. Family farms make good communities

Leon C. Neher

For years after being born, each child must be nurtured by others. Even as adults, we find we cannot live a full life without the help of other people and without being in touch with the fruit of our natural and spiritual environment. We cannot pull ourselves up by our own bootstraps. To be truly human is to live in relationship with other people, with our God, and with God's creation.

At the heart of meaningful human living is relationship. Indeed, to live or not to live in the context of human and/or environmental relationships is not a choice we make. It was made for us—by our Creator. We accept that fact, and live. We can refuse it, and die. Or, we can try to choose some kind of middle ground and live in unending frustration.

Everything affects every other thing

All of life is tied together as if it were a giant web. No part hangs by itself. Everything is a part of every other thing. Nothing can be changed without all other parts of the web being touched, be it ever so small or seemingly unimportant. Change agriculture and every other part of society will in turn be changed.

An example of the impact of seemingly small events on cultures and lifestyles is the invention of barbed wire.[1] That seemed of no importance, but it made the fencing of the North American Great Plains possible. Barbed wire closed the open range and set property boundaries in place. It made agriculture on the Plains possible. This, in turn, tolled the death knell of the way of life of the nomadic Plains Indians, forcing them into a

---

1. W. P. Webb, *The Great Plains* (Chicago: Ginn & Co., 1931), pp. 270 ff.

degrading existence on the reservations.

Ironically, as John Collier reminds us, the Indians had an ingredient that "the world must have again, lest it die."[2] That lost item is "reverence and passion for human personality, joined with the ancient lost reverence and passion for the earth and its web of life."[3]

Human need supplied by farming

Jesus said something about relationships in John 10:10, "I came that they may have life, and have it abundantly."

That is what human culture, with all its values, norms, and folkways, is about. Through relationships, we form families, transfer information, establish and maintain order, produce and distribute economic goods, and find purpose in our lives. If we mess up at any one of these points, the whole cultural nest is fouled. If we do it right, the whole world is made a little better.

One of the purposes of the farm and its related institutions is quite simple: they produce food and fiber and see that these products are distributed to all points of human need. Without agriculture's proper functioning, people suffer.

This fact may seem so trite as to deserve no mention. Yet such basic facts have often been forgotten and thus the evils of famine and war have come to us. We highly trained specialists who learn more and more about less and less may be in the midst of such a period today!

As long as our society thinks milk comes from cartons, meat from coolers, or bread from supermarkets, we need to go back to our kindergarten lesson on relationships. As long as we think it does not matter who owns the land, how it is tilled, what is grown, or how food is processed and distributed, we are headed for colossal chaos and death. A Chinese proverb says, "If you do not change your course of direction, you are liable to get to where you are headed." Let us change course!

Our brokenness of wrong ideas

While well formed and good working relationships provide the basis for wholeness of life, relationships that don't work can lead to sickness in society and personal tragedy. These can stifle the human spirit, marring our very likeness to God. Relational ties, with the almost supernatural powers of tradition, *can* destroy as well as give life. When this happens within a society, the culture can pass on, from one generation to another,

2. John Collier, *Indians of the Americas* (New York: New American Library, 1947), p. 7.
3. Collier, p. 7.

the myths of nationalism, racism, sexism, militarism, and materialism that dull the human spirit.

The Middle Ages was a time when the power and strength of cultural errors smothered individual identity. One response to that heresy was the Protestant Reformation. A part of that movement brought on the Protestant ethic, which in turn became the base for today's system of capitalism, including American agriculture.

In correcting the medieval view of salvation by works, John Calvin, viewed by many as the creator of the Protestant ethic, stressed the doctrine of salvation by the grace of God. But that created a problem for some of his followers. If they were not saved by their good works, how could they, then, know that they were saved? That is still a problem for many people today. Calvin's response was that the elect would probably share the following likenesses:[4]

1. *Labor.* They would work hard and not be slothful like the masses who had grown weary under the feudal system.

2. *Individualism.* Each person is a child of God in his or her own right and a person's behavior is worked out in terms of his or her relationship to God rather than in terms of what the community and/or church said.

3. *Asceticism.* They would live the simple, frugal life with no room for conspicuous consumption; they would save their money.

4. *Rationality.* They would use their *own* thinking rather than going by tradition in making goals and forming patterns of behavior.

This Protestant ethic was a good corrective to medieval darkness and theological error. It also laid the basis for the rise of capitalism as an economic and eventually political system.

Push the Protestant ethic too far, though, and you have another heresy. *Now* it has evolved into the heresy of too much individualism, the breakdown of community and personal relationships. Competition is stressed more than cooperation. Greater value is placed on production than on production's effects on the environment. Freedom is valued more highly than responsibility. The piling up of material wealth is often taken as proof of Christian faithfulness. If people are poor, we tend to see them as spiritual sloths. Bigger is often defined as better, be it in diamond rings, cattle, or even churches. If the earth gets raped in the process of subduing it, who cares?

We begin to live under the fantasy of having pulled ourselves up by our

4. Max Weber, *The Protestant Ethic and the Spirit of Capitalism*, translated by Talcott Parson (London: Allen & Unwin, 1930). See also R. H. Tawney, *Religion and the Rise of Capitalism* (New York: Harcourt, Brace, and World, 1926) as well as Hans Gerth and C. Wright Mills, *Character and Social Structures* (New York: Harcourt, Brace and World, 1953).

own bootstraps, without realizing that our neighbors may have no boots. In so doing, we go full circle, back to the feudal structures of the Middle Ages with the same works-salvation ethic. Only now *we* may be the lords and will vote for the conservative political parties and policies that will protect our interests from the serfs who live in the shacks behind our mansions.

Or we may be among the new growing class of American farm refugees, desperately searching for ways to put some meaning back into life. It comes as a shock to some when they discover that capitalism is *not* a New Testament ethic.

The current rural crisis is rooted in the brokenness of wrong ideas and relationships. Our hope, however, will not be found in cursing the darkness. Rather we need to renew our relationships and give new purpose to our lives. In so doing, we may find times for remembering the birds of the air and the lilies of the field, as well as recognizing the potential need for overturning the tables of the money changers (Matt. 6:26,28; 21:12).

We must examine our own motives. To be sure, when in captivity, we are promised release—escape from our Egypts, manna in our wildernesses. But judgment cautions us: "Woe to those who . . . add field to field" and "build larger barns" (Isa. 5:8; Luke 12:18).

Having gained some understanding into the nature of relationships, i.e., how everything affects every other thing, we are ready to explore in more detail how what happens on the farm and in agribusiness impacts the entire society.

Power rooted in the land

Land use has been at the heart of every culture since the Stone Age. From the earth's surface, including both what is above and beneath it, comes *all* new material wealth. It comes in the form of food, fiber, minerals, and energy. Out of these, everything else is made. Even a bank note is written on paper that came from earth resources.

As a result, those who own and/or control the land and its produce are the major power holders in modern society. When one desires more power over others, it can be achieved by gaining still more material resources. Those with power may enslave others and wage war for that end. Without the ownership and/or control of some property, one has little control over most of his or her life.

North Americans with European ancestry should know this well, for many of our ancestors were landless peasants. Hope for land and the freedoms that go with it enticed them to the western hemisphere. Thomas Jefferson argued that ownership of land by the masses would be the best basis for a democratic form of government.

Those with African or American Indian ancestry should know the importance of land control as well, for their ancestors were deprived of land ownership and/or control. They became the American victims of social and economic injustice, just as many of our white ancestors had been European victims.

In spite of its inconsistencies, the pattern of land ownership by the masses that evolved throughout much of North America may well be viewed as one of the most significant social, economic, and political experiments in the history of civilization. *Experiment* is the proper word, because it is not yet certain if such a pattern of land ownership can long endure. Marxism says it cannot. Trends of the past 100 years would seem to be against it. The very policies of the United States government often seem to lead toward its destruction. Even so, some of us have dedicated ourselves to preserving the dream of land ownership and its husbandry by the largest possible number of people.

Fewer people living on fewer farms

It is no secret that the numbers of farms and farmers have declined dramatically in the United States during most of the twentieth century. Using the current definition of a farm (product sales of $1,000 or more, regardless of acreage), farms have now decreased to less than one-third of

Table No. 1. Land in farms, selected years, 1900-78[5]

Year	Land in farms* (million acres)	Change (percent)
1900	839	—
1910	879	+4.8
1920	956	+8.8
1930	987	+3.2
1940	1,061	+7.5
1950	1,159	+9.2
1954	1,158	0.0
1959	1,120	−3.3
1964	1,110	−0.9
1969	1,062	−4.3
1974	1.017	−4.2
1978	1,031	+1.4

Source: ESS/USDA and 1978 Census of Agriculture
*Data not adjusted for changes in enumeration methods and farm definitions.

5. *A Time to Choose*, p. 55.

their peak number of 6.8 million in 1935.[6] As the numbers continue to go down, estimates are that in the year 2000 the present number of farms (about 2.2 million in 1986) will be reduced by half. By that time, only 50,000 farms could produce 75 percent of the U.S. agricultural goods.[7]

Despite fewer farms, the amount of land being farmed in the United States has remained relatively constant during this century, in fact, increasing in total acreage during each decade until 1950 and declining slightly during most periods since then.[8] (See Table 1.)

This means that the average size of farms has grown. According to Figure 1, farm size has increased from about 150 acres in 1920 to almost 450 acres in 1978, an increase of 200 percent.

Figure No. 1 Number and Average Size of Farms.[9]

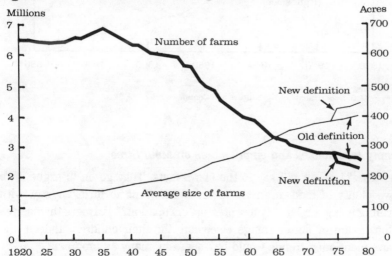

Sources: Average size of farms 1920-50 from 1964 Census of Agriculture. All other data from Crop Reporting Board, USDA.

These changes, of course, brought on a decline in farm population. Figure 2 shows the change from 32 million people living on farms in 1920 to 6.2 million in 1979. Thus, we can clearly see that land ownership and/or control is in the hands of a decreasing number of people.

6. Shantilal P. Bhagat, *The Family Farm: Can It Be Saved?* (Elgin, Illinois: Brethren Press, 1985), p. 27.
7. Knight-Ridder News Service, *The Sun* (March 18, 1986), p. 3A.
8. United States Department of Agriculture, *A Time to Choose* (Jan. 1981), p. 55.
9. *A Time to Choose*, p. 42.

Figure No. 2   Farm Population, 1920 to 1980.[10]

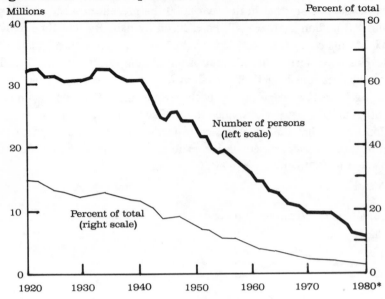

*Preliminary.
Source: U. S. Departments of Agriculture and Commerce.

Empty farmhouses and empty stores on Main Street

"So what?" many will say to the above facts. They go on to argue, "We have plenty of food—even too much. Who wants to farm anyway, with farming being a relatively low prestige occupation?" Farmers themselves often dream of better things elsewhere for their children. Indeed, the above-mentioned trends would be viewed by many as progress.

Not many young people choose farming for a career today, even though many may eventually become significant property holders with some form of agribusiness investments in their portfolios. That says something profound—like the proverbial chicks who were more than willing to eat the cakes, but would have nothing to do with making them. Again, this shows how every part of society is in some way tied to agriculture.

We need no special survey to show that what happens on the farm affects the entire rural community, and even the urban community. Every time a community loses six farm families, another business on Main Street is forced to close for economic reasons. As the countryside depopulates, so do the Main Streets of its towns.

10. *A Time to Choose*, p. 34.

To be sure, many fine rural communities continue to thrive, but rural areas are not immune to social problems. In many rural areas, social decay of almost every kind can be found. Not unlike the inner city, except in terms of population density, they have empty storefronts with broken windows, boarded-up schools, drug and alcohol abuse, family disorder, and crime.

Empty farmsteads abound. Indeed, property is often more valuable if no buildings stand on it, for then no money has to be spent to tear such structures down.

At the other end of the continuum is the social decay of the inner city. From where do these poor people come? They used to be newly arrived immigrants from other countries. Today, vast numbers are the descendants of people squeezed out of farming or small towns. If those people would have been given the means of a livelihood in the communities of their origin, *both* rural and urban areas would have fewer social tragedies. Indeed, the place to fight future urban blight is probably in the rural hinterland.

Better living on small farms and in small towns

Even though the impact of farms on the total community seems obvious, a number of social researchers have studied the matter in an objective, scientific way.

1. *Arvin and Dinuba*. One of the classic studies was done by Walter Goldschmidt in the Central Valley in California, in 1944.[11]

He compared two communities: Arvin, a large-scale corporate farming area; and Dinuba, a small-scale family farming area. Both communities have similar growing seasons and have the same type of soil. Both rely on irrigation, as the area has only ten inches of annual rainfall.

His study showed that the rural areas around Arvin and Dinuba had similar numbers of acres under cultivation, with similar amounts of income. The distribution of that wealth, however, was vastly different, along with the resulting class structure of the two communities. In the large-farm community of Arvin, wealth was concentrated with the landowners and professional classes, while in the power-diffused, small- farm community of Dinuba, wealth was more widely shared.

The difference between the two towns was striking. Dinuba with its small farms had more schools, with a lower rate of teacher turnover. It also had more churches, with a high percentage of people attending.

11. Walter Goldschmidt, *As You Sow* (Montclair, New Jersey: Allanheld, Osmun and Co., 1947, 1978).

Dinuba had more than twice as many businesses with almost double the gross sales.[12]

Arvin and Dinuba were studied again by other scientists in the early and mid-1970s.[13] The same differences still existed. Dinuba with its small farms was still a much better place to live and the community provided more services.

2. *130 Towns in San Joaquin*. Also in the 1970s, Isao Fujimoto made a much larger study in the San Joaquin Valley, one that included 130 towns.[14] He tested the link between the quality of community life and the control of major farming resources—specifically land and water. Fujimoto confirmed Goldschmidt's earlier findings.

Areas with large scale farms had fewer towns and a much smaller range of services. On the other hand, places with smaller farms had more schools, churches, service clubs, cafes, doctors, and other community services.

3. *Arizona, California, Florida, and Texas Study*. In 1985, Dean Mac-Cannell and Edward Dolber-Smith reported on what may be the most extensive study yet on the relationship of changing agricultural patterns and community structures.[15] They looked at ninety-eight counties in California, Arizona, Texas, and Florida.

Forty counties in the study ranked among the top 100 counties in agricultural sales in the nation. The other counties in the study were less advanced technically and had lower sales. But the rural communities in the counties with the high sales did not share in the economic benefits. While farm sales increase, "the rural community stagnates or declines."[16]

More and more, the large corporate farms in these counties came to depend on foreign labor. These agribusiness areas do not take part in American social and cultural traditions. "They resemble more Honduran plantation communities, or Laotian communities, rather than rural counterparts in other areas of the United States," said these researchers. "We

12. Goldschmidt.

13. William D. Heffernan, "Structure of Agriculture and Quality of Life," in Don A. Dillman and Daryl J. Hobb, *Rural Society in the United States: Issues for the 1980s* (Boulder, Colo.: Westview Press, 1981), p. 339.

14. Isao Fujimoto, "The Communities of the San Joaquin Valley," in *Priorities in Agricultural Research of the United States Department of Agriculture*, Subcommittee on Administrative Practice and Procedure of the Committee on the Judiciary, United States Senate, 95th Congress, second session, 1978, Appendix, part 2, pp. 1374-96.

15. Dean MacCannell and Edward Dolber-Smith, "Report on the Structure of Agriculture and Impacts of New Technologies on Rural Communities in Arizona, California, Florida, and Texas," draft manuscript, University of California, Davis (March 8, 1985).

16. MacCannell and Dolber-Smith, p. 23.

have, in effect, imported Third-World social and economic relations in order to maintain the World Market position of [large scale, industrialized] agriculture."[17]

MacCannell and Dolber-Smith's analysis of farm size and technology strongly agrees with Goldschmidt's large industrial farm versus small farm thesis. From their study they conclude that "there is already advanced community deterioration in those ... counties which have achieved the highest levels of agricultural-industrial development."[18]

They link this decay directly to the ownership pattern and dependence on technology. "The current trend toward increasing farm size, concentration of ownership, and dependence on new technologies will accelerate the social degradation of these communities unless there is substantial programming aimed directly at correcting these pathologies."[19]

These findings raise public policy questions regarding projected changes in technology and their effect on rural communities. American agriculture may well be on the brink of another upheaval. "There is some concern already expressed that this technological revolution may have unforeseen and undesired negative impacts on soil, air, and water quality, wildlife and human health," they say. The rural community and rural family should also be added to this list.[20]

4. *Other Studies.* A number of other scientists, using varied methods, have studied various parts of the linkage between agricultural structure and quality of life in rural communities. "No single study or set of studies can answer all of the research questions," says William D. Heffernan, one of the social scientists involved in this work, "but it seems significant that a dozen studies, spanning four decades and all regions of the nation and performed by researchers using different methodologies, have rather consistently shown that a change toward corporate agriculture produces social consequences that reduce the quality of life in rural communities."[21]

In testimony before the Nebraska Unicameral, Don Reeves said, "It does not take any sophisticated study to see that the industrial model for agriculture is not good for a community. It is disastrous."[22] But, the studies *do* confirm the casual observations. Reeves sums it up well.

17. MacCannell and Dolber-Smith, pp. 23-24.
18. MacCannell and Dolber-Smith, p. 51.
19. MacCannell and Dolber-Smith, p. 52.
20. MacCannell and Dolber-Smith, p. 52.
21. W. D. Heffernan, pp. 340-41.
22. Don Reeves, "Testimony Before Agriculture and Environment Committee, Nebraska Unicameral" (February 8, 1985), p. 2

In total, and by almost every single indicator used, communities set in the midst of large farms with absentee and corporate ownership are poorer than those set in the midst of resident owner-operated farms: fewer businesses, fewer community services, fewer amenities, less schooling, lower average incomes, fewer churches with less members, fewer civic organizations, clubs and volunteer groups, fewer recreational opportunities, lower voting rates, higher incidence of poverty. The pattern is consistent, and well documented.[23]

Bigger farms for a profit that costs too much

If the trend toward ever larger farms is so negative in terms of human costs, why do we continue down that road? That's a question we must ask ourselves loudly and clearly. It's a question that reflects the fact that decisions are often made without regard for the good of the society.

The most common response, however, is that we do it in the name of efficiency: to provide our ever-growing population with plenty of cheap food. Also, it is argued, we need surplus production for export sales to help balance our national trade deficit. And then, technology sets the standards. Bigger tractors, for example, can farm more acres per hour. That makes the operator feel he is doing much more than the Amish neighbor with his horses. We have defined that as progress. In all likelihood that is a cultural error: we are probably wrong.

In reality, our *progress* has come up with *less* efficiency. James Wessel points out that by the late 1960s, the upper limit of efficiency had already been reached on the farms that produce most of our food. Recent growth in farm size has not brought any greater efficiency. "Above about $40,000-$50,000 in gross sales—a size that is at the bottom end of the medium-size sales category," says Wessel, quoting a USDA study, "there are no greater efficiencies of scale."[24]

We need to realize that efficiency is not the same as increased production. Ingolf Vogeler explains this clearly:

> Large-scale farmers measured in number of acres, produce more agricultural goods and higher *yields per worker.* Yet all published data indicate that the larger the farm operation, the lower the *yields per acre.* Proponents of agribusiness measure the success of farming by using output per farmer, but this index confuses agricultural

23. Reeves, p. 2.
24. James Wessel, *Trading the Future* (San Francisco: Institute for Food and Development Policy). The study cited is *Economies of Size in U.S. Field Crop Farming* by Tom Miller.

efficiency with productivity. Large-scale farmers *seem* more efficient, but they actually only produce more in quantity and value with fewer workers and more land.[25]

The primary reason for bigger farms can be stated in one word: *profit*. Even though big farms may not be more efficient, they *do* produce more wealth and/or power for the owner. Couple this with the values that tend to link spiritual virtues with the gaining of wealth (Protestant ethic) and we have a most powerful force propelling us in the direction of larger and larger farms. Human greed and covetousness add to the speed of the trend. Again and again in our economy, what produces profit is what gets done; not what benefits the public. A tension exists between the public good and certain individuals or corporations earning profits.

Passion for the earth versus the bottom line

Agriculture is more of an art than a science. It has much to do with relationships between human beings, the soil, water, plants, animals, air, and other human beings. It needs to reflect the Native American "reverence and passion for human personality, joined with the ancient lost reverence and passion for the earth and its web of life."[26] Ultimately, it is dependent on God!

On the other hand, business is business. When you change agriculture into agribusiness you have an entirely different set of values. To large corporate agribusinesses, farms and farmers are natural resources to use and/or to use up. Farmers are seen more as potential markets for the products of technology than as human beings seeking a quality life. Decisions have to be made in terms of profit, debt service, and cash flow projections rather than conservation and ecology.

The mindset of this type of agribusiness as opposed to agriculture is deeply ingrained in us. Some argue that the very concept of family farms is now an illusion. Vogeler says, "Even though family farmers work their own land, they are manipulated by agribusiness through its control of processing, storage facilities, transportation, and financial capital. The small holder can therefore be considered a worker in an agricultural system controlled by urban financial interests."[27]

The widespread notion that family farms and competition are the rule in

25. Ingolf Vogeler, *The Myth of the Family Farm: Agribusiness Dominance of the Family Farm: Agribusiness Dominance of United States Agriculture* (Boulder, Colo.: Westview Press, 1981), p. 90.
26. Collier, p. 7.
27. Vogeler, pp. 290-91.

U. S. agriculture is indeed an illusion, says Vogeler, and "obscures the deep-seated corporate and governmental forces that have concentrated the bulk of agricultural production in the hands of large-scale farmers while family farmers are destroying themselves in fierce competition."[28]

Victims of world colonial powers

This crisis on the farm and in the rural community has a ripple effect reaching into the larger urban society. How do we make sense out it?

Albert Memmi, a Tunisian, provides some solid theory to undergird our understanding of the situation in his detailed analysis of colonialism.[29] Colonialism is that system whereby one group or government gains control over another in most of the important parts of the colonized's life. Economic exploitation is at the heart of the system. Remember the Boston Tea Party?

Colonialism has been one of the dominant economic and political themes of the past three centuries. The form of colonialism most visible right now, I contend, has to do with the exploitation of farmers in every part of the world by agribusiness and energy monopolies.

The colonized provide the labor and raw products for the colonizers who in turn process and sell them at great profits—even to the colonized. Justification for this exploitive system is found in defining the colonized as lazy, weak, or stupid, that is, inferior beings who deserve to be exploited. They are believed not capable of self-control or rule of their destiny.

Needed: a second revolution

Human beings have been made to live in relationship both with each other and with the larger cultural and ecological environment. When we break relationship, we get into trouble. All of life is tied together as a giant web. Nothing can change without impacting the total social structure.

The current farm crisis is a product of many cultural errors and human greed. What happens to our farms is changing the quality of life all across our nation. Indeed, it has global consequences!

Ingolf Vogeler has stated prophetically:

> The first American Revolution resulted in political freedoms; the second will be for economic freedoms. Democracy based on individual political rights is meaningless for people without economic

28. Vogeler, p. 194.
29. Albert Memmi, *The Colonizer and the Colonized* (Boston: Beacon Press, 1967).

rights, and civil rights are granted in liberal democracies only when they do not threaten the basic economic system. The next revolution in the U.S. will require the expansion of political democracy to include economic democracy; only then can agrarian capitalism give way to agrarian democracy. Because of the increasingly contradictory forces U.S. family farmers face in the 1980s, they need to work toward this democratic and economic revolution.[30]

What will be the conclusion of the North American experiment of land ownership by the many? Will it lead toward wholeness in relationship? The answer will come partly in how we build our future.

For study and discussion

1. With all of life functioning as a giant web, with every part or happening affecting all other parts and happenings, what are *you* doing that will impact the future?

2. If capitalism is not a New Testament ethic, is there any other economic system that would be?

3. How is a Christian to know whether it is time to remember the birds of the air *or* to upset the tables of the money changers in the temple? List some things for which we should be content, as well as some tables that you feel need upsetting.

4. Do you believe the ownership and/or control of at least some material goods is necessary for the enhancement of human welfare? If so, what can *you* do to make sure *everyone* has some?

5. Has life become better or worse in your community as farms have gotten larger?

6. Why is it that some rural and/or farming communities attract their youth back and others do not?

7. Do you view the exploitation of rural people and resources as a form of colonialism? Why?

8. How can you, your church, or your community minister both creatively and dynamically to the needs of your town or area—today? in the future?

9. Do you agree or disagree with Ingolf Vogeler when he calls for a second American Revolution to expand political democracy to include economic democracy? Why?

---

30. Vogeler, pp. 294-95.

Hutterite colony

People who have
community live in it in
the way one wears a
comfortable old coat.
They aren't even aware
they 'have it on.' But, if,
on a cold winter's day,
someone were to take it
away from them, they
would know full well it
was gone.
—Joe Paddock

8. Models for family farms

Freeman: formed by its family farms

Lois Janzen Preheim

Freeman is a farming community set in the heart of some of South Dakota's richest farmland. Typical of rural communities across the nation, Freeman was built by family farmers whose relationship with the land and with one another shaped the area.[1]

The larger Freeman community includes people living in Hutchinson, Turner, and McCook counties. These three southeastern counties lead in crop and livestock production. In 1985, for example, all three counties were near the top in oats, corn, and soybean yields for the state. Farming is diversified with grain and livestock operations—beef, dairy, hogs, and sheep. Hutchinson County has led the state in hog production. The major livestock enterprises in Turner and Hutchinson counties prompted Turner County Extension Agent Merlin Pietz to refer to the two counties as the state's livestock belt.

According to figures from the county agents, Hutchinson County has about 1,000 farmers with the average-sized farm around 380 acres. Turner County with about 1,100 operators averages about 324 acres per holding. In McCook County, 650 farmers work farms averaging about 520 acres each.

Most of the people who settled in the Freeman area in the mid-1870s came from Russia, but were not Russian. They were of German and Swiss

---

1. Tim Waltner, editor of the *Freeman Courier*, assisted in writing this profile of the Freeman community.

origin and had moved to Russia a century before with promises of special privileges, offered because of their reputations as good farmers. However, when many of those privileges were revoked in the 1870s, many left. The resulting immigration brought some to the plains of South Dakota.

Among the people settling in the Freeman area were those of Mennonite, Lutheran, Catholic, Evangelical, and Separatist confessions. They tended to settle as groups in different parts of the tri-county area centered in the town of Freeman: for example, the Low German Mennonites to the north of Freeman, the former Hutterite Mennonites to the north and west, and the Swiss Mennonites to the east and south.

Their heritage is important to the Freeman people. Schmeckfest, an annual three-day spring festival sponsored by the Freeman College Women's Auxiliary, features the foods, handicrafts, art, and musical traditions of the community.

The land on which these German-Russian immigrants and others settled in the 1870s has been productive. It has been so in large part because of the good farming practices and strong will of these immigrants. The forces of nature have not always been kind. Grass fires, grasshoppers, and drought plagued the early settlers. Today, unpredictable rainfall continues as an ongoing concern; few farms in the area are irrigated.

But the strength of the people and the richness of the soil have helped form a strong rural community. The town of Freeman has enjoyed growth and progress since its founding in 1879. The 1980 census placed Freeman's population at 1,462, forty-ninth in the state. While integrally connected with the agricultural community which it serves, the town has become a business, professional service, educational, and cultural center for the area.

Basic, of course, is agriculture. Two farm implement dealerships, more than half a dozen grain and feed operations, three fertilizer plants, a large milk-handling plant and several manufacturing operations producing ag-related equipment are essential elements of the local economy. They reflect the important relationship between the farm and the larger community.

Recent decades have seen significant shifts in the farm community. The number of farms has been decreasing and while Freeman's population has grown—a notable exception to most small towns in the state—the combined population of Hutchinson, Turner, and McCook counties dropped from 32,351 to 25,049 in the past thirty years, a decline of 23 percent.

That decline has changed the larger community. Non-agricultural manufacturing has shown some growth. The median age of the population has become older as farm families have retired and farms have been merged with other farms rather than passed on to another generation. The resulting larger farms have altered certain farming practices as well.

Expansion has resulted in more individualism and independence and less reliance upon labor-intensive practices. For some, this has raised questions about what it means to be a family farm community.

The national economic pressures on U.S. agriculture in the early 1980s have been felt in Freeman also. These have in turn raised questions of farm ethics, practices, and priorities.

The more conservative nature of farmers in the area has provided some protection from the larger economic forces. Still, the impact of high interest, low prices, poor markets, and the ever-present vagaries of the weather have combined to make farming more demanding and, for some families, no longer feasible.

The impact of the economic pressures can be seen in a slowing of growth in Freeman's business community. It was a factor in the decision to close Freeman Junior College at the close of the 1985-86 school year. The weakened financial base of the Mennonite school, nearly totally dependent on the ag-based community for support, prompted the school to decide to concentrate on its secondary education program, an effort seen as more manageable.

Recently, several area farmers started Faith and Farming, a group to help community farmers meet needs as they face financial crisis. Believing that American life encourages people to isolate various parts of their lives, they hope to stimulate Freeman area farmers to more clearly consider the connections between their faith and the way they farm.

In the face of these diverse factors—a rich heritage, a strong agricultural tradition, and ever-changing economic, sociological, and technological conditions—four Freeman farm families share their views on integrating their faith with their farming.

The Epps: hard work from the whole family

In 1945, Walter and Emma Epp started farming on rented land with $4,000 Walter had saved and "a few critters" his father had given him. For each of the first five years, their best fields flooded and they lost half the crop.

When his father had a heart attack in 1951, Walter bought eighty acres adjoining the home place, and he and his brother Willard farmed the two acreages together. Walter's eighty acres had small, dilapidated buildings with no running water. In 1956, the Epps' net income was less than $1,000. "We had no money, but we lived with what we had, and we made it," Walter says. "And we had seven kids then!"

The Epps' finances improved when they moved to Walt's Uncle John's farm and Walt farmed for him. When the youngest of Walter and Emma's ten children was born, the Epps returned to the eighty that they owned.

At last Walter had a chance to develop his dream of starting a hog operation on his own place. He rebuilt the farm buildings, enlarged the house, and installed running water. "When we got a little income, we put it into the hog facilities or the machinery. But we didn't buy the latest stuff; I did a lot of welding to make things work."

When the youngest child was five, Emma died suddenly. Three years later, in 1971, Walter married Catherine Epp, a Canadian Mennonite nurse who had been a missionary in Nigeria for fifteen years.

On the Epp farm, the children helped in both the hog operation and the field work. Catherine, too, enjoyed the outdoor work, although she was primarily needed to manage the household. "It took a lot of hard work from the whole family to make the farm productive," Walter says.

For Walter Epp, good stewardship and conservation are an important part of applying the Christian faith. Care of the land is a concern that goes back to his youth. "When I was young, we farmed up and down the hill, and every year the gullies got deeper," he says. "We were destroying our land. Corn at the bottom of the hills was six feet high; on top, half of that. The tops of the hills, where there used to be six inches of black soil, turned yellow.

"My dad and I decided that we had to stop this water running down the hills. So I got involved with the Soil Conservation Service and we put in terraces. The worst land we seeded into pasture." A smile of satisfaction crosses his face. "We got that land back into shape, into production. I feel very good about that." Although it takes three times as long to farm the terraces as it does to go up and down the hills, Walter says he wants to "be a quality steward on a small piece of land."

The children are scattered now in various communities across the country. Two of the daughters are farming with their husbands. One son, John, is at home, having recently returned to the farm to work with his father. Walter looks to the future with a hope that John will share his values of stewardship and love of farming. "But I know," he says, "I can't force my values on him."

The Hofers: father and two sons on three farms

LeRoy and Sarah Hofer began farming in 1950. Today the Hofer farm is a modern pork and beef operation. Everything about the farm—its layout, the house, the buildings, the machines—speaks of efficiency, organization, and careful management.

LeRoy's initial investment was for machinery, since his father had bought a farm for him to work. In 1965, when the elder Hofer retired, LeRoy and Sarah moved onto the home place.

LeRoy renovated the buildings. He outfitted the livestock barns with pit and slat floors. He built two additional facilities for his hog finishing operation. And he installed conveyer belts to speed up the cattle feeding chores. In 1979, the Hofers built a modern ranch style house.

Except for the house, the improvements were done only when LeRoy felt sure that he would get a return on his investment. Prices for farm products were good when he built the house and he figured that he could repay the loan within five years. "Well, things didn't turn out that way," he says with a sigh. "If we wouldn't have built the house. . . ."

LeRoy helped his sons, Bruce and Carlos, begin their farm enterprises like his father had helped him, but it was an expensive proposition to start farming in the '70s. Their three farms created a 1,440-acre unit in which each of the men run separate livestock programs. Because they are neighbors, all three use many of LeRoy's machines, although LeRoy's income from his own 480 acres no longer quite covers the machinery needs. "The ideal situation would be if we split the cost of new machinery three ways, but neither son can do it yet," he says. "And since we built the house, I haven't bought any machinery either."

LeRoy wants his third son, Stan, who is now in high school, to have the same choice as Bruce and Carlos, if he wants a farm of his own. But it may be more feasible economically for Stan to take over the family farm instead.

From his father, LeRoy learned prudence. His father believed that he survived the '30s because he did not enter those years with borrowed money. To LeRoy, being prudent not only means being careful with money. It also means paying attention to the soil and to weed control. He uses herbicides and fertilizers, but as he has learned about groundwater contamination, he has become more careful in how he uses them. His concern for weed control led him to become active on the county Weed and Pest Board.

In the early years of their farming, LeRoy's wife Sarah had a poultry business of 500 broilers. They also had some sheep. But they quit the smaller enterprises when changing markets and government controls began to make them unprofitable. Now Sarah does volunteer work in town.

LeRoy supports his family's interests off the farm. He is proud that his daughter Geraldine has a good job in Denver as a saleswoman. He wistfully notes, however, the changes that have come to church and family life. "You can see the result of so many women working in town by looking at choir," he says. "And kids aren't available for church activities, either, as they once were. We even have trouble eating meals together now, because we're not all at home at the same time."

The Mieraus: getting the soil back into shape

Joe and Lorena Mierau started farming in 1972 when Joe's father Hugo died. Newly married, Joe and Lorena had just begun a Mennonite Voluntary Service assignment in Denver, but as the oldest son in a family of five, Joe felt responsible to return home and farm.

The 260-acre Mierau farm presented a challenge to Joe and Lorena. Buildings were in disrepair, fields were weedy, and yields were down. Hugo Mierau had believed that Christian farmers should use biological rather than technological solutions. But he couldn't keep up with the work that was required to farm with smaller equipment and without chemicals. "If you are going to farm without chemicals," Joe says, "then you have to be constantly checking your fields."

Joe wanted to retain his father's philosophy of farming, but he also wanted it to pay. Full of energy and dreams, Joe and Lorena plunged in. Their first goal was to restore the soil to a good production level. They decided to drop corn from their rotation and go to wheat and soybeans. "None of our neighbors had this arrangement," says Lorena. "We lay awake at nights, wondering if it would work."

Mieraus also decided to idle 15 to 20 percent of the land every year, to give the soil a chance to renew itself. Their decision is consistent with their belief that the soils should not be violated in order for them to make more money. Joe recognizes that he does not get the maximum yields that would be possible with chemicals, but it is more important to him "not to mine extra bushels out of the ground." The soil has responded to the Mieraus' care. "We've met our goal of getting the soil into good shape," Lorena says with satisfaction.

Every fall, Joe invites townspeople to bring him the leaves they rake up in their yards. In 1985, Joe had enough leaves to fertilize 14 acres. Joe regards this project as a service to the townspeople and one small way he can stimulate ecological awareness.

For Joe, part of the challenge of farming is keeping his old machines working. More importantly, keeping his machinery costs down is a way of cutting his production costs. He believes that the present farm debt crisis resulted in part from farmers buying machinery that could not pay for itself.

Joe and Lorena believe also that American agriculture's commitment to mechanical and chemical technologies comes out of a repressed scorn of physical labor. "People look down on those walking beans to pull weeds instead of using a bean buggy," says Joe. "Even though this task is good exercise, many look for ways to get out of it."

Fortunately, the '70s were years of good yields and good prices. Joe was able to build new farm buildings and to begin to renovate their house, doing much of the labor himself. Lorena earned money selling carrots, onions, and potatoes from her huge garden. They took sweet corn to a cooperative in Sioux Falls. And they sold flour milled from their wheat.

In the early '80s, the Mierau farm, like many others, began to lose money. Joe added to the number of carpentry jobs that he was already doing in the community. By this time, their children Kristi and David were in school, so Lorena took a job at the local print shop.

Now Joe and Lorena are classified as part-time farmers. Nonetheless, they consider the farm their number one commitment. For them, the bottom line is not how much money they can make from the land, but whether their way of farming is healthy for both humans and soil. They believe that their own well-being is in direct proportion to the soil's well-being.

The Brockmuellers: loving the animals they work with

In 1970, after several years of overseas experience with the U.S. Agency for International Development, Gordon and Shirley Brockmueller returned with their children to farm 880 acres of their parents' and grandparents' land south of Freeman. Gordon credits the years abroad with giving them an appreciation for other agricultural systems and for seeing what they do on their farm in light of global conditions. Their son Lee has similar interests, having recently spent a winter in Burma on an agricultural assignment with Ohio State University and earlier working in a Mennonite Central Committee agricultural development project in Bangladesh.

Lee and his brother Joe both farm with Gordon. They divide their responsibilities according to their interests: Gordon is in charge of the livestock, Lee is the agronomist, and Joe manages the business and accounting.

Gordon has always made a conscious choice to involve everyone in the family in some aspect of the farm. He recognizes that Shirley's supportive backup role is an essential contribution. The children's work, even when they were young, was not just a matter of following his orders, but in developing a sense of responsibility. "Suzanne, our youngest, took care of the calves through their first year when she was a little girl," he said. "It was up to her to do the choring and to report to me when something was wrong. I wanted her to determine what to do if there was a problem."

"I look at my vocation as animal husbandry," Gordon says, referring to his care of his eighty purebred Shorthorns and his eighty sows. "I especially like the word 'husbandry' rather than 'animal scientist' because I love the animals I work with.

"When I speak about loving my animals, I'm thinking about what it feels like when I discover a newborn calf out in a pasture in a cold driving rain. I pick up this slimy ninety-pound calf, put him on my back, trudge the mile and a half home with the mother cow following me, and take the calf into the barn to comfort him."

Does livestock confinement clash with the notion of loving one's animals, as some animal rightist groups claim? Gordon decided that it does not negate his concern for the health and comfort of his animals. "The advantage of confinement is that you can control the environment of the animals," he says.

Although animals are his first love in farming, Gordon intentionally developed a diversified farm. He has a three-year crop rotation program of corn, small grain, and soybeans. To help his cash flow, he sells certified seed and soybeans.

Committed to pull together

The Epps, the Hofers, the Mieraus, and the Brockmuellers represent different backgrounds, interests, and lifestyles in their varied farming practices, but they are all Christians who see the land as an inheritance, a place that needs their best wisdom, care, and responsibility. Together, their stories illustrate changes in family farming in the last fifty years. Their words speak of hope for the next generation and of their own struggle not to squander the efforts of the generation before them.

Like many other communities across North America that have been formed by the family farms which gave them shape, Freeman is a place where relationships matter. The commitment to pull together provides a strong sense of identity, and offers its members purpose and a secure place to be. Sometimes this commitment to present a united front collides with individual preferences and differences. But the creative tension between community and private life has produced a community concerned to pass on its joy and values to the next generation.

Faith and farming meet and prosper

Burton Buller

The Amish: farming for the life of it

For the Amish, the earthly experience is a spiritual journey. Plowing the soil, caring for animals, helping a neighbor in need, and attending Sunday meetings all have spiritual meaning. Both the community and the farm are gifts from God to be nurtured and preserved. Anything which holds the potential to damage or destroy these gifts should be avoided. Technology which has clear benefits must be introduced slowly so that the community has time to integrate the effects of new methods.

Soil, the Amish read in Genesis, belongs to God. The farmer's duty is to dress the garden, to manage and work it for pleasure and fulfillment. In the psalms and in the parables, humans are seen as stewards of the soil.

For most Amish, responsible stewardship has come to mean limited use of nitrogen, liberal use of animal manure, concern for soil fertility, and the pursuit of diversified farming. By maintaining a variety of crops and livestock, income is diversified. Efficiency and convenience do not dictate work and family priorities. The Amish aim to be unaffected by outside worldly trends and fads.

Dependence on fossil fuels translates into reliance on structures the Amish don't understand and basically mistrust. Growing oats for draft horses on one's own land and returning the manure to the soil represents a more closed system, one that is sustainable and productive in spite of outside economic pressures. Likewise, direct government subsidies are refused, for they increase dependence on outside resources and reduce the incentive to care properly for God's creation.

To the Amish, profit is not the most important factor. Farming is done in a way that preserves and promotes social and religious values. These methods have a leveling effect. No one Amish family becomes exceedingly wealthy, and all, with frugality and initiative, have a chance to meet life's basic needs. Having reached this plateau of well-being, to strive for more would put them at odds with their Amish community.

But a relatively self-sufficient way of life does not insulate the Amish from all outside pressures. Amish tend to have large families. And each son, ideally, is given a chance to become a farm operator. But land prices have skyrocketed in some Amish communities, creating financial problems for some families.

They have met with this crisis by setting up large dairy and poultry operations which require small land bases. Although this creates more off-farm dependence for feed and marketing, it allows families to farm without incurring the high cost of land purchases.

The Amish model, although sustainable over a longer period of time, is still subject to many of the same pressures which force neighboring farms into foreclosure. But when farming is done for the life it provides, and the values and community it promotes, rather than for the wealth it can create, the pressures on the land to produce are lessened. This may point the way toward a more acceptable form of stewardship.

The Hutterites: life enough from a small land base

Among the world's oldest communitarians, the Hutterites are the pragmatic cousins of the philosophical Amish. While starting from the same theological premise, they make radically different assumptions about how agriculture is to be done. The Hutterites, who live communally on corporately owned lands in rural regions of Canada and the United States, are effectively isolated from the surrounding population. Radios, newspapers, and television are not allowed, since these are devices through which alien foreign philosophies could be introduced to the detriment of the community.

Although living with much the same beliefs as in the sixteenth century, the Hutterites farm with the most sophisticated techniques and equipment available. Herbicides, pesticides, commercial fertilizers, state-of-the-art tractors and combines, and experimental production techniques are equally embraced.

As much as possible, their colonies are self-sufficient in the basic needs of life. Each colony of 80 to 120 people maintains a large garden and a modern facility for food processing and preservation. This provides plenty of work for the young people and limits contact with the outside world.

In addition to tilling the soil, nearly all colonies operate one or more large livestock production units. Turkey, swine, egg and chicken production are favorites, with dairy operations providing needed milk. The accountant at one colony claimed that egg profits alone paid all household expenses for his entire colony.

By disavowing private property, Hutterites have been able to farm on the cutting edge of Western agriculture, but do it more efficiently than most. Because their per capita land base is much smaller than that of their neighbors, the Hutterites have to farm more efficiently. To remain competitive, they rely on technological efficiencies and highly diversified farming.

Pragmatism rather than ideology seems to be at the base of many colony decisions. Where the Amish see all of life as a spiritual experience, the Hutterites clearly delineate between metaphysical and physical. "We do not try to modernize the Bible," says a minister in South Dakota. "But the Bible has nothing to say about how we farm."

Some colonists openly admit that one of the reasons for entering the spiral of ever larger and more sophisticated equipment is to keep their young men satisfied at the colony. Over the years, a love for well-designed equipment has grown, partly from the experience of home manufacture in their own blacksmith shops. They have an intense pride in their ability to build, rebuild, and repair technologically advanced equipment. They are highly conscious of the color and size of the machinery used by the colony down the road or in the next state.

But one group of Hutterites looks at it differently. In Saskatchewan, a colony farms with old, almost antiquated equipment. When asked about this, the minister reflected that if they bought newer and more efficient machines, their young men would not have enough work to do and they would begin to get into mischief. More land would be needed to offset the increased efficiency and to pay for the equipment. He couldn't see the value in that. Like the Amish, this group had reached a plateau of well-being, and saw no need to move beyond it.

As a result of the greater efficiencies of their communal social structure, some Hutterites have managed to keep costs down and still have the most modern machinery available. Others successfully practice a more sustainable, self-sufficient form of agriculture akin to what all Hutterites used to practice. This says much for the versatility of their communal lifestyle.

Plow Creek: land that nurtures family

Conrad Wetzel

"Strawberries will be ripe in a couple of days!"
"Sweet corn is ready; come and get some for your family!"
"Plenty of melons; help yourself!"

Such phrases are welcome signals each summer to the folks at Plow Creek Fellowship that the seasonal firstfruits of the labors of many friends are ready to be enjoyed. From the first asparagus shoots in the spring to the tomatoes that yield to the frosts of autumn, the gardens of Plow Creek symbolize the shared experience of planting and gathering in, working and celebrating that shapes the relationship of the community to the land.

Plow Creek Fellowship is a church community of Christians who have joined in a common search for the kingdom of God. Their home is a 189-acre farm of richly varied terrain near the old village of Tiskilwa in north-central Illinois. The Fellowship derives its name from the winding creek that flows through Plow Hollow, a beautiful valley with wide gardens, old barns, and tree-lined slopes, making this creek the most striking feature of the farm.

To these low-lying fields, wooded hillsides, and broad expanse of sky came a small group of persons in the summer of 1971, sent out from their parent community, Reba Place Fellowship of Evanston, Illinois, to establish a new community. The Fellowship was influenced in its formation by Mennonite, Hutterite, Quaker, and Brethren values, and since 1978, it has been affiliated with both the Mennonite Church and the General Conference Mennonite Church.

Working the land is a shared experience at Plow Creek. The farm is used in a variety of ways: crops of corn and soybeans for cash income, fields of alfalfa to make hay for the milk cows, a commercial garden including pick-your-own strawberries, a common garden yielding many vegetables for using fresh and for stocking up, and wooded hillsides for firewood to use by the community and to sell.

Two of the brothers devote full time to the farming and commercial gardening, a brother or sister supervises the common garden, and one of the sisters oversees the canning and freezing. The remainder of the members are involved in a variety of ways in getting the work done. Adults and children are assigned to work projects on Saturday mornings; children work in supervised groups as part of their summer program and are on call for a weekly evening of weeding strawberries, freezing corn, or canning tomatoes. Twice weekly common meals generally include foods produced at Plow Creek.

Farming and gardening provide but one portion of the income of the Fellowship, additional support coming both from fellowship-owned businesses and outside jobs: construction, law, social work, teaching, medicine, and other work. Decisions regarding the use of the land are initiated by the farming-gardening committee, processed through the coordinating council, and finalized at the members' weekly business meeting. The work is then carried out in the knowledge that it has been planned with the care and encouragement of the whole community. And just as any field or garden needs weeding and cultivating for proper growth, so the relationships in the community need "weeding and cultivating" so that the common decisions are made with charity and forthrightness.

While farming is not the main reason for Plow Creek's existence, those of us who are a part of the community see the proper use and care of the land as important features of our life together. In forming our theology of the common life, the Old Testament concepts of shalom and Jubilee take on lively meaning as we engage in the planning, working, and decision making that go into putting the land to work in our mutual care of one another and for sharing with others. Especially important for us is the integrative experience for our children in working together with many adults who are wise and gentle models of work made visible. These adults are the Christian friends with whom the children not only work, but also play and worship and celebrate in the weekly, yearly round of the common life.

Homesteaders: people growing their own food

Maynard Kaufman

Homesteaders are small-scale family farmers who emphasize production for household use, unlike conventional farmers who produce for sale to the market. The new homesteading movement is a classic example of a *prosumer*[2] activity as people produce more of what they consume.

Emphasizing organic or natural techniques of farming and a simple lifestyle, modern homesteading emerged from the back-to-the-land movement of the 1960s. It matured in the migration reversal of the 1970s when, for the first time in U.S. national history, more people—over three million more—moved from urban to rural areas than from rural to urban areas.[3]

Since the Census Bureau does not gather data on production for household use, the size of the homesteading movement can only be inferred. We do know that at the end of the 1970s, 44 percent of the farms were classified as rural farm residences with gross annual sales of under $5,000. We can assume that many of these farm families concentrated on production for household use.

Another indicator of the size of the homesteading movement is the boom in home gardening. Surveys by the National Gardening Association, a non-profit organization, show that in recent years 40 to 50 percent of American households were growing some of their own food. The retail value of this production for household use was estimated at 13 to 19

2. See Alvin Toffler, *The Third Wave* (New York: Bantam Books, 1981), Chapter 20.

3. Calvin Beale, "Demographic Aspects of·Agricultural Structures," in *Structure Issues in American Agriculture* (United States Department of Agriculture, 1979), Agricultural Economic Report 438, p. 84.

billion dollars annually, roughly equal to the value of the nation's corn crop each year.[4]

So much for the economic side. The values embodied in the new homesteading movement are more important than its dollar-and-cents yield. Given its back-to-the-land origins and its link to a growing ecological awareness in the 1960s, the homesteading movement stressed organic methods of production. Organic methods which avoid the use of chemicals are preferred by those who raise food for themselves. Even now only a few farmers who produce for the market use organic methods.

In fact, production for household use with organic methods is as close as it is possible to get to living within natural energy flows. Production for the market, even with organic methods, is heavily subsidized by fossil fuels—for mechanical power, manufacture of machinery, and transportation—and thus contributes to pollution and is vulnerable to energy scarcity. If, or when, energy costs more than labor, many more of us in industrial societies will be moving toward a post-industrial mode of food production on the household level.

Not only is household food production ecologically sustainable, but it can also help hard-pressed farm families and rural residents toward economic viability. Wendell Berry, an eloquent advocate of homesteading, estimates that household production of food and firewood can cut a family's need for income by $5,000 per year.[5] And the cash value is less important than the strengthening of family life as the entire household cooperates in the provision of a high quality food supply.

Finally, widespread production for household use would weaken an industrial food-growing system which destroys rural culture and exploits both soil and consumers. The long-term import of the homesteading movement may lie in the fact that it expresses an alternative to the industrial model of agribusiness and production for the market economy. In this respect, homesteading is an expression of the pastoral ideal in which the goal is sufficiency rather than growth.[6] This may seem like a visionary ideal now, but it may become a practical necessity as we move beyond the frontier mentality which exploits nature toward a steady state system in harmony with nature.

4. The National Gardening Association, 180 Flynn Ave., Burlington VT 05401, reports annually on backyard and community gardening activity.

5. Wendell Berry, *The Gift of Good Land* (San Francisco: North Point Press, 1981), Chapter 20, "The Economics of Subsistence."

6. Leo Marx, *The Machine in the Garden: Technology and the Pastoral Ideal in America* (New York: Oxford University Press, 1969), p. 127.

Farmland trusts: an end to buying and selling

Bill Minter

Mennonites in North America have been a people deeply rooted in the land. Is this still our ideal? Or has society's view of land ownership caused us to discard those principles that we once accepted as having been established by God when he led the children of Israel into the land of Canaan?

Should the church begin to take an active role in redefining those principles? Should we look again at the biblical message prohibiting buying and selling land? Should the church provide an alternative to private land ownership so that land can be accessible to those who wish to begin farming or who need another option simply to continue farming?

If so, perhaps we need to look to a broad-based church organization, such as Mennonite Foundation, to oversee a land trust that would make such an alternative possible.[7]

A farmland trust is a democratic, nonprofit corporation that acquires land through purchase or donation, intending to retain title in perpetuity. Trust land is removed from the speculative market and leased to persons who agree to farm it in ways responsible to the environment and to society. A broad-based church group could oversee a land trust.

A board of trustees representing the interests of agriculture, real estate, finance, and natural resources could be set up to manage this trust. The donor's family and heirs would have the first option to continue farming the land. These farming rights would be annually leased from the land trust for an amount equal to the property taxes, plus an administrative fee. If the donor was still living and wanted a lifetime annuity, the lease rate could be increased to provide the annuity. When the heirs no longer wished to farm, the rights could be leased at the current land rental market rates.

Any additional lease income above that needed for taxes and administrative costs would be placed in a land improvement fund. In order to protect the value of the capital resource base, the lessee would be required to implement and/or maintain conservation practices recommended by local conservation agencies. Practices that improve the inherent productivity of the land could be financed by the fund.

---

7. Currently, Mennonite Foundation accepts gifts of farmland which it often sells, distributing the proceeds according to the wishes of the donor. By giving the land, the donor may receive tax deductions, avoid most capital gains taxes, and reduce future estate taxes paid by heirs.

Four objectives would be accomplished by the church's involvement in a land trust. First, the opportunity would be provided to Mennonite farmers to pass on their land stewardship ethic to others willing to continue practicing it. Second, future generations would be assured access to land without paying for it time and time again. Third, farmland would be removed from the pressures of the speculative development market, which could result in a decrease of the property tax assessment. Fourth, the long-term land stewardship view would be maintained, as part of the work of the church, regardless of market conditions.

Is this a solution to the current problems faced by our rural communities? It will not remedy the effects but could address some of the causes. A proposal such as this brings to light many questions that will need to be addressed if it is to become a reality. But it may reveal an opportunity to call some of God's people back to the basic principles God established.

For study and discussion

1. Each of the stories in the first part of the chapter indicates a personal concern for the next generation. How does your community reach to the future? What efforts in your own life are done in behalf of someone else's future?

2. Is farming today practiced by the majority of North Americans for the lifestyle and values it perpetuates, or is farming done for the wealth which it is expected to create? Are attitudes and expectations different today than they were twenty or forty years ago?

3. When an Amish farmer faces foreclosure, the church intercepts the process by taking control of the checkbook and formulating a debt repayment program which is presented to the bank for approval. An Amish foreclosure never gets to civil proceedings. Would this be a workable model for other churches? How might it work in your own community?

4. In what ways has the trend toward independence in North American agriculture raised the cost of doing business? Has this trend been a result of changing social and religious values, or has it been the result of increasingly sophisticated farm technology and the pressures associated with paying for it?

5. In what circumstances might community life as practiced by the Hutterites be advantageous or desirable?

6. Do you think that the shared decision making and shared labor in the farm work by members of the Plow Creek Fellowship help them to apply the concepts of shalom and Jubilee to their relationships with one another and with the land? Do individual farm families that you know sometimes

have a similar sense of relationship with their neighbors and/or their land?

7. Natural energy flows imply a food production system modeled on an ecosystem. Under what conditions is this a possibility?

8. Production for household use implies growth in the non-monetized, informal economy at the expense of the formal or market economy. What moral and religious value is there in thus bypassing the market economy?

9. Is the ownership of land an inalienable personal right? How is your answer to that question reflected in your view of land trusts?

10. What specific guidelines given by God in Leviticus 25 and Exodus 23 would be addressed by the proposal for a land trust described in this chapter?

11. The writer states that there are questions that need to be considered if his land trust proposal is to be workable. Given current farm management patterns, what would some of those be?

Planting rice in Sri Lanka

A genuine public life
would begin with the
premise that there are
victories for the whole
which are greater than a
victory for any of its
parts. We would
understand that we are
members of one another;
that the social order will
be secure for our own
life, liberty and pursuit
of happiness only if it is
secure for others as well.
The foundation of public
life is the tenacious faith
that we are in this
together and can find
ways for everyone to win.
—Parker J. Palmer

9. Family farmers linked to others

Jocele Thut Meyer & LaVonne Godwin Platt

As Christians, we see ourselves in community. The way we relate to other people shows how we interpret the Bible's words, "Love your neighbor as yourself" (Matt. 22:39). Along with those who do not claim to be Christian, we find that today's world forces us to see our welfare tied closely both to local people and to others around the world.

Yet when we think of North American farmers, independence and individualism and not community come first to mind. Individual or family ownership of land and a sense of independent decision making are certainly important to most farmers. At the same time, most rural people have a sense of community. They see themselves in light of their relation to the people among whom they live and work, as well as to those people beyond their local area.

Farmers know that their lives are linked to the people who provide goods and services on which they depend for equipment, fuel, seeds, and financial advice. They also see their lives bound up with those who buy and use their products. Let's look at some of the ways in which North American family farmers express their ties with other rural people and with urban people whose lives intertwine with theirs.

Family farmers linked to other rural people

When rural people see how interdependent they are with one another, they begin to strengthen their bonds in helpful ways. Linking their lives with others in a variety of ways has advantages at several levels—social, economic, political, and spiritual.

Where people help each other

The value of this interaction is seen most vividly in times of crisis. Farmers caught in the present economic downturn often find that they receive emotional and spiritual strength, as well as needed economic and legal advice, when they become part of *support groups* in their churches or communities. These groups put farmers in touch with others who have similar concerns or with those who have expertise to advise them on particular problems.

A Mennonite group in Manitoba, formed to work with farmers in financial crisis, also addresses underlying causes of soil degradation and encourages responsible use of land. Farmers who cooperate with the Soil Conservation Service, County Extension Service, or other *organizations that focus on conservation and good farming practices* have similar sharing and learning experiences. The Center for Rural Affairs in Nebraska and the Land Stewardship Project in Minnesota are two groups whose work links farmers with similar concerns.

A number of associations work with southern farmers to help them improve their chances for survival. The Rural Advancement Fund in North Carolina works with both black and white farmers, helping them understand the need for interdependence in solving farm problems. The Federation of Southern Cooperatives, now merged with the Emergency Land Fund, has helped farmers form co-ops where members buy supplies, market products, receive information, develop skills, and gain access to funds.

Which farm organizations should we choose to work with? Mark Epp (who develops principles of good farming in chapter 6) believes that farmers should become active in those groups whose members help each other improve their farming practices and their use of the land. Also important are those groups that give social, emotional, and spiritual support to their members.

He also believes farmers should join national and regional farm organizations. Such groups build political awareness and provide a place to raise issues for others to hear and understand. Christian farmers should not choose single-issue associations but instead join organizations that recognize value in other groups (such as labor unions) that are different from their own. Both in a biblical sense and in an economic sense, Christian farmers can be helped, through their organizations, to identify with urban industrial workers as brothers and sisters. Some organizations focus on international links, helping farmers to see the tie between large military budgets and low farm prices, to recognize injustice, and to identify with

the powerless, as Jesus did. Epp also suggests that farmers should participate in groups that see peace and fairness as goals, both within the
organization and in society.

Co-ops that get the job done

Farmer cooperatives are integral to family farms in many parts of America. Co-ops provide a major channel through which farmers can work
together for the good of all. Ray Regier, a farmer in central Kansas,
describes the role of cooperatives in his farming:

> I market all of my wheat, corn, and soybeans through my local
> cooperative, the Mid-Kansas Cooperative at Moundridge. My local
> co-op markets much of the wheat through Union Equity Cooperative
> Exchange, a regional cooperative owned and controlled by local co-
> ops throughout the winter wheat producing area.
>
> I buy my fuel, fertilizer, tires, and agricultural chemicals at my local
> co-op, which buys them from Farmland Industries, a regional coop-
> erative owned and controlled by its member co-ops, including the
> Mid-Kansas Co-op. Farmland Industries owns fertilizer plants and,
> together with other regional co-ops, owns refineries where it pro-
> duces its own products designed to meet my specific needs as a
> farmer.
>
> I use the services of the Mid-Kansas Credit Union which, like all
> credit unions, is also a co-op. When we bought our farm we borrowed
> from the Federal Land Bank which, along with the Bank for Cooper-
> atives and the Production Credit Association, makes up the coopera-
> tive Farm Credit System.
>
> We get electricity on our farm from a privately owned company, but it
> was because of pressure from the cooperative Rural Electric Associ-
> ation that private companies were "forced" to provide service to
> rural areas such as ours.[1]

Regier points out that a cooperative is a democratic institution which
seeks to serve the best interests of its members, each of whom has one
vote—and only one—in the decisions of the cooperative, regardless of the
amount of investment. Co-ops distribute profits in the form of patronage
refunds determined by the value of a member's transactions. By contrast,
the main purpose of a business corporation is to make profits for stock-

1. Ray Regier, unpublished paper, 1986.

holders who control the business in proportion to the amount of their investment. Cooperatives maintain local control of capital and allow producers greater control in marketing and processing.

Regier says that "farmer cooperatives are valuable institutions that enable farm communities to exist, and they will flourish or die along with the communities themselves." He goes on to say that "while co-ops are essential for small farmers, they do not harm large farmers. There is room for all sizes within cooperatives."[2]

Some cooperatives aim to help small producers and family farmers improve farm practices and marketing procedures. Thomas Vaughns, extension horticulturist at the University of Arkansas, assisted more than a thousand vegetable growers and small farmers in a vegetable cooperative in Arkansas. With a corps of horticulture aides, he set up a program to share information regarding growing, harvesting, and marketing. Now, with cooperation among producers, businesses, and the extension service, families who otherwise would have had to leave their farms are able to make a decent living. The co-op has been sensitive to the needs of the local people, enabling them to use resources at hand and showing them where to find help to solve their problems.[3]

Helping farmers who need a hand

When we look at the links that connect rural people with one another, we must consider the relationships between the advantaged and the disadvantaged among North American rural society. To understand the economic linkages in agriculture, we must recognize that those who are family farmers in the mainstream of North American rural life are meshed with rural people who are alienated from power in our society—especially black farmers, Native American farmers, and migrant farm workers. As more and more family farmers experience the sense of powerlessness that comes from being isolated from control of the factors of production, they may see more clearly how they are bound together with other rural people who have always lacked that control in their own practice of agriculture.

Black farmers. Land ownership by black people in the United States reached a peak in 1910, when they were full or part owners of 15 million acres of farmland. In the years that followed, black ownership of land declined to 12 million acres by 1950, 5.5 million acres by 1969, and 4.2 million acres by 1978. The numbers of black farmers declined from nearly

2. Regier.
3. Thomas Vaughns, "Vegetable Cooperative," *Catholic Rural Life* (July 1984), pp. 16-17.

a million in 1920 to only 33,000 in 1982. If present trends continue, by the year 2000, there will be no black farmers in the United States.[4]

Other destructive influences have heightened the current economic crisis for black farmers. These include "restrictive property tax and inheritance laws; discriminatory schemes of local governments and rival landowners that cheated owners and their heirs; unavailability of credit; mechanization and other new technology that encouraged debt and expansion; and the black-owned farm's traditional small size and less secure financial status."[5]

Chester Jones, a United Methodist minister, suggests that because racial discrimination has much to do with this situation among black farmers, churches should respond to the need. Especially critical has been the discrimination against black farmers seeking to obtain credit. Jones believes that if churches would make funds available to black farmers, it could also be a way for the churches to re-establish commitment to values that place the rural economy and its people above material gains and profit.[6]

Native Americans and the land. We speak glibly of Europeans discovering North America. This land was inhabited by a people whom the European settlers pushed from their homes to the least desirable areas of the continent. Those of us whose ancestors settled virgin farmland must recognize that we, in a sense, participated in displacing native peoples. Knowing this should move us to work for the rights of native people today.

Even now, Native Americans do not receive full income from the products of their lands. In the 1970s, products grown on land considered by the Bureau of Indian Affairs to be Indian land were marketed for nearly $400 million. However, non-Indian farmers who leased the land from Indian owners received 73 percent of that $400 million income.[7] Most of the leased land is the better land. The native people are left with marginally productive farms and rangeland. In addition, as with other small minority farmers, Native Americans lack access to credit and government farm aid.

We can learn much from Native Americans concerning stewardship of the land and partnership with the creation. Lawrence Hart, a Mennonite leader and Cheyenne chief, says that the Cheyenne have a sense of

4. Chester Jones, "The Plight of Black Farmers Driven From Their Land," *Engage/Social Action* (June 1985), pp. 20-25.
5. "Family Farm Networker," Interfaith Action for Economic Justice, Washington, D.C. (April 1986).
6. Chester Jones.
7. David A. Larsen, "A Poor Harvest," *The View From the Land*, Vol. I, 1979, p. 17.

closeness to the earth and to all of nature. Their desire to live in harmony with the earth and its progeny expresses this respect for all of creation.[8] This concept of land stewardship would have been understood by the psalmist who sang, "The earth is the Lord's and the fullness thereof, the world and those who dwell therein" (Ps. 24:1).

Migrants and seasonal workers. Maria is a migrant worker who, with her husband Juan and other farm workers, came to a National Farm Workers Ministry Conference in Ohio several years ago to tell of their efforts to bring growers and workers together for negotiations.

Maria's English was halting, but she communicated well. Her story was of farm workers who may have only enough food to keep themselves alive, yet provide for others strawberries in January, broccoli all year, and orange juice every day for breakfast. Living in squalid shacks and traveling at night between jobs, the migrant and seasonal workers are hired to work at a farm for a few weeks or months and then move on to another part of the country as the growing seasons change.

When Art and Jocele Meyer lived in Grenada, West Indies, they met persons who were seasonal farm workers in North America. Morgan Lewis, a local taxi driver for five months of the year, works seven months each year with a farm crew in Ontario. Each year, he leaves his wife and five children and returns to the same farm to plant, cultivate, and harvest.

At extremely low pay, the Caribbean workers do jobs that most North Americans won't do. For example, a Jamaican farm worker at a Virginia orchard is paid thirty cents to pick a forty-five-pound box of Red Delicious apples which retails for $22.50.[9] Rarely are migrant farm laborers covered by workers' compensation, unemployment benefits, or other fringe benefits.

All too often our society treats these workers as commodities rather than as people with pride, feelings, and needs. Robert Coles tells the poignant stories of migrant children and their disrupted families in *Children of Crisis: Migrants, Sharecroppers, Mountaineers*. The book highlights ways the loss of hope and oppression destroy initiative.[10]

We are linked almost daily and in important ways to the Marias and Juans and Morgan Lewises of our society. They provide our farms with needed workers. Without much effort on our part, we enjoy the products

8. Lawrence Hart, "The Message from the Native American People," Symposium II Conservation/Ecology: A Mennonite Mandate, Laurelville, Pa., December 1982.

9. Ingolf Vogeler, *The Myth of the Family Farm: Agribusiness Dominance of U. S. Agriculture* (Boulder: Westview Press, 1981), p. 219.

10. Robert Coles, *Volume II Children of Crisis: Migrants, Sharecroppers and Mountaineers* (Boston: Little Brown and Co., 1967).

of their labor. Can we find ways to make that link benefit them as well as us?

The National Farm Worker Ministry of the National Council of Churches and the United Farm Workers work at strengthening the relationship. They organized consumers to boycott certain products until producers agreed to provide improved working conditions and more equitable wages to the migrant farm workers.

The effectiveness of this type of effort was shown when the Farm Labor Organizing Committee's seven-year boycott of Campbell products was suspended in February 1986, after workers, growers, and the corporation agreed to meet to address the needs of all the parties concerned. Under the agreement, the Campbell Company continues to hold profitable contracts with the tomato and cucumber growers in Ohio and Michigan; the food processing company in that area is assured of a steady source of tomatoes and cucumbers picked on time; and workers now have guaranteed jobs, improved housing, better working conditions, health care and wage raises. Only 600 workers in Ohio and Michigan's tomato and cucumber fields were covered by the new contract, but efforts to include other workers, producers, and food processing companies looked favorable at the time of the agreement.[11]

Family farmers often have not seen seasonal migrant farm workers in a positive light. Whether or not they have hired migrant workers on their farms, many family farmers have not supported the right of farm workers to organize.

Others, however, see similarities in the powerlessness of seasonal farm laborers and their own lack of control in setting prices for their products. These farmers believe that difficulties in the present system of hiring farm labor could be overcome if different options could be considered that would be mutually beneficial and would bring dignity and power to the farm worker as well as to the farmer. They recognize that, ideally, people who work the land should share the benefits and the fruits of their labor.

Links between rural and urban people

Rural and urban people depend on each other in many ways. This relationship, both on the local and national level, needs constant nurture. The linkage is seen most clearly in the role of farmers who supply food and other products for everyone.

11. *FLOC Update*, Toledo (April 1986).

Farm and city need each other

The apostle Paul wrote, "If one member suffers, all suffer together; if one member is honored, all rejoice together" (1 Cor. 12:26). Rural people, who today face the loss of their land and, along with it, a way of life, can also feel the hurts and fears of people in urban areas who suffer from unemployment, loss of purchasing power, and hopelessness.

Traditionally, rural life has fostered values that have been highly regarded. Communion with God, the Creator, has been sustained by daily work with the creation, through dealing with the uncertainties of the weather, and depending on the unfailing changes of the seasons. Positive social values contributing to the welfare of society have been strengthened in rural family and community settings.

"A rejuvenation of rural America is essential to the welfare of our whole society," says James Pierce, executive director of National Sharecroppers/Rural Advancement Fund. "Unless the problems of rural areas are solved, the problems of cities will be intensified. A prosperous rural America will mean a healthier economy in the nation and the world."[12]

Moving to and from the city

Hard times in rural areas have generally increased migration to the cities, increasing existing urban problems. The 1982 Report of the U.S. Commission on Civil Rights lists problems readily seen in urban areas today. "Virtually every aspect of urban crisis—poverty, welfare, unemployment, crime, housing, health," says the report, can be attributed to rural migrations to the city. Too many people are forced into too little space. "The result is a national crisis of the environment—the relationship between the people and the land—and from this crisis others have erupted all around us."[13]

Following World War II, many people moved from rural areas to cities. A reverse migration slowed that trend during the 1960s and '70s in a "back to the land movement" which saw people moving to rural areas to make their homes, if not their livelihoods, on the land. Such crisscrossing, whether for economic or cultural reasons, can help break barriers and strengthen links between urban and rural people. The new homesteading movement, which Maynard Kaufman describes in chapter 8, has given a positive direction to these relationships.

12. James M. Pierce, *The Condition of Farmworkers and Small America*, Report to National Board, National Sharecroppers / Rural Advancement Fund, 1982.
13. A Report of the U. S. Commission on Civil Rights, *The Decline of Black Farming in America*, 1982, p. 6.

Farming's shadow on the factory

Michigan Congressman Levin, in testimony before the U.S. House of Representatives in March 1985, showed how the present agricultural crisis touches all citizens. Agriculture, with a work force of 23 million people, is the largest industry and largest employer in the nation. Every major industrial state also has a major agricultural sector. Michigan, for example, lists manufacturing as its first industry and agriculture as its second.

Agriculture is also a major consumer of industrial products. Farm equipment factories face slowdowns, consolidation, or loss of their businesses whenever the farm economy declines and farmers purchase less equipment. Levin also said that the overvalued dollar and high interest rates have decreased farm exports in the same way that exports from the industrial sector have been affected.[14]

City workers and farmers with common woes

A common misunderstanding exists between farmers and urban laborers. Persons in each group believe the other group to be causing economic problems for them. Some urban workers point fingers at farmers, blaming them for the increase of food costs at the grocery store. They do not know that the farmer receives only seven cents of the dollar cost of a loaf of bread, for instance, and that the farm-to-retail price spread has increased steadily throughout the 1980s. Each year, the farm value of food goes down, while the retail price goes up.[15]

On the other hand, some farmers blame urban workers, saying that high wages raise the cost of farm inputs. This charge, too, is off the mark. The data show something different. Between 1972 and 1981, "the purchasing power of the average worker earnings declined by 16 percent," says the Institute for Labor Education and Research. "The country's gross national product (GNP) more than doubled during the 1970s, but the standard of living provided by the average worker's earnings was lower in 1981 than it was in 1956."[16]

In fact, per worker hour costs rose much more slowly than in any other industrial country. Therefore, in terms of labor costs, U.S. corporations were actually gaining relative advantage over corporations in other countries.[17] A closer look at the facts shows the more precise causes of in-

14. *Congressional Record*, House of Representatives H 1043, March 5, 1985.
15. Dirck Steimel, "A Thinner Slice," *Wichita Eagle-Beacon*, December 14, 1986, p. B-1.
16. Institute for Labor Education and Research, *What's Wrong with the U. S. Economy?* (Boston: South End Press, 1982), p. 2.
17. *What's Wrong With the U. S. Economy*, p. 348.

creased prices: 1) top heavy corporation bureaucracy, that is, steady increase in the ratio of the number of supervisory personnel to production workers; 2) corporate work in the cost of mergers (paper assets) and the cost of increased investments overseas.[18]

Citing this data, Nebraska farmer Mark Epp says, "Farmers and urban laborers should see themselves in solidarity with one another. We should not be antagonistic toward one another, but rather see each other as allies."

Hunger at home a common cause

In the United States, agricultural legislation links food producers and people who receive food assistance. Charles Lutz finds three reasons why farmers and low-income food-aid recipients have a common self-interest that is strengthened by the fact that federal food programs are a part of the Department of Agriculture.

First, he says, "Farmers need the support of non-farm members of Congress to get favorable farm legislation passed . . . [and] the food programs need support from representatives who do not have large concentrations of the poor." Secondly, Lutz points to the education that takes place through the implementation of the program. "It helps nonfarm populations to learn about and gain empathy for the situations of farmers. The widespread concerns about hunger in America and overseas have also provided some education about farming and farm economics in the United States. Farmers have been a major part of that process of educating the rest of us," Lutz says. Finally, he suggests that the alliance between food producers and food-assistance recipients can remind both "that they share a kind of economic vulnerability in our social system. The nature of the risk is different, but both face economic insecurities."[19]

Back to the land in the city

Cities result from agriculture that produces surplus at the expense of limited resources. In the process, many people are separated from the land. Urban gardening and farmers' markets are two ways that urban people can link themselves to the land once again. Creating opportunities for urban young adults to spend summers in rural areas—living and working with farm families—is another type of experience that can help people form ties to rural values as well as to the land.

18. *What's Wrong With the U. S. Economy,* p. 358.
19. Charles P. Lutz, ed., *Farming the Lord's Land: Christian Perspectives on American Agriculture* (Minneapolis: Augsburg Publishing House, 1980), Chapter 2.

Gardening. Nearly half the households in the United States have gardens. In 1982, home gardens produced fruits and vegetables valued at an estimated $18 billion.[20] Even in urban areas people often have access to land to grow some of their own food.

Several years ago Jocele visited a community gardening project in Newark, New Jersey. The gardens were located in an area surrounded by heavy traffic and signs of urban decay. It was late in the season and only a few fall crops remained. It was evident that the half dozen men preparing their plots for winter felt a sense of responsibility and ownership for the gardens.

The county horticulturist who supervised the project pointed to an experimental geodesic, solar greenhouse that was a part of the cooperative endeavor. Under a wooden frame covered with plastic were steel drums, painted black and filled with water to serve as a heat bank for the cucumbers, lettuce, and tomatoes that were growing in the greenhouse. This venture had potential to provide fresh vegetables in winter and seedlings for spring planting.

In rural areas near cities, pick-your-own gardens provide consumers with another enjoyable way to relate to the land. A few producers accept regular customers who pay on a yearly basis for the opportunity to pick.

Obviously, farmers will continue to be responsible for the major production of food crops. Nonetheless, urban consumers and nonfarm rural residents who produce some of their food will have a greater appreciation of the food producing system.

The connection of people to growing things in soil goes deeper than developing an understanding and appreciation of a rural way of life. When people garden, the nurturing and caring qualities that are in each of us emerge. It is a useful contrast for urban people who are caught up in the competitive work of most urban jobs.

Direct Marketing. Direct marketing is an age-old tradition of farmers being revived today. It may be a one-truck tailgate operation, a roadside stand, door-to-door sales on a regular route, or a group of farmers setting up produce stands in a central location on a weekly basis.

In addition to providing new outlets for produce, direct marketing helps to conserve diminishing farmland, through continuing to use land near cities for agriculture instead of developing it for industry and housing. Shoppers who purchase food directly from producers save an average of 20 percent on their grocery bills. Farmers receive an average of 44 per-

20. Dana Jackson, "The Sustainable Garden," in Wes Jackson and others, *Meeting the Expectations of the Land* (San Francisco: North Point Press, 1984), p. 106.

cent more than through regular wholesale channels.[21] Moreover, direct marketing gives farmers an opportunity to control factors of both production and marketing, something that is often not possible if the farmer is under contract with wholesalers to deliver particular products.

In many parts of the country, vegetable and fruit stands in front yards of farmsteads provide local produce in season. Most are family enterprises. Larger markets have grown from some of these small stands.

Farmers' markets have played an important role in the development of small-scale ethnic farming in the United States. One of the oldest farmers' markets in the nation is described in a 1985 issue of the journal, *Agriculture and Human Values*.

> Pike Place Market in Seattle, Washington, began in 1907. It provided an alternative marketing outlet to small farmers who were receiving low prices from wholesale houses.

> Although the Market has grown from a few wagons parked along the side of Pike Place to a seven acre historical district with over 200 retail shops and restaurants, it still retains its identity as a farmers' market. The Pike Place Market has retained its basic aim to provide fresh local produce to the citizens of Seattle. Currently, 85 farmers sell their produce in the Market.

> Market farmers arrived here in waves of immigration. First the Europeans, then the Japanese, later the Filipinos, and recently the Hmong and Mien Highlanders from Laos.

> Ethnic farmers have always been important to the survival of the Pike Place Market and, by the same token, the Market has been important to the survival of ethnic farming in western Washington. Traditionally, ethnic farms are small and have limited access to marketing outlets. Direct marketing methods, like those used at the Pike Place Market, are one of the few ways small farmers have to sell their produce.[22]

Not operated by farmers but giving them an alternate outlet for their produce, Greenmarket is a well-organized and profitable market for farm produce at twelve locations in New York City. Individuals, shopkeepers

---

21. "Help to Write a New Law," Rodale Press, undated paper.
22. Steven Evans, "Ethnic Farmers and the Pike Place Market: a Brief History of Ethnic Farming in Western Washington," *Agriculture and Human Values* (Summer 1985), Vol. II, No. 3, p. 57.

and restaurant owners regularly patronize Greenmarket stalls for fresh produce.[23]

Alternative markets for local products and ethnic foods are being started in small cities and towns all across the nation. One new retail store in Wichita, Kansas, specializes in baked goods and hormone-free meat. The store provides a wider market to several small ethnic bakeries and butcher shops in nearby rural towns. Alternative markets such as this offer a variety of choices to the consumer, along with local control in decision making by the food producer and the small store owner. They represent a healthy relationship between rural and urban people.

Gaining control over our food supply

Consumer cooperatives build a sense of community and foster an understanding of the interdependence of consumers and producers as they work together. Growing out of the social activism of the 1930s, consumer cooperatives have varied in popularity as the acceptability of social programs in the United States has ebbed and flowed. Like the producer cooperative to which they are closely akin, consumer co-ops help to increase the self-reliance of their members by helping them gain greater control over a major aspect of their lifestyle.

Among the various types of consumer cooperatives, food buying co-ops have been the most active in recent years. Many persons participated in food co-ops during the 1960s and 1970s when the back-to-the-land movement and a responsible lifestyle emphasis were popular. People were interested in eating the less processed foods that were commonly available at co-ops. Because co-ops buy in bulk (often from local producers), save on advertising and packaging, have low overhead costs, and provide their own labor, prices are usually kept low.

The Bluestem Cooperative in Newton, Kansas, is typical of small food co-ops that offer alternatives to supermarket shopping, providing quality food at prices equal to or lower than supermarkets, but more importantly, maintaining the principles of interdependency and cooperation that link producers and consumers. The Bluestem Co-op sells locally produced cheese, eggs, flour, honey, and hormone-free beef.

It is one of several dozen cooperatives and food buying clubs in the Midwest affiliated with the Ozark Cooperative Warehouse that provides local member co-ops with basic products, mostly in bulk packaging. Many

---

23. "Case Study: Greenmarket," *Food Marketing Alternatives for the Inner City*, Community Nutrition Institute, 1982, pp. 54-64.

of the warehouse suppliers are producer cooperatives from across the nation. A women's trucking co-op distributes the warehouse orders to local co-ops on a regular basis. At the beginning, the Bluestem Co-op banked at a credit union in a nearby small rural town, forging yet another tie to a sense of community.

The Bluestem Co-op, like other cooperatives, represents a spirit that is built around the concept of working together with other people to develop community interdependency. One of the founders of the Bluestem Cooperative stresses the links that are formed in cooperatives:

Many of us in buying our food may reflect very little on where it comes from. We need not concern ourselves with the sweat or fatigue or frustration of the people who helped produce it. That the weather or seasonal changes affect availability of food hardly enters our consciousness as supermarket shoppers, . . . but haven't we lost something in all this convenience? What we may have lost is a sense of our dependence on the land and of our interdependence with the people who cultivate it. If that sense is worth regaining, then a co-op might help us do it. Working at the co-op, talking with other members, learning about the sources of supply for the co-op—all might help us appreciate again these interdependencies.[24]

Holding on to rural values

The American public realizes the need for a strong agriculture base and is willing to work toward saving the "culture of the land." A newspaper poll, taken in February 1986, revealed that 55 percent of those surveyed were willing to pay higher taxes to sponsor programs that help farmers save their land.[25]

Individual efforts to strengthen relationships and understanding between urban and rural people must be channeled into political, economic, and social systems that give direction to today's agricultural and industrial sectors. Preservation of a way of life that is efficient, interdependent, just, and sustainable requires the best efforts of all working in the best interest of all humankind.

For study and discussion

1. How can the migrant worker situation best be addressed today? Are

24. Dwight Krehbiel, draft copy of report of Bluestem Cooperative, Newton, Kansas, undated.
25. Report of *New York Times*-CBS Poll, *Christian Science Monitor,* (Feb. 26, 1986).

boycotts of specific fruits and vegetables by consumers the best way? If you know migrant workers and/or farmers who hire them, discuss the situation with them and hear their views.

2. Native Americans in certain areas are being moved today with the possible intent of making their homeland available for coal and other mineral mining. How do you think this issue should be resolved?

3. Do you feel that the government and church agencies assume as much responsibility for minority farmers who are losing their land as for other small farmers?

4. Some members of the urban church which the Meyers attended in Ohio came to the city from rural southern areas. Many of them prospered financially. They had left hard work and low financial return in the South. Now many of them are having problems as the city has an unemployment rate double the national average because steel industry and related industries are depressed. How can the church relate to these urban people in a depressed economic setting and to farmers in similar financial straits? What is the relationship between the two settings?

5. List various foods served at breakfast (or another meal). Trace one or more of them from producer to consumer. How many steps and different persons were involved? Evaluate this food system.

6. What are the advantages of local food production and distribution? Could you purchase more locally grown foods?

Stavely, Alberta

Public policy has in the past determined the shape of agriculture and farming in this country. It has provided a political and economic environment within which individual farmers could function. Public policy will be an even more dominant factor in shaping agriculture in the future—even determining whether there will still be family farms. Involvement by concerned individuals and groups in shaping our future public policy would seem to be appropriate.
—Raymond Regier

10. Make public policy work for justice

Roger Claassen

Because of its benefits to society, family farm agriculture is a reasonable goal for government public policy.

Family farms provide society with a food production system that is stable, economically resilient, adaptable, and efficient. The decentralized nature of family farming ensures that our food supply is not concentrated in the hands of a few decision makers. On a local level, family farming contributes greatly to the economic and social development of rural communities.

Past farm policy shaped the present

Throughout U.S. history, public policies have strongly influenced agriculture. Most helpful in building family farm agriculture in the Midwest and Plains states was the 1862 Homestead Act. This law limited farm size and encouraged owner-operators to live on their land.

In the 1930s, farm policy turned toward promoting efficiency and production in agriculture, as well as correcting the disparity between farm and nonfarm incomes. Federal farm credit policies made credit available for farmers to adopt new technologies. Farm commodity programs helped control surpluses and compensated farmers for low prices.

Policy choices harmful to the family farm

Over the past fifty years, U.S. agriculture has undergone basic changes. The number of farms has been reduced by two-thirds. The distribution of production and farm income has become skewed more and more toward a few large farms. About 5 percent of farms now account for almost 50 percent of production. Absentee ownership of farmland and other agricultural resources is increasingly common. Beginning farmers have found it more and more difficult to get started in agriculture. Farms have become more specialized and have replaced labor with capital investment.

Public policies have exerted divergent influences on the farm sector. For the most part, however, they have encouraged concentration of farm resources into fewer hands. Benefits from farm programs are doled out on the basis of production volume, almost without regard to farm size. Tax breaks gain value as a taxpayer's net income and tax bracket increases, making agricultural investments more lucrative to wealthy farmers and high-income, nonfarm investors. Even federal credit programs designed to help beginning farmers or those with limited resources often provide credit to larger, expanding farms instead.

At the same time, policy makers, regardless of their political views, have supported the family farm in their public statements. The 1977 Food and Agricultural Act (the farm bill) is a good example:

> Congress hereby reaffirms the historical policy of the United States to foster and encourage the family farm system of agriculture . . . it is the policy and the express intent of Congress [that] no such [agriculture or agriculture related] program be administered in a manner that will place the family farm at an unfair economic disadvantage.[1]

Often, however, *family farm* is a vague term used to evoke a nostalgic response and gain support for whatever farm policies a particular person advocates. A clear definition, advanced by Interfaith Action for Economic Justice and stated in the Introduction of this book, bears repeating here:

> A family farm is an agricultural production unit in which the management, economic risk, and most of the labor—peak seasons excepted—are provided by a given family, and from which that family derives the bulk of its income.

Thus, family farms can vary in size, type, and practices. Historically, family farms have generally been diversified, with a relatively low level of capital investment (and debt)—factors which spread out risk and allow maximum flexibility in adjusting to changing economic conditions.

Even when a definition is agreed upon, however, catch phrases such as *the family farm* may carry a variety of meanings. Because of the many concerns involved, it may be more helpful for the most part to think of

---

1. Quoted from "Family Farming and the Common Good," Interreligious Taskforce on U.S. Food Policy, February 1977.

specific traits desirable in agriculture rather than a particular definition of family farm.

The decline of the family farm reflects changes in the structure of most farms. It is not simply a matter of farm families being replaced by industrial agribusiness corporations. Farmers—who are by all standards family farmers—may choose to do things that damage the family farm system.

In some cases, farmers must choose between self-interest and what is in the interest of family farm agriculture. For example, the push to expand farm size has reduced opportunities for beginning farmers. Yet many established farmers feel that expansion was and is necessary for them to stay in business. Public policies, unfortunately, have heightened the tension between self-interest and maintaining the family farm system. Often, they encourage choices harmful to family farm agriculture and enhance the competitive position of industrial agribusiness corporations relative to family farms.

In this sense, reorienting policy toward family farm agriculture is less an issue of picking out which farms fit a particular definition than designing programs to support particular trends, actions, or activities that strengthen the *family farm system*. Stated another way, farm policies should meet the legitimate needs of family farm agriculture. They should avoid encouraging or subsidizing trends which work against that system of agriculture.

The purposes of a public policy oriented toward the family farm would be to meet some of the legitimate needs of family farm agriculture:

- to help assure stable, fair incomes on efficient, well-managed moderate-sized family farms;
- to foster widely distributed ownership of land and other agricultural resources by farm operators;
- to help beginning farmers realize opportunities in agriculture;
- to conserve food producing resources;
- to encourage diversified farming systems.

Learning from the farm crisis

Like many past downturns in the farm economy, the current crisis is the result of a boom-and-bust cycle in which the financially weak lost control of agricultural resources and the financially strong gained control of even more. During the 1970s, the export boom, extremely low real interest rates (the nominal rate minus inflation), and government incentives brought rapid and massive investment to agriculture. Farms expanded production rapidly to meet an increased world demand for U.S. commodities. These investment patterns continued and perhaps speeded up trends moving toward the demise of family farm agriculture.

The price of farmland, in particular, reflected the increased expectations of agriculture made possible by the profits of the '70s. In the competition to increase acreage, many farmers took on greater debt to expand their farms or make other capital investments, using inflated land values as collateral. Increasingly, land had speculative value, as well as being valuable for its production of farm income. By the late '70s, ties were cut between the price of the land and its income producing capacity.

Through increased net worth and borrowing power, those who already owned land benefited from higher land prices. Wealthy farmers and investors could use the tax code to shelter other income or gain control of even more land. For tenant farmers, beginning farmers, or those who relied on current income from farming and could not successfully exploit the tax code, land purchases were expensive and difficult. Inflated land prices blocked opportunity for many would-be farmers.

In the dramatically altered economic environment of the 1980s, an overcapitalized and overproductive agriculture now faces massive readjustments. In 1986, an estimated one-fourth of farm debt could not be repaid, and as many as one-third of farmers may face bankruptcy in the next few years.

Farm survival depends largely on debt load. Farmers who carry debt loads low enough or who can subsidize agricultural investments with other income will survive. Efficiency and productivity are, at most, minor factors. Farm size does not tell which farms are likely to have problems. Farmers that began during the 1970s, and those that expanded most rapidly then, taking on large debt loads, are having the most financial difficulty—not small or large farms, as such. However, small or moderate-sized family farms without substantial nonfarm resources or income may ultimately have greater difficulty in dealing with financial problems.

Alleviating the effects of the farm crisis—the boom years as well as the bust—is extremely important to the future of family farm agriculture. A family farm oriented public policy must not only help indebted farmers recover; it should also help to reverse past structural trends that have been harmful to family farm agriculture. In particular, policy should:

- retire excess debt without displacing and/or dispossessing farmers. Debt loads should be adjusted to be more closely in line with the income producing capacity of agricultural resources, especially land. Per farm levels of assistance should be limited, so that more moderate-sized family farms may receive realistic levels of assistance and large concentrations of farmland may be broken up. A coordinated approach, where similar options are available to farm borrowers regardless of credit source, should be developed.

- start rebuilding family farm agriculture by helping beginning and reentry farmers take advantage of new opportunity created by low prices for land and machinery. Land that has been foreclosed by banks or other lenders is a large resource pool that could be directed toward beginning and reentry farmers. To make such purchases, qualified farmers must have access to reasonably priced credit.

Finally, the long-term prospects for family farm agriculture depend on reforming a variety of public policies including tax laws, farm commodity programs, farm credit policies, and research priorities. The role of trade in U.S. agriculture policy should also be closely examined. State governments must take on an expanded role in forming agricultural policies at the state level.

Tax policy as a form of farm policy[2]

Federal tax policy is one of the most powerful influences shaping U.S. agriculture today. In recent years, a complex web of tax breaks have tended to distort investment decisions, attracting overinvestment and resulting in increased economic concentration in the farm sector.

Agriculture has been among the most tax-favored of all U.S. industries. In general, a tax break is realized any time current income can be understated for tax purposes. Both general business and special farm tax provisions offer ways to shelter income through agricultural investments. These include rapid depreciation of assets, cash accounting, favorable corporate tax rates, and deductibility of some capital expenditures as cash expenses.

Most tax breaks increase in value as income increases (regardless of source). Thus, the competitive position of persons who are in higher tax brackets is strongly enhanced through tax breaks. Out of a $1,000 deductible expense, a corporation in the 34 percent bracket realizes a $340 reduction in taxes, while a farmer in the 15 percent bracket realizes only a $150 reduction.

Tax policy is another form of farm policy. In many instances, however, the tax code has worked at cross purposes to other farm policies and

2. This section on tax policy relied heavily on information provided by Chuck Hassebrook, Center for Rural Affairs, Walthill, Nebraska.

programs. It increased federal budget costs (especially revenue losses due to tax sheltering) and encouraged overproduction, while farm commodity programs try to control surplus production. Beyond any doubt, tax laws have hastened the decline of family farm agriculture. Although the strength of tax policy effects on agriculture cannot be reliably measured, the general direction of their influence is clear:

- Tax policy contributed to the recent boom-and-bust cycles in land prices. Tax benefits promoted demand for farmland from both farmer and investor, placing upward pressure on land prices. When farm profits fell and land prices leveled off or began to decline, tax speculators stopped buying land, worsening the bust.

- Tax policy stimulated overproduction of some commodities (resulting in lower prices and reducing overall profits), encouraged the expansion of existing farms, and encouraged farmers to replace labor with capital.

- Tax policy until recently encouraged environmentally damaging practices such as sodbusting or swampbusting (the conversion of highly erosion prone rangelands or wetlands to crop production). Special allowances continue to actually subsidize depletion of water resources in some areas.

A major positive change in the influence of tax policy on agriculture came with the passage of the 1986 tax reform law by the U.S. Congress. Although the bill retained certain tax breaks that grant competitive advantages to large corporate farms, this new tax law will reduce the negative effects of tax policy on the family farm.

The new law ended the deduction of some (but not all) capital expenditures as cash expenses. It eliminated altogether such tax advantages as investment tax credit and preferential treatment of capital gains. Nonfarm investors will not be able to deduct farm losses from other income unless they take part in the management of the farm, and limits will be set on the amount of farm debt interest that can be deducted for tax purposes.

Estate and gift taxes are other issues of concern to family farmers. Laws governing these taxes were first enacted to prevent undue concentration of wealth in a few families, or, in agricultural terms, the development of a land owning class.

During the 1970s, farm expansion and inflation sharply increased the value of many farms. The estate tax came under frequent criticism as a hindrance to passing on the family farm to the next generation. Rather than preventing economic concentration, estate taxes were seen as a threat to family farms.

As written, estate tax laws encourage nonfarmers to hold onto inherited land and prompt wealthy investors to build farm estates. Thus estate tax rules, like income tax laws, have encouraged fewer and larger farms and absentee ownership.

Focusing commodity programs on farm income

Commodity programs, commonly referred to as farm programs, were enacted in the 1930s to help correct the imbalance between farm and nonfarm incomes. Basically unchanged over the past fifty years, commodity programs have concentrated on controlling surpluses and supporting commodity prices.

These programs have several features: price support loans, deficiency payments, and acreage reduction programs. In most cases, price support loans and deficiency payments are extended to farmers who agree to participate in acreage reduction programs. Loan size is based on a per bushel loan rate. Farmers may opt to forfeit grain to the government in lieu of repayment. Deficiency payments are direct government-to-farmer payments that make up the difference between the loan and an established target price.

Despite their original purposes, commodity programs have failed to focus clearly on supporting farm incomes. Benefit levels have always been tied to volume of production—paid on a per bushel basis to anyone who controls production of supported commodities (wheat, feed grains, cotton, rice, dairy products). Farm program recipients are not required to be farmers or to depend on agriculture for their income.

Small and moderate-sized farms receive a relatively small amount of support in the farm programs. Direct payment limitations at $50,000 per producer are overly generous. At that level, the limitation does little to redress program imbalances—10 percent of farmers receive about 50 percent of government payments in most years. Even then, the largest producers benefit from loopholes that exempt a portion of payments from limitation.

Moreover, the amount of a price support loan that a producer can receive has no limit. In past years, even if farmers did not take part in acreage reduction, the loan program held market prices up and allowed nonparticipants to ride free on the price enhancing effects of such programs. The 1985 farm bill lowered the price support loan rate, so that a large portion of support is made through direct payments, forcing a higher percentage of farmers to participate in the programs.

Furthermore, prior to the 1985 farm bill, commodity loans and payments were made without regard to conservation practices. The new sodbuster law will eventually cut off farm program payments to farmers who produce commodities on highly erodible land. In a similar way, swampbuster provisions will cut off payments to farmers who fill in wetlands for the purpose of agricultural production.

As currently structured, farm commodity programs have often been criticized for doing too little to support farm incomes and of having unintended side effects. Support levels have failed to keep pace with production costs, keeping farm incomes relatively low and encouraging farmers to make up in production what is lost on price. Moreover, by reducing price risk on a nearly unlimited volume of production, commodity programs have also reduced the risks of nearly unlimited farm expansion. By granting benefits according to land ownership, commodity programs have tended to further stimulate the overvaluation of land and capital relative to labor and management inputs.

Simply improving per bushel support rates, or lowering limitations on the size of farms eligible for payments are, by themselves, inadequate solutions. To truly support the goal of fair incomes for farm families, support rates should be raised and benefits extended only on a level of production necessary to provide fair family incomes from efficient, well-run, moderate-sized farms. Eligibility requirements should ensure that program benefits go to persons who depend on farm income, not investors or speculators. Such limitations would help ensure that labor and management are valued more highly relative to land and capital. Farm incomes would be raised without encouraging farm expansion or higher land prices.

The key drawback to such an approach is the perceived lack of participation in supply management programs by larger producers and landowners. As the structure of agriculture shifts toward a system dominated by relatively few large farms, this problem will increase. For wheat and feedgrain farmers, however, realistic, fiscally sound proposals that would target benefits towards small and moderate-sized farms could be shaped to improve support and, thus, participation incentives for about 99 percent of farms covering 80-85 percent of acres. For other crops, such as cotton or rice, industry concentration already makes targeting of benefits more difficult in practical and political terms.

Credit for the farmers most needing it

Commercial banks, the federally chartered, borrower-owned Farm Credit System, Farmers Home Administration, life insurance companies, and the Small Business Administration all provide credit to agriculture. Readily available credit has allowed farmers to adopt new technologies and enlarge farms, often improving operating efficiency and reducing the heavy burdens of farm labor.

Many believe, however, that easy, subsidized credit terms may have helped propel these changes too far, too fast. The ready availability of emergency loans cushioned the risk of farm expansion and large debt loads, encouraging individual farms to expand.

On the other hand, credit *access* often determines who will have the opportunity to farm and whether land offered for sale will be added to an expanding farm or used to create opportunity for a new farmer. In distributing credit among farmers, lenders have much to say about which would-be farmers will eventually succeed. Over the years, credit access has been a difficult problem for beginning, minority, and small acreage farmers who lack assets to pledge as collateral against loans, yet need additional resources to build viable farm operations.

Farmers Home Administration (FmHA) was created in 1946 to help beginning, limited resource, and tenant farmers, who could not get credit elsewhere, to become viable owner-operators. FmHA also served as a lender of last resort to family-sized farms, especially in the event of natural disaster. As such, FmHA has played a key role in helping to maintain the family farm.

In recent years, however, loans have been granted in ever larger chunks to more established producers, often cushioning the risks of farm expansion. During the late '70s, as farm debt mounted, heavily indebted farmers were less able to withstand the instability of weather or price changes.

FmHA emergency loans were given to help farmers through what was then considered a temporary downturn. These programs included disaster loans which extended credit to farmers in the event of natural disaster and economic emergency loans designed to cushion established farmers from the impact of low commodity prices. The high loan ceilings and broader terms of eligibility were suited to larger farms that could not qualify for regular FmHA farm loan programs.

Gradually, FmHA became a lender of last resort to the entire farm economy. "FmHA credit assistance to farmers has generally and gradually evolved toward providing credit to all farmers who for various reasons are unable to obtain credit elsewhere," says the U.S. Department of Agriculture.[3] "The subsistence and large-scale operations are equally eligible

3. "Federal Credit Programs for Agriculture," *Agriculture Information Bulletin*, No. 783 (United States Department of Agriculture, November 1984), p. 16.

as long as credit is not available elsewhere at reasonable terms."

Even regular FmHA programs, which once earmarked funds exclusively for low-equity, limited resource borrowers, have been broadened through increased loan ceilings, and changes in eligibility requirements. Most recently, the 1985 farm bill shifts FmHA loan programs away from providing direct government-to-farmer loans toward guaranteeing commercial loans. Previous experience with guaranteed loan programs indicates that loans will be fewer in number and granted in larger chunks to relatively large farms.

Another sign of change is the shift of loan funds among FmHA activities. Since 1981, loan funds earmarked for farm ownership have declined from roughly one-half to one-sixth of regular (non-emergency) loan funds. Today, largely because of farm debt restructuring, farm operating loans dominate FmHA lending. The lack of loan funds further reduces the opportunity for beginning or limited resource farms to obtain land. Farm ownership loans will become increasingly important in coming years as lenders put foreclosed farmland back on the market.

These actions raise fundamental questions about the role of federal farm credit programs: to whom, for what purpose, and under what terms should credit be extended to the nation's farm sector? The current farm crisis has increased the need for a lender of last resort to keep financially troubled, yet viable farms in operation. And, ironically, lower prices for land and machinery also mean greater opportunity for beginning or reentry farmers—if reasonably priced credit is available to them. If FmHA is to fulfill these functions, lending practices must reflect a commitment to these particular types of farm borrowers and be tailored to their specific needs:

- loan eligibility criteria and loan ceilings should effectively direct lending toward beginning and limited resource family farm borrowers;[4]
- FmHA should return to its traditional emphasis on direct government to farmer loans;
- loans for farmland purchases should be retained and funding significantly increased.

4. The 1985 farm bill brings emergency loans, as well as regular farm loan programs, under the family-sized limitation. Family-sized farms, as defined by FmHA regulation, are 1) managed by the borrower and 2) have a substantial portion of the labor provided by the borrower and his or her family. Thus, a family-sized farm is the size of farm that can be run primarily by family members.

Self-reliant family farms through research[5]

State agricultural experiment stations and other land grant college re-search projects have influenced American family farms in the past and have a role in their future direction. Traditionally, the primary objective of research, particularly crop and livestock research, has been to increase production and reduce labor. The increased production has appeared to increase farm efficiency as well, because of higher yield per acre and per farmer. This assessment, however, has failed to consider the greater reliance on fossil fuels, outside capital, and the decline in long-term inherent productivity of the land. As farm surpluses increased and prices of farms lowered, costs of inputs per acre or per animal unit increased. In essence, family farmers became victims of the research programs that were intended to help them.

Research programs should consider first the needs of the family farms they are trying to assist. Priorities of research should include developing and sustaining the inherent productivity of the land without the use of large amounts of resources for external inputs. This type of research will help farmers become more self-reliant and less dependent on inputs bought from commercial agribusiness companies. Labor will replace capital rather than the other way around.

This new approach would be done best by a broad-based coalition of researchers representing many disciplines within the agricultural colleges. Not only agronomists and soil scientists, but also economists, sociologists, and ecologists should be involved in agricultural research. The research should be organized around an interdisciplinary approach that includes concern for the land, the families that farm the land, the rural communities to which they belong, and the long-term ability of the system to sustain itself.

Stable markets abroad for better world trade?

World competition is a major issue of the 1980s. Many U.S. industries, including agriculture, have suffered much from foreign imports or in-creased competition for other world markets. To some extent, for the last thirty years, U.S. farm policy has focused on foreign markets as a way to handle surplus production. More recently, the 1985 farm bill placed export competition in its most central role ever in the history of agriculture policy.

During the massive trade boom of the 1970s, U.S. farm exports in-

---

5. This section on research written by David Gerber, Agriculture Department, Hesston College, Hesston, Kansas.

creased fourfold. Since 1981, they have declined by about 30 percent. Worldwide recession and record grain production, especially in developing countries where markets grew most rapidly in the 1970s, have led to a shrinking world grain trade. Intensified international competition, a strong U.S. dollar, and, according to some, the overpricing of U.S. commodities have reduced the U.S. share of world markets.

Price support levels were targeted by the Reagan administration and some agricultural trade advocates in Congress. The 1985 farm bill sharply reduced price support levels, thereby lowering commodity prices in an attempt to recapture lost markets. Target price levels (from which direct payments are determined) will be lowered by 10 percent over the five year life of the bill. In theory, this attempt to save money and to expose farmers more and more to world markets forces investment and production decisions to reflect world market conditions.

It may be several years before the trade implications of the 1985 farm bill become fully clear. In the meantime, farm exports continue on their downward trend. Ultimately, the expansion of U.S. exports may be more a matter of expanding market share than capturing new markets in an overall expansion of world grain trade. If so, already heated competition among developed grain exporting nations could get even hotter.

In the midst of the rush to export, several observations can be made. First, even though nearly 500 million people—one-quarter of the world population—are malnourished, it is doubtful that U.S. food (or commercial or concessional food exports from any country) can solve hunger problems. People are hungry because they are poor. They cannot afford food or do not have the means to grow it. And many hungry people live in relatively wealthy countries, including the United States and Canada, or in poorer countries with a so-called exportable surplus of food, such as India. Hunger is a justice issue that can be solved through equitable economic and agricultural development, not through increases in food imports.

Nor is food aid a solution, although it can be helpful if properly used. In emergency situations, such as the recent famine in sub-Saharan Africa, food aid can be of great value. And, when applied carefully, food aid may also help to foster development. However, even in its most virtuous roles, food is an inefficient form of aid, difficult (and expensive) to transport and limited in use. In many, if not most cases, contributions of cash or needed nonfood resources would be more helpful.

Secondly, domestic policy goals, such as maintaining family farm agriculture or conserving food producing resources should not be compromised for the sake of trade. Trade should be viewed as a tool by which legitimate policy objectives may be achieved. Even if new market-oriented policies prove effective, heavy reliance on trade as the solution to farm problems is a questionable policy. The agricultural success enjoyed by an increasing number of nations makes trade a less and less plausible solution to surplus production. Moreover, the fickle nature of world demand will increase the risk of future boom and bust cycles in agriculture.

In the long term, increasing food security in developing countries and improving trade opportunities for U.S. agriculture will depend on broad-based increases in income through equitable economic development. For now, U.S. trade policy should call for greater stability in world commodity markets and improved international cooperation in supply management, reserve holding, and export subsidy restraint. Such action would be a considerable departure from current policy which, rather blatantly, pursues world domination. Multilateral negotiations toward agreements on agricultural trade should begin as soon as possible, even though the short-term prospects for meaningful agreements are not good.

States handle conservation, crises, corporations

Public policy at the state level generally focuses on conservation, use of natural resources, and laws relating to land ownership. Concern for such legislation is usually highest where public policy advocacy groups are active.

Conservation legislation. Concerns about soil erosion and the wise use of other natural resources have influenced legislation in some states. These state laws augment the work of the federal Soil Conservation Service. The strength of such programs is often a sign of the land stewardship ethics of the people of the state at a particular juncture in its history.

A recent example of strong conservation legislation on the state level is Minnesota's 1986 law. This law requires nonfamily farm corporations to include in their lease agreements a provision that prohibits damage to conservation practices. Under the new law, corporations which destroy conservation practices put on the land with cost-share funds from the state are required to repay the state at 12 percent interest, even if a previous owner had received the state funds to initiate the conservation practice.

Counseling and advocacy efforts. At least ten states have programs that provide counseling and advocacy services to financially troubled farmers. About half of these programs are fully or partially funded by state governments. The programs vary in services provided, but generally help farmers in financial difficulty to work through options and exercise rights. Some state programs refer farmers to appropriate legal or emotional help.

Homestead exemption reform. All state bankruptcy codes include homestead exemptions that protect a certain amount of property from being sold under foreclosure proceedings, unless the exemption is waived in a mortgage agreement—a standard practice. Some states are now expanding the amount of property exempted. Other proposals would limit the waiver of homestead exemptions on second mortgages.

Mandatory mediation. A few states (for example, Minnesota and Iowa) have instituted programs that, upon the borrower's request, require foreclosure proceedings to be suspended while a mediated solution is sought. The process includes a credit analyst review of the situation and mediated meetings between the lender and borrower. Other states have similar programs under voluntary plans.

Dwelling redemption. For farmers who can come up with ample cash or financing, dwelling redemption laws allow a farmer who is undergoing foreclosure to retain the family home, farm buildings, and a few acres. These provisions are designed to keep families in the community and help them retain resources that can be used to begin rebuilding toward an eventual recovery of the farm.

Debt restructuring. A number of different plans are being tried, generally focusing on lowering debt payments through interest rate reduction. Initial experiences with such plans in some states showed mixed results. In linked deposit programs, state cash reserves are deposited in agriculture banks at reduced rates of return with the understanding that banks will pass reduced costs on to qualifying farmers. In many cases, however, the eligibility requirements were so loose that almost any farmer could receive lower priced loans.

Restrictions on corporate farming. At least thirteen states have laws restricting the agricultural activities of corporations. One of the strongest such statutes is Nebraska's Initiative 300. This is an amendment to the Nebraska state constitution prohibiting the further purchase of farmland or establishment of farming operations by nonfamily corporations and limited partnerships.

Farmers can shape their futures

Farmers themselves make many of the decisions that will determine the future of U.S. agriculture, even though the influence of corporations and investors cannot be ignored. Public policies are instrumental in determining the climate in which crucial decisions are made. Beyond any doubt, public policies need reform if the family farm system is to survive. And those involved in agriculture will have much to say about crucial decisions in the public policy arena.

Even though farmers are a small portion of the population, they hold significant power in farm policy decisions. Substantial federal resources are poured into farm programs and agricultural tax subsidies every year. How these resources are allocated—whether to enrich the largest farms and wealthiest investors or to support a family farm system of agriculture—is largely up to farmers. Farmers need to recognize that they can influence policy at local, state, and national levels.

Any successful effort at changing public policy needs grassroots support as well as a Washington and state capitol presence to communicate with elected officials. Just as attitudes and values will determine farm management choices that are key to the survival of the family farm system, those same attitudes and values should be reflected at the ballot box and in work through public policy organizations. Together, family farmers and concerned citizens *can* make a difference, and *now* is the time to begin.

For study and discussion

1. What public policies do you believe have influenced agriculture the most?

2. How have changes in the structure of agriculture been determined by public policy?

3. How do the 1986 tax reforms make a difference to U.S. agriculture? What have been the short-term effects for you personally? Will the changes be good for you in the long run? How do you think they will affect the stability of the family farm?

4. Of the public policies discussed in this chapter, which are the most important in assuring economic justice for all citizens?

5. What do you think should be the primary goal for agricultural research?

6. Which public policy decisions are the most important ones for your state or province? Is your province or state working on these issues?

7. If you agree that farmers themselves make many of the decisions that will determine the future of agriculture, what responsibility does that place on you?

Global questions require global answers. . . . The shaping of our common future is much too important to be left to governments and experts alone. Therefore, our appeal goes to youth; to women's and labor movements; to political, intellectual and religious leaders; to scientists and educators; to technicians and managers; to members of the rural and business communities. May they all try to understand and to conduct their affairs in the light of this new challenge.
—The Brandt Commission

11. Farmers of the world connected

Farmers everywhere burdened by militarism

Robert O. Epp

The horse-drawn disk that day in the late '30s was weaving back and forth, leaving a crooked trail of dark brown freshly turned soil. Any good Mennonite farmer driving by would have thought, "That boy on the disk will never make a farmer."

The boy was so engrossed in watching the black-headed gulls around him that he was oblivious to all else. "Are they sea gulls?" he wondered. "What are they doing here on the plains of Nebraska? Where do they come from? Where are they going?" He pondered the questions as he watched the birds swoop so low they almost touched the horses' ears, then drop to the ground behind him and pick up the fat white grubs the moving disk had exposed.

At his earliest opportunity the boy sought the help of a guidebook that identified the birds as Franklin's Gulls. "They nest in the northern United States and Canada and winter along the coast of Mexico and Central America," he read.

"Central America. These birds have come from Central America," the boy said. It was a pleasant link to a faraway place he only vaguely pictured in his mind.

Since that early spring day when the brilliant blue sky and cumulus clouds provided a peaceful background for the ever-moving gulls, the links between my Nebraska farm and the lands of Central America have become sharper in my mind and many of them less benign than they seemed fifty years ago when I first saw the gulls.

Prosperity built on military spending

Most United States citizens see their country as a peaceful nation desiring no foreign territory and promoting free enterprise as it helps smaller nations to join the family of democracies. A closer examination, however, shows a different reality.

At the close of World War II, the United States was the most powerful nation in the world. Agriculture and industry seemed to be prospering. It appeared that we were able to supply both "guns and butter."

Fearing that a sudden shift from a wartime to a peacetime economy would bring a return to chronic unemployment and economic doldrums, policymakers continued high military spending, coupled with a search for ever-expanding markets for our industrial and agricultural products. They also feared Soviet Union expansion, so a plan to keep raw materials and resources from falling to the Soviets seemed a natural part of the first requirement of keeping our economy strong. The anticommunist stance became the primary argument advanced to the public to gain support for the military budget.

The rationale of gaining prosperity through military spending has created a dilemma for those of us who advocate peaceful coexistence and a nonviolent approach to international disputes. We publicly deplore our nation's militaristic policy and avoid openly admitting that we have benefited from it. We have not done what we could to present a united voice against it.

"Though the mills of God grind slowly, yet they grind exceeding small" is an old proverb we need to learn anew. We need to take seriously the straightforward biblical maxim: "Such are the ways of all who get gain by violence; it takes away the life of its possessors" (Prov. 1:19).

The United States history since World War II parallels the history of Israel during the reign of Jereboam II, who capitalized on the powerlessness of Israel's war-torn neighbors and pursued a policy of foreign expansion. Israel gained control of major trade routes which brought great affluence to the country. (See Amos 6:4-6.) At the same time, according to Amos 3:10, the people stored up "violence and robbery in their strongholds" because their wealth was based on exploitation of the poor.[1]

Farmers hurt by military spending

We are now feeling the effects of a policy that has been pouring resources, capital, labor, and brain power into the military-industrial sector which

---

1. Jack A. Nelson, *Hunger for Justice* (Maryknoll, N.Y.: Orbis Books, 1980), p. 58.

produces nothing useful to the economy.[2] High military expenditures hit hardest those regions with few defense industries, since these areas pay more into the federal treasury than is received in return. Rural areas are heavy losers in this system.[3]

From 1980 to 1985, the federal deficit went from $60 billion to an estimated $203 billion, an increase of $143 billion. During the same period, military spending rose from $136 billion to $287 billion, an increase of $149 billion.[4] It is readily clear that the military budget, coupled with reduced income from taxes, is primarily responsible for the current deficit.

To translate these figures into familiar terms, consider what could happen if the cost of only one MX missile were invested in the farm community. If the $120 million spent on building an MX missile were used instead for agriculture, it would buy two hundred L-3 Gleaner combines at $89,787; four hundred 7045 Allis Chalmers tractors at $43,328; thirty thousand acres of irrigated land at $2,300 per acre; and forty thousand feeder calves at $325; with $2,355,700 pocket money left over. When we consider that Congress has voted to deploy fifty of these MX missiles in only one part of the military budget, can we doubt that the military has an effect on U.S. agriculture?[5]

To meet the rising costs of these parasitic expenditures, the government has to borrow one-third of all the available capital in this country.[6] Competing thus with all other users for the limited amount of capital tends to keep real interest rates high and hurts farmers who are heavy users of capital in our present system of farming.

The high interest rate creates an overvalued dollar which in turn hurts our ability to export products. Export markets for U.S. manufactured goods were the first to feel the pinch when industry either lost out in the competition or moved overseas in search of cheap labor. For a time, our farm exports were the only bright spot in our balance of trade. Now the foreign markets for our agricultural products have been lost also.

Our exports of cereal grains affect Third World countries, raising serious ethical questions for us. At the same time, the system of agriculture

---

2. Lloyd J. Dumas, "Why Buying Guns Raises the Price of Our Butter," *Christianity and Crisis* (Nov. 27, 1978).

3. James R. Anderson, *Bankrupting America: The Tax Burden and Expenditures of the Pentagon by Congressional Districts* (Lansing. Mich.: Employment Research Associates, 1982).

4. Data from Congressional Budget Office, Washington, D.C., 1985.

5. Jeff Tracy, *No M-X*, Nebraskans for Peace, undated pamphlet.

6. Jeff Tracy, unpublished paper.

that we have adopted has been severely hurt by the loss of export markets. This situation is deepening the farm crisis and, as we have tried to show, is a direct result of our bloated military expenditures. To add insult to injury, the Reagan administration tried to recapture the foreign grain market and thus improve the balance of trade by meeting the world market price, while at the same time cutting the federal budget for agriculture programs. This policy has been a disaster for family farmers.

Profits for agribusiness in military contracts

So, does anyone, particularly anyone engaged in agriculture, benefit from the present situation? Yes. The Tenneco Corporation, which has invested capital in a broad spectrum of the economy, is a prime example. In 1983, Newport News, a subsidiary to Tenneco, had $7.5 billion in military contracts, mostly with the navy. Tenneco itself showed 17.9 percent profit with its navy contracts. They made over $2.5 billion profits from 1981 to '83 and yet reported $189 million in tax refunds from the government. This was done by taking advantage of corporate tax laws to invest profits in business ventures that provide tax-loss shelters.

As most farmers know, Tenneco recently bought International Harvester Company's farm equipment division and merged it with J. I. Case, which they already owned. In addition, through a subsidiary company, Tenneco West, they own 1,129,398 acres of land in the United States. Tenneco itself farms 29,500 acres and the rest is leased to farmers.[7]

Corporations grow fat while peasants go hungry

We have seen that U.S. military policy has developed to satisfy pragmatic and ideological goals. What effect has it had on the rest of the world? In 1969, American forces staffed 399 major and 1,930 minor overseas installations with approximately 1,222,000 soldiers. Since 1945, the United States has conducted a major military campaign or paramilitary CIA sponsored operation at an average rate of one every eight months. These military interventions included Greece (1948), Iran (1952), Guatemala (1954), Indonesia (1958), Lebanon (1958), Laos (1960), Cuba (1961), Congo (1964), British Guiana (1964), the Dominican Republic (1965), Vietnam (1964-68), and Grenada (1983). In addition, the United States has provided billions of dollars in military assistance to governments of poor countries hoping to insure stability and a proper investment climate for U.S. companies.

In the Caribbean basin and in Central and South America, the United

7. Jeff Tracy *Nebraska Report* Vol. 13, No. 4, April 1986.

States maintains a strong influence. This general area was first colonized by Spain. The *conquistadors* came looking for gold to take back to Spain. The land itself was parceled out to explorers and members of the aristocracy, who developed it in plantation style. An elite landed gentry, who continued to extract wealth by exploiting the labor of the indigenous people, became the dominant social and power structure. When the Spanish empire declined, the British began to fill the vacuum, until the United States, under the impetus of its Manifest Destiny doctrine, replaced the British through military and political intervention. American entrepreneurs gained control of millions of acres in Central America, where they could grow bananas for export to supply the demand of the North American consumer.

As a Nebraska farmer I saw this link between my life and the lives of people in the small countries to the South when I went to Nicaragua with a Witness for Peace delegation in March 1984. There I saw the effects of the economic invasion of Central American countries by American interests.

A hundred years ago, Nicaragua was self-sufficient in basic grains and cereal crops. Then corporations with outside capital took over the land and shifted production to cash crops (cotton, coffee, sugar) for export. After this happened, cereal grains needed to be imported. But the small farmers who had been displaced had very little income and could not afford the imported food. Malnutrition spread among much of the peasant population, who eventually revolted. In 1912, the United States sent marines into Nicaragua to maintain order. Thus began a twenty-year occupation of Nicaragua by U.S. armed forces and control of the economy by U.S. bankers.

Recent U.S. policies in Central America have also favored financial interests at the expense of human interests. During the last twenty years, Central America has increased its beef production dramatically with the help of low interest loans to huge consortiums. The loans were subsidized by U.S. taxpayers under the Alliance for Progress, but the beef production did not benefit the people of Central America. During this time, for example, Guatemalans ate 50 percent less beef and Costa Ricans ate 41.2 percent less beef than before the program started.[8]

The largest owner of grazing land in Central America is the Latin America Agribusiness Development Corporation (LAAD).[9] LAAD is a holding company with fifteen members, including Chase Manhattan

8. Jeff Tracy *Nebraska Report* Vol. 13, No. 2, February 1986.
9. *Nebraska Report*, Vol. 13, No. 2.

Bank, Bank of America, Borden, Cargill, CPC International, John Deere, Gerber, Goodyear, Castle and Cooke, and Ralston Purina. LAAD is also responsible for funding many meat processing plants in Central America. It has received U.S.-AID loans on several occasions, at 3 to 4 percent interest, to expand its projects in Central America.

In addition to LAAD, other large corporations or consortiums raise cattle in Central America. The largest single exporter of beef from Central America seems to be Agrodinamica, a company based in Honduras and Costa Rica. This company is heavily financed by ADELA, an investment consortium of 222 shareholders who represent the largest international firms and banks in the world. U.S. corporations active in ADELA are Citicorp, Caterpillar Tractor, Bank of America, IBM, Coca Cola, and Castle and Cooke.

Low interest loans subsidized by U.S. taxpayers finance these operations which compete directly with U.S. livestock producers. The citizens of the Central American countries concerned do not benefit from them. Instead, their lands are taken and basic foodstuffs are no longer available to them. In addition, these operations affect the environment by destroying the rain forests and replanting the areas with grass. When the grasslands are no longer productive, they are abandoned or retired, with the corporations retaining ownership.

It is sometimes difficult to determine what our official national policy is toward Central America, since our actions are often inconsistent with public pronouncements. Whether or not economic invasion of these countries is intended, our government policy fosters a political climate which makes it possible. Our Witness for Peace delegation had an hour-long interview with Roger Gamble, the deputy chief of mission at the U.S. Embassy in Managua, who supported this policy. In part, he said,

> The only way the U.S. can relate to Central American countries is from a position of dominance. As a superpower we do have a dominant factor. It is a fact of life. It is our right as a superpower. Our interests are not economic. Our security interests are such that a political openness to revolution is a threat to our security. This is not a policy easy to sell to anyone. Right or wrong, we will do all in our power economically, politically, and *finally militarily* to insure our right to dominance. (Emphasis added.)

Oppression spreads to our own farmsteads

The Third World resembles, in many ways, the U.S. farm sector. Recently, some have referred to our agricultural economy as the domestic Third

World.

Some states have established policies to help family farms survive by legislating restrictions on corporate farming. In 1982, Nebraska voters placed a restrictive clause on corporate farming into the state constitution. Prudential Life Insurance had poured $450,000 into the campaign in an effort to defeat the initiative, but failed. Since then, legislators attempting to repeal or modify the amendment have used arguments that sound suspiciously like the Manifest Destiny concept being refashioned to apply to corporate agriculture in the United States. The struggle for control of raw materials and land faces the family farmer here as well as the *campesino* in Central America.

Military machine takes aim at land ownership

The military policies pursued by our nation are draining the productive sector of the economy. The cost is not only in capital and natural resources, but also in human resources. The greatest costs may be in their effects on our attitudes which cannot be supported by an ethical world-view. Those who gain materially apply relentless pressure to continue these policies, with no regard to the human and social costs involved. The balance of the policies are heavily weighted against the rural areas, both at home and abroad. The resulting military machine is used to insure that resources of the world, especially in Third World countries, are at our nation's disposal.

In this country, one of the last natural resources as yet widely dispersed in ownership is land. The struggle for the control of this resource provides a common link between the *campesino* of Central America and the family farmer of the United States.

Each spring, Franklin's Gulls will return to the Plains on their annual migration to their nesting grounds, as they have for untold centuries, a visible link between the Americas, a symbol of enduring and symbiotic connections. Just as I sought information years ago about the migratory gulls, so today I seek information about the forces at work in our society so that I can make morally sound judgments.

It is clear that the violence inherent in the military buildup inevitably "takes away the life of its possessors," as the writer of Proverbs warned. We must work to forge symbiotic relationships that can be sustaining and enduring, both ecologically and in human relationships.

World farmers cope with hunger

Gordon I. Hunsberger

A visitor to our southern Ontario farm one summer day some years ago stood with me on the hill where our buildings are located. We looked at the pond and crops in the fields below, and he said, "You people are living in the Garden of Eden."

His remark surprised me. I had lived in the area all of my life and had not traveled widely at that time. I naively assumed that many of the world's people lived somewhat like we did. We were just ordinary people.

Some years later I stood on another kind of hill in the mountains of Haiti and looked across the valley to a barren mountain. The old man at my side explained how conditions had changed for the worse since his youth. Now the mountains had lost more forest, and the land was less productive.

Seeing the contrast in living conditions between these two scenes, I understood much better why I had been told that I had grown up in the Garden of Eden.

Some questions face us: Are there links between these two places? And how can we work at correcting the disparity to our mutual benefit?

After colonialism: new oppressors

International development is a recent effort. Only since World War II, and largely during the past twenty years, has much attention been given to it. During the colonial era, most of the so-called Third World countries were possessions of European colonial powers. They were primarily sources of cheap raw materials for the rapidly growing industrialized nations.

Modern communication and transportation systems brought about changes that led to international development programs. Travel, once restricted to the wealthy, now became possible for more people. Via radio and, later, television, people around the world became more aware of how others lived. The oppressed were no longer satisfied to be exploited for the benefit of the oppressors. They began to demand and to get political freedom. But their newfound political freedom did not bring them the instant wealth and luxury they had expected. In some cases, it did little to improve their economic well-being. Sometimes the power elite in the newly independent countries became the new oppressors and life changed little for the ordinary citizen.

Development agencies take aim at hunger

As concerned people in the industrialized world sought ways to help others less fortunate than themselves, they soon discovered that they needed to do more than just give food to the hungry. They began to see ways to help create self-sufficient and self-reliant societies and communities. They formed development agencies to work at eliminating the causes of hunger. Some of them chose to work against systems that are exploitive.

Goals and purposes of development agencies also vary. Government agencies such as the Canadian International Development Agency (CIDA) and the United States Agency for International Development (U.S.-AID) always have as one of their goals the benefit of their own country as well as the recipient countries. Nongovernmental organizations (NGOs), on the other hand, are usually moved by concern and a sense of justice for those they are trying to help without seeking benefit for themselves. Since many international development agencies are involved in meeting the food needs of people, their efforts affect agriculture throughout the world.

Food is a basic human need, but many people suffer from hunger and malnutrition. Development agencies aim to correct this injustice. But they have learned that simply increasing food production does not resolve the problem of hunger. Perhaps the best illustration is the United States, which has the world's largest supply of surplus food. At the same time, according to the report of the President's Commission on Hunger in the U.S.A, the country has many hungry and malnourished residents. People throughout the world are suffering from hunger, not because of a lack of food, but because they do not have access to it. "The inequality of power, not scarcity of food resources, is the true cause of hunger," says Frances Moore Lappe.[10]

Changing the face of farming across the world

While international development efforts have not yet been able to bring about any significant change in this imbalance of power, their work has had a noticeable effect on world agriculture. India, for example, has long been known as a country with much hunger, malnutrition, and, at times, starvation. In recent years, however, partly as a result of the green revolution and other improved farming methods, India has become largely self-sufficient in basic food grains, and in some years even an exporter. Nonetheless, hunger and malnutrition are still widespread among the poor in India.

Even though national self-sufficiency in food supplies does not by itself assure the elimination of hunger within a country, it is still a worthwhile

10. Frances Moore Lappe, *Food First News*, No. 23, Fall 1985.

goal. One reason is that it helps assure dependability of supply. Food importing countries have learned that in times of shortages due to drought or other disasters, food exporters always look after their own needs first. The importing countries who depend on the surpluses of other nations cannot be assured of a supply.

Another recent development is the dramatic increase in the debt of Third World countries. Many of these countries have become so heavily indebted to wealthy nations, the World Bank, and the International Monetary Fund, that it is difficult for them to buy needed food supplies. Because Third World countries are already so heavily in debt, exporters are reluctant to extend further credit. Countries which are self-sufficient in basic food supplies can eliminate some of these hazards.

Many development agencies help countries work toward food self-sufficiency, but the goal is not always easy to attain. In some cases, control of the land resource is a major problem. Where large areas of food producing land are controlled by a few wealthy people or by foreign corporations who produce cash crops for export, it is difficult to increase food production for domestic use. Foreign development agencies can do little to change such situations. When the problem is lack of technical expertise or inputs of various kinds, they can be of much more help. An important ingredient for success in increasing food production is that the government of the host country be committed to such a goal. If they are not, worthwhile results are difficult to achieve.

A major problem in some countries is rapid population growth which has sometimes exceeded growth in food production. This is happening in Egypt, one of the largest recipients of American food aid. Egyptian leaders need to face the question of feeding their rapidly growing population should foreign food aid be cut off.

Food trade drying up as farming succeeds

In spite of problems, progress toward food self-sufficiency is being made and is having an effect on agriculture in other countries. It has had a marked effect on trading patterns. Former food importers have become exporters and vice versa. Government policies have been an important factor in these changing patterns as well.

The United States, Canada, and Australia have for years been the world's major food exporting countries. Buyers have been the densely populated countries of Europe, the Middle East, and Asia. In recent years, as the Soviet Union turned to increased livestock production it has become an important buyer of feed grain. It is likely that with its vast land resource, the Soviet Union will become self-sufficient in the not-too-distant future.

Because its agricultural sector has been heavily subsidized, the European Economic Community has now become a major food exporter rather than an importer. Many African countries, on the other hand, who for years had produced surplus food grain, have now become major importers.

Ever since the colonial era slave trade, much of Africa had been sparsely populated. However, foreign missionaries and international development agencies have introduced better health care systems and populations have mushroomed.[11] More people increased the need for food and firewood. Forests were cleared, droughts became more frequent and more severe, and crop failures and famine more commonplace.

Well meaning development agencies have in some cases inadvertently added to the problems by drilling wells in the Sahel. More water meant an increase in the size of the nomads' cattle herds. The cattle then overgrazed the sparse vegetation, causing the deserts to spread. Now many African countries find it necessary to import food.

On the other hand, some Asian countries that in the past have been large importers of food grains, are moving toward or have achieved self-sufficiency in basic foods. India is a prime example.

Even Bangladesh, a country about the size of the state of Wisconsin with a population of more than 100 million people, is moving toward self-sufficiency in food grains. Development agencies like the Mennonite Central Committee and many others are helping in the process. Using low cost, labor intensive appropriate technologies, they have introduced improved varieties of seeds, new crops, double cropping systems, and simple low cost irrigation pumps to help increase food production.

China, the world's most populous country, has also become self-sufficient in food, although there it has been done through internal government policy decisions rather than by international development. assistance. This change has had an effect in world agriculture because China has in the past been a major food importer. It still imports food such as wheat at times, but also exports rice, so that it is no longer a large net food importing country.

Feeding the world with surplus grain won't work

Historically, agriculture has gone through three stages—from subsistence agriculture (each family producing enough to feed itself), to market agriculture (producing more than enough for the family and selling the sur-

11. Paul Nelson, *Roots of the African Crisis* (Washington, D.C.: Bread for the World), background paper, No. 79.

plus to others within the country), to export agriculture (producing to sell to other countries). Large-scale export and import trade only became possible with development of modern transportation systems. Transportation and communication systems, agricultural technology, and dissemination of information are having a major impact on world food production patterns.

The market for food exports expanded with a growing world population which has been most rapid during the last century. But this, too, is changing. While population growth is still rapid in some countries, particularly in Africa and Latin America, in others it has slowed considerably, and in some it has stabilized. As development agencies succeed in helping people to achieve greater economic security, they no longer need the security of large families.

In a small way, the effect of economic security on population growth is illustrated by the Mirpur Wheat Straw Project, begun by the Mennonite Central Committee in Dhaka, Bangladesh, which I visited in the winter of 1986. About 450 economically disadvantaged young women are employed to make handicrafts using wheat straw. As the economic situation of the women has improved, they have delayed marriage until they are older and those who are married have been open to family planning suggestions, resulting in a lowered birth rate.

The export of agricultural commodities has become important to countries like the United States, Canada, and Australia. U.S. farm exports increased greatly during the 1970s. In Canada, thirty-two cents of every dollar the farmer receives for his produce comes from exports. In 1985, total cash receipts from Canadian farming operations was nearly $20 billion. Exports of agricultural products alone earn Canada nearly $9 billion.[12]

In Australia, I recently saw wheat stored on the ground in huge plastic-covered piles of up to 50,000 tons, awaiting a presently nonexistent export market. The farming communities in Australia, as well as in Canada and the United States, are feeling the effects of this change in export markets.

During the decades of the sixties and seventies, North American farmers were encouraged to produce all the food they could to feed a hungry world. It now appears that some farmers have produced themselves right out of business by producing more than they could market.

This picture could change quickly, as it has in the past. Weather, political upheaval and policy changes, wars, and changing economic condi-

12. From an address by the Honorable John Wise, Canadian Minister of Agriculture, June 4, 1986.

tions all affect food production and the farm economy. Crops must be suited to the climate. Canada, obviously, will never be able to produce its own citrus fruits, bananas, or coffee, but it can supply high quality wheat and dairy products to other countries. Food will always be exported and imported. Nevertheless, the old concept of feeding the world with North American food surpluses is changing.

Looking toward self-sufficiency in food production

Many agricultural experts believe that most countries have the resources to be self-sufficient in food. As international development agencies try to make that happen, farmers in traditional food exporting countries will need to make adjustments in their production planning.

Government policies are an important part in the process. Farmers have often shown their capacity to increase production when given the incentive. The present surpluses in the European Economic Community are the result of excessively high subsidies. During the first half of the seventies, when world grain reserves declined to dangerously low levels, it seemed to some world leaders that population growth had finally caught up to food production.

American farmers were encouraged by the U.S. Secretary of Agriculture to plant fence row to fence row and to produce all they could. In only a few years, grain elevators were again overflowing. In the Diefenbaker years in Canada, the government established floor prices for certain agricultural products at which the government would buy surplus products to maintain the price. This had to be discontinued after a few years, as the government became inundated with surpluses.

There is little doubt that with present-day technology, world food production could be greatly increased. The more difficult question is: where should it be produced and by whom? As I write this, in the spring of 1986, reports say that the world wheat price will drop sharply this year. The future looks gloomy for wheat producers in Canada, the United States, and Australia. The time has come to reevaluate.

Should the trend toward ever larger farming units, more specialization, more mechanization using fewer and fewer people be continued? Should water and fertilizer resources be used up to produce crops for which there is no market? Instead of simply focusing on production, perhaps we should again think first of feeding the family as our ancestors did, and as many producers in the less developed world still do, and then think of where we can market the rest of our production. The trend toward self-sufficiency in food production will likely continue, and it should.

Cooperation in God's worldview

Concerned farmers in countries like the United States and Canada are faced with a real dilemma. One of our major problems at present is overproduction. The surpluses result in depressed prices. In some cases government response is to pay farmers not to produce certain crops.

Farmers often ask whether something can be done to get our surplus food to needy people in other parts of the world. They don't feel right about curtailing production when the world has many hungry people.

But we need to remind ourselves again that hunger is the result of poverty. The hungry are too poor to buy our surplus food. Giving it to the needy does nothing to resolve the North American farmers' problems, nor does it resolve the problems of the poverty-stricken, Third-World farmers.

I remember a Haitian community where a Food for Work program was introduced by a foreign development agency. Peasant farmers found it easier to live from the food being supplied than to plant their own land. Furthermore, the influx of foreign food destroyed the market for the food they could produce beyond their own families' needs. When the Food for Work program ended they found themselves worse off than before, since they had not planted their own land.

From a world perspective, the answer would seem to lie in cooperation instead of confrontation. International development and trade directed toward improving the economy of poor nations would in the long run benefit wealthy nations as well. That is the thrust of the book, *North-South: A Program for Survival*. Willy Brandt writes in the Introduction, "To diminish the distance between 'rich' and 'poor' nations, to do away with discrimination, to approach equality of opportunity step by step is not only a matter of striving for justice which in itself would be important. It is also sound self-interest, not only for the poor and very poor nations but for the better-off as well."[13]

It is important for our Christian communities to develop a worldview. As we work at overcoming narrow individualism and nationalism, we need to become increasingly aware that God, who created the world and its resources, has always had a worldview.

For study and discussion

1. How have Americans who oppose militarism benefited from a war

---

13. The Brandt Commission, *A Report of the Independent Commission on International Development Issues* (Cambridge, Mass.: MIT Press, 1980).

economy? How have Americans who oppose militarism been hurt by a war economy?

2. How do military expenditures hurt the economy? Who is hurt the most? Who benefits?

3. What is meant by pragmatic and ideological reasons for military expansion? Which has the greatest emotional appeal?

4. Would you say the U.S. relationship to Central America is colonial, neocolonial, imperialistic, or paternalistic? Or is it a combination? Why?

5. What is meant by manifest destiny as a concept of national policy?

6. What is meant by a symbiotic relationship? Can you think of ways to foster symbiotic relationships both intranationally and internationally?

7. Do you see the work of international development agencies as having any noticeable effects on North American agriculture? on world agriculture? If so, what are they?

8. Is the goal of basic food self-sufficiency for all nations a valid one?

9. In light of the present economic crisis in North American agriculture, should the goals of international development be reconsidered?

10. Are government subsidies a help or a hindrance in resolving the problems of a depressed agriculture economy?

11. As a concerned Christian community, what should be our priorities in a world where in one part food surpluses are causing farm bankruptcies, and in others people are dying from malnutrition and starvation?

"Anabaptist Family near Berne," by Auré Le Robert

I believe a re-examination of our inherited philosophic and biological interpretations of human nature—*as well as greater trust in our own experience*—will lead to one conclusion: individual well-being is impossible outside of the well-being of others.
—Frances Moore Lappe

12. Responding to our rural crisis

Working together makes a difference

LaVonne Godwin Platt

Rural America is experiencing a crisis of major proportion. More and more families are being forced out of farming, businesses in rural towns are closing, and support services are being cut just when they are needed most. The statistics are there whenever we pick up a newspaper.

Most of us, however, do not measure the crisis by statistics. Instead, we see the crisis as David and Susan reorganizing their Pennsylvania farm under a Chapter 11 bankruptcy proceeding to save the land where David's ancestors settled seven generations ago. Or, we see it as Sharon and Alan farming as tenants on the Minnesota land they had owned for twenty-five years until a foreclosure sale in 1986 transferred the title to an insurance company.

We see the rural crisis in farm couples who have been able to keep on farming only because the wife, and sometimes the husband, too, took a second job in town. We see it in farm families who have left the rural community to find work and in urban workers who risk losing their jobs as an increased labor supply competes in the marketplace.

Some measure the farm crisis in terms of emotional tragedy—they see families torn apart by economic stresses; children and teenagers forced to face an uncertain future once thought secure; a neighbor whose feeling of isolation and inability to cope with the loss of his farm led to his suicide; the friend who lost not only his farm but also his faith when he gave in to the propaganda of a group promoting hate and violence as its answer to the farm crisis.

What have the churches and communities done for the families hit hardest by the farm crisis? How have their friends and extended families reacted? The response has been mixed. Sometimes relatives have rallied round to help at the first sign of trouble, friends have been supportive, churches have been sensitive to their needs, and communities have been quick to provide services to help the family make decisions that may carry them through the crisis.

Often, however, responses have not been positive or helpful, not compassionate or understanding. Many families undergoing these hardships have been ignored by people closest to them. In other cases, the responses have been negative, and families facing the loss of their farms felt blamed for situations which in large measure they could not control. Rural people, known for meeting emergency needs of neighbors and providing relief to people in distant lands, seemed unable to help when the persons in trouble were facing the loss of their family farm.

The examples are far too common. A young farmer is scolded almost daily by a relative who blames him for losing the family farm. A family, active in the church, receives no pastoral call even after their foreclosure sale is announced in the newspaper. A farmer with heavy debts faces serious surgery alone because his wife must remain at home to do the chores since he can no longer afford help with the farm work. A family finds that they cannot use their checking account while a bankruptcy proceeding is underway, and they have no cash to buy groceries. The list could go on and on.

Guidelines for our response to the rural crisis

Why so many people have reacted in negative ways to their neighbors in distress is not clear. Whatever the reasons, most of rural America seems now to be looking for better ways to respond. Many people have become aware that their lives *are* linked with their neighbors and their community, indeed, with the larger American society and the world.

Now they are looking at the ongoing crisis in rural America and asking how they can respond in creative, helpful ways. Let us look for some guidelines that may lead to positive, creative answers.

Persons and communities caught in the present rural crisis need to see their situation in a historical, economic perspective. This view frees them from blaming themselves or others. It can provide a context in which to find creative solutions to their problems. Thus, an important step toward wholeness is to *become aware of what happened and why it happened, without assigning fault.* (Margaret Hiebner deals with these concerns in chapter 5.)

Because a crisis gives rise to change, facing it allows individuals, families, and communities to look anew at their goals and priorities. To *assess and recover our basic values* is a second step to a new beginning based on an enduring foundation. (Ron Guengerich, Roy Kaufman, and Mark Epp help us test our values.)

Decisions of government at all levels shape farming practices and rural communities. Designing farm policies that will lead to economic recovery and promote family farm values can't be left to government officials alone. Rather, the *reshaping of public policy* is important for all who look for ways to turn the rural crisis into a time of opportunity. (Roger Claassen and others suggest helpful ways to assess public policy.)

The rural crisis has struck all of us, no matter where we work or where we live. It gives all of us a unique opportunity to respond to one another in creative ways. But it hits hardest those who face the loss of family farms, particularly when the farm has been in the family for several generations. When one's sense of place and self-identity is tied closely to vocation, as it often is for these farmers, the struggle can be difficult beyond measure. To be a supportive friend, to make sure that sound financial and legal advice are available to families under stress are important ways we can *affirm and minister to one another.*[1] We need to find helpful ways to respond as individuals, as churches, and as communities to the needs of our neighbors and friends who are hurting.

Finding ways to help people in trouble

No individual or family should endure the effects of the rural crisis alone. No one's needs should be faced in isolation.

During the mid-1980s, as the rural crisis deepened, many new groups were formed to focus on its causes and meet the needs of rural people at local, state, and national levels. Organizations that already worked with rural people added new services. Coalitions of churches, using networks already set up, were in the forefront of this movement. They held conferences and workshops throughout the farm states. They produced educational materials and issued statements of concern. Using telephone hotlines, they set up support networks for emotional, financial, and legal counseling for those in distress. In some states, they administered relief funds.

In addition to church-related groups, other state and regional associations responded. State governments enacted reforms aimed at easing

---

1. The four kinds of response in this essay were adapted from an article by Don Reeves, "Responding to the Farm Crisis," in *Quaker Life* (April 1986).

problems in farm communities. They provided farmer/creditor mediation services (as in Iowa) and counseling hotlines (as in Kansas) where such programs were not already in place.

Following the lead of Bethel College in Kansas, several colleges and universities developed plans to provide tuition-free education for retraining members of families forced to leave farming. Community colleges began job training services (as in Kirkwood Community College in Cedar Rapids, Iowa) and financial management programs (as in a statewide effort in Nebraska). Extension services in some states developed materials on stress counseling, in cooperation with community mental health centers. Community support groups took the lead in bringing in speakers to discuss such widely varied topics as the ethics of bankruptcy, helping a neighbor cope with stress, understanding the economic background of the farm crisis, and theology of the land.

Words and deeds for the churches

Responding to the rural crisis requires clarity of purpose and the commitment of people. In "Concerned for the Land and Its People" that follows, the Kansas Mennonite Farm Crisis Committee has called upon churches and government to take specific actions in response to the needs of rural America. Among the many groups committed to meeting those needs is the Mennonite Central Committee Farm Task Force, appointed to coordinate a response to the needs of farm communities. Following the Kansas group's statement, a profile of the task force members and their work continues to focus our concern on responding to rural America in crisis.

Concerned for the land and its people

Kansas Mennonite Farm Crisis Committee

Members of the committee that prepared the following statement of concern in August 1985 were: David Habegger, Bill Voth, Tom Graber, Raymond Regier, Armin Samuelson, Larry Goering, Annette Voth, Daryl Regier, Ervin Ediger, Jim Graber, Johnnie M. Bartel, Bruce Janzen, Griselda Shelly, and Gladys Regier.

As people with a strong rural heritage and a commitment to live out our Christian faith in practical ways, we are deeply concerned about the stress and pain being experienced by those families who make a living by farming, especially those on small or moderate-sized farms. It is our faith that land is a God-given resource to be cherished and that a proper stewardship of the earth's resources is a concern for all people.

An economic crisis in agriculture is adversely affecting many farmers and their surrounding communities. The scope of the problem facing them can be imagined when we learn that over four million farms have vanished over the past half century and America is still losing 30,000 a year.

The stress being experienced by farmers in our country has many complex roots. Among the major causes are the decades of agricultural and tax policies that encouraged the development of larger farms, an era of high interest rates linked with current declining land values, the decline in prices of farm commodities, ever-mounting debt loads, and unfavorable weather. The rapidly rising national debt and the increased appropriations for military expenditures are causes directly related to the rural economic crisis that few have been ready to acknowledge.

The net effect is that family farmers have little or no control over the means of their livelihood. The resulting stress affects both the physical and mental well-being of farm families. Financial stress takes its toll in strained and broken marriages, in spouse and child abuse, and in the misuse of alcohol and drugs. Grief and depression over threatened or impending loss of a farm and displacement from the land, in all too many cases, has led to suicide. There is a sense of alienation in the church and community as farmers are seen, by persons unaware of the problem, as inadequate planners and poor managers. The church has been seen as particularly unsympathetic and judgmental by many farmers.

We call upon our churches, as communities of faith, hope, and love, to do the following:

1. Affirm the following principles as basic:

• Ownership of agricultural land should be widespread and family farms encouraged in order to assure a democratic character to rural communities, the careful use of agricultural resources, and the welfare of society in general.

• Farming should provide a meaningful opportunity to earn an adequate living.

• Owning farmland for speculative purposes should be discouraged.

• Stewardship of natural resources is both a legitimate public policy objective and a responsibility of land ownership. Land is the common heritage of humankind; therefore, public policy should support and farmers practice conservation.

2. Affirm and cooperate with the various interchurch and governmental agencies that are taking action to be supportive of farm families. Among the agencies that are active, we note:

- [several Mennonite conferences and committees]
- [Kansas] Interfaith Rural Life Committee
- Interchurch Ministries of Nebraska
- [Kansas] Farm Assistance, Counseling and Training Service (FACTS)

3. Strengthen their ministries to those in stress by:

- Being present to all who are hurting, listening in nonjudgmental ways, seeking understanding and empathy, organizing support groups, and offering financial support for families to obtain professional counseling for stress management, marital and family tensions, and/or financial management.
- Organizing emergency responses to material needs in rural communities and offer—where appropriate and feasible—food purchases, health insurance premiums, and temporary financial assistance to cover cost of planting crops.
- Providing increased leadership and support for:

   a. forums for sharing hurts and struggles within communities and in the larger setting.
   b. organizations and coalitions that are committed to the preservation of family farm agriculture in the United States.
   c. programs, projects, and organizations seeking to stop the loss of minority-owned land in the United States and enhance opportunities for minority farmers to earn a livelihood from agriculture.
   d. means of educating and informing church members about farm issues.

We call upon our state governments to do the following:

1. Undertake studies to determine if state tax policies are having an adverse effect on family farm ownership, and act to distribute tax burdens more equitably in proportion to income.

2. Establish through legislation a family farm development fund to provide low interest loans to young beginning farmers.

3. Require through legislation that all state supported programs of agricultural research and education focus on small and moderate-sized family farm operations, and that such programs be especially targeted to minority farmers and landowners in those areas where they constitute a significant proportion of the population.

4. Expand local markets for farm products by opening market opportunities and providing market information and training activities to farmers.

5. Actively support the family farm by advocating the federal government provide a fair price for farm products.

We call upon the federal government to do the following:

1. Establish as a major priority of farm programs the support of family owned and operated moderate-sized farms.

2. Reduce military spending, [an action] which would benefit all of America by reducing the national deficit. This would allow increased exports and the replacement of funds for farm support and humanitarian programs.

3. Revise tax policies that now attract agricultural investment by nonfarmers seeking tax shelters and that disproportionately benefit large and well financed farming operations.

4. Correct the inequitable distribution of benefits in farm programs by limiting eligibility for subsidized credit and support payments to moderate-sized farms.

5. Strengthen Congressional oversight of the Farmers Home Administration (FmHA) to ensure that the FmHA carries out its historic role and mandate as a lender of last resort and as an aid to beginning farmers making initial land purchases and to further ensure that the limits on loans meet the needs of moderate-sized farms.

6. Recognize that agriculture needs a farm credit system that provides fair and equitable service.

7. Provide new research initiatives and programs that assure the development of long-term, sustainable agriculture in the United States, protect the natural resource base from further loss and contamination, and provide small and moderate-sized family farmers the opportunity to make an adequate living from the land.

People being there for others

Wilmer Heisey

In 1985, as a response to North America's rural crisis, the Mennonite Central Committee appointed the Farm Task Force: Don Gingerich (Iowa); Walton Hackman, (Pennsylvania; now deceased); Marvin Penner (Nebraska); Dwight Stoltzfus (Indiana), and Robert Yoder (Illinois). Additional appointments in 1986 were Mark Epp (Nebraska) and Elvin Stolzfus (Pennsylvania). In 1986, Mennonite Mutual Aid and Mennonite Economic Development Associates began to share in this response to the needs of farm communities by supporting the work of the farm issues coordinators and developing resources for persons taking on new employment. This section profiles the efforts of some of the task force members.

Finding the energy of the rural life

Riding with Robert Yoder from Peoria to Tiskilwa, Illinois, in early spring was quite an experience. A man of the soil, Bob sees his home country in Illinois with eyes and insights that the passerby cannot fathom. He talks freely of the people, their land, their crops. He knows how events have affected his people over past generations and reflects on what is happening to them now. He pays attention to how world affairs impact this farming community in the heartland of America.

In his work as congregational stewardship secretary with the Mennonite Board of Congregational Ministries, Bob knows many other communities. He has seen the pattern of people's lives and has shared in their joy and their pain.

While giving a running commentary on soils, crops, and terrain, this community leader—a student of philosophy, sociology, and economics—reveals the wider crosscurrents that plague him. A way of life is passing. Forces of change have been unleashed. But driving across that rich farmland, he shows his broad worldview when he suggests that the rising self-sufficiency in grain production outside North America is a good thing.

The creative energy released by the people who turned the frontier into productive farmland is a force not well understood. Rural America has offered many generations room to grow. That space has molded their independent characters. Even as the trend away from rural life increases, farm communities continue as a vital source of values and virtues.

Caring for the land and doing justice

This American way of life had profound influence on Mennonites as a people. But Christians of any persuasion must discriminate between their way of life and the kingdom of God. One of the sharpest points of tension between the American way and the kingdom of God is the tension between the daily work of production and the nurturing of God's creation.

Mark Epp spent five years with Mennonite Central Committee in Bolivia where he lived and worked in a resettlement project, teaching agriculture and community development. That exposure to life from another point of view was followed by four years as a staff person for the Rural Advancement Fund among poor farmers in southern United States. By the time he returned to Nebraska to farm in 1983, his experiences and faith journey had led him to seek a biblical perspective on the tension between agricultural production and the nurture of resources. Mark and Cathy Wismer, whom he married in 1985, are holding faith/justice issues in creative tension with present economic realities as they farm some of the land where his great-grandfather broke the sod more than a century ago.

In addition, Mark works with the Center for Rural Affairs in Walthill, Nebraska, on issues affecting family farms. Recently, he worked in an organizing effort to preserve the state's constitutional amendment that prohibits nonfamily corporations from owning land and operating enterprises that compete with family farmers. Through his frequent talks to church and community groups, Mark helps people gain a broader vision of the relationships we share with other people and with God's creation.

Prepared to give useful counsel

The beckoning of the American frontier gave birth to a myth. According to this myth, almost everyone could be successful if she or he worked hard enough and had enough courage to endure hardship. Even if one venture failed, another opportunity would come. That myth became doctrine, not openly preached from the pulpit, but taught in American homes and society for generations. Such teaching has molded the thought patterns of rural America, as its people pursued material success rather than practicing stewardship of the resources of a bountiful God.

Walton Hackman has been an exception. He practiced stewardship rather than pursuing material success. His Guernseys, his field work, the weekly north Philadelphia farmers' market stand which he ran with his wife Karin, and his endless involvement in community and church projects should have used up all of his time and energy. Yet he was always up on the latest news. He analyzed issues ahead of his neighbors. He related kingdom issues to both the mundane and the momentous events of the day. In hard times, he was a ready source of counsel and encouragement to those around him. For Walt, understanding economics was a part of the discipline of living under the lordship of Christ.

With prophetic insight, he entered into the throes of the crisis of rural America ahead of his contemporaries. One phone call about a farm family in financial crisis in a neighboring state caused him to do research, plan a visit to the farm, and follow up with more research so that he could give useful counsel to that family. Until he died in December 1985, at the age of forty-eight he modeled what it means to do all to the honor and glory of God.

The church that couldn't stay silent

Too often an artificial separation of spiritual and secular issues has set economic concerns apart from active dialogue within the Christian community.

One evidence of this separation is the distance between farmers and their pastors. In many churches, farmers neither expect nor receive understanding or helpful counsel from their pastors. Pastors complain, "My people don't want me to speak on economic issues." But the avalanche of woes that has engulfed rural America in the past few years is changing the climate.

Few issues demonstrate that spiritual/secular dilemma more clearly than the matter of going into debt. Church people have been taught that integrity in business relations is the foundation of one's testimony in the community. But in modern times, contracting debts has become a normal way for people to take advantage of economic opportunity. During the rapid expansion of the 1970s, farmers were thrust into business ventures for which many were not well prepared. Success and failure depended on good cash flow charts and a sharp pencil as much as hard work, the weather, and common sense. But, as has always been the case, farmers did not control the economic forces of the marketplace.

The business failures that have come with the reversal in the farm economy since 1980 strike at the heart of what has made American farmers the self-reliant citizens they perceive themselves to be. At the collapse of the agricultural prosperity of the 1970s, American farmers were caught off guard. In the first wave of crisis, heads wagged over greedy farmers who got caught in their attempts to make a financial killing. But, at the same time, many farmers of peerless reputation spent sleepless nights and anxious days trying to avert financial disaster.

During the years of expansion, counsel on business-related matters from the financial community took the place of the counsel from the community of faith. But when the crunch came, lenders and borrowers sometimes became adversaries. With no one to talk to, the pressure mounted. In some cases, husbands and wives walked this lonely road together; in other cases, they drifted away from each other.

The church's silence on the issues facing the rural communities seemed to imply censure of those getting caught. And the church's failure to see a neighbor's need was a profound denial of the Christian faith.

Not always was the church silent, however. Pastor Eugene Garber, from

Mount Pleasant, Iowa, was one who challenged the notion that Christian compassion should extend only to people in need in other parts of the world, or to victims of fire, flood, and storm but not to people in need in our communities. That business matters of individuals are cared for largely outside the congregation underscores a lapse in genuine Christian community. Garber argued that the faith community can and must respond to all brothers and sisters in need. His concern prompted Mennonite Central Committee to respond in ways that brought the Farm Task Force into being.

A voice to those facing loss

The members of the Farm Task Force saw that many people facing financial crisis were unable to take the first steps toward openness, either because of pride or fear. The Task Force found various ways to introduce a third party, bringing about a less threatening situation. As people in financial distress find open channels of communication through a farm hotline, a newsletter, and regional meetings, they are put in touch with sources of support that help them cope.

Helping other rural Mennonites through the Farm Hotline are Nancy and John Halder. Nancy Kinsinger met and married John Halder while she was serving with the Mennonite Board of Missions in England during the 1970s. In 1979, the Halders returned to Nancy's home community of Parnell, Iowa, to farm. They were not yet well-established when the economic crisis was upon them and they could not afford to stay in farming.

In 1985, John and Nancy agreed to have the Farm Hotline placed in their home to be available to callers facing the same kind of problems they themselves were facing. Nancy's skills in writing and speaking soon gave her opportunities across the country to give a voice to those facing the loss of their farms. Her message is one of hope amid the crisis of change.

Faith meets economics on the new agenda

New leadership in farm communities has helped people break free of the paralysis that first strikes a suffering community. People begin to talk to each other. Giving and receiving happen on a basis of genuine need and unselfish love. People discover that they can trust each other.

Counseling with neighboring farmers, going with them to meetings with lenders, and sharing in the pain of lost dreams, Don and Karen Gingerich have cried with their eastern Iowa neighbors. These experiences have taught them the meaning of Paul's admonition: "Do nothing from selfishness or conceit, but in humility count others better than yourselves. Let each of you look not only to his own interests, but also to the interests of others" (Phil. 2:3-4). In addition to sharing with their neighbors, Don relates to policymakers on both the state and national level, working with them to search for ways to bring relief to the rural economy.

Economic forces on the international level and government policies on the national level dominate the marketplace on which American farms depend. Access to persons carrying decision-making responsibility in government is possible in free societies. The perspective and informed judgment of Christian farmers who place kingdom values ahead of selfish advantage is a needed resource to persons in government. Such officials need the contributions of experienced representatives of the farm community. The Christian community has spokespersons well qualified to be a valuable resource to policymakers.

Believing that God's provisions are adequate for a changing environment, the Gingeriches see promise in bringing the issues of economics back into the agenda of the church. They speak with confidence about Christian farm families in the future. In January 1986, at the annual meeting of the Mennonite Central Committee, they said, "The values we have clung to in the past will still endure. Honesty, integrity, sharing, compassion, and even hard work will fit into the rejuvenation of agriculture, as much or more than it ever has."

Agriculture today is one part of a web of interrelated economic forces in the world. The independence and isolation of the American frontier no longer exist, but one is better off as a part of the Christian community than in trying to find one's way alone. Where Christian faith is vital, the issues of economics and faith will come together again as they were understood in both the Old and New Testament times. What that will mean for church agendas of congregations and conferences is yet to be seen. But a vision is emerging within the Mennonite community of some things that can be done now.

All one body in Christ

The primary arena for response to the crisis in rural America is within the Christian community itself. Mutual sharing and interdependence have always worked well among poor people throughout the world. Secular history and biblical teaching confirm this. In the present rural crisis, it is reassuring to discover that most of the resources needed for survival are still available in affected communities. Experience, wisdom, courage, and wealth are usually present where trouble strikes. When a community finds ways to release those resources, a step has been taken for the survival of its people.

Dwight Stoltzfus has a growing vision to help people in local rural communities begin to share with each other. For many years an Ohio dairy farmer, Dwight has given the later years of his career to the mutual aid ministries of the church. Retiring recently from leadership of Mennonite Mutual Aid, he is helping to sharpen a new vision for mutual sharing in local communities.

Emerging networks of caring people bring hope to communities whose members have lost security and self-confidence. As people are open with each other, they become active players in the drama for survival. The pain of each hurting family becomes the concern of all, and the joys of recovery are also shared.

Answers cannot be imported, but a community group or congregation can invite a sensitive person from outside to open conversation. Invariably they find more people interested and willing to help than they realized. Special leadership gifts in one community can be shared also with neighboring communities.

Lester and Winifred Ewy farmed in central Kansas through the era when American farmers were called upon to feed a hungry world. But the harsh realities of the '80s took them through the stages of disillusion, crisis, and loss. Now Lester and Winifred have accepted another challenge—to work with the Farm Task Force to help local communities respond to each others' needs during times of crisis. As farm community issues coordinators, the Ewys share from personal experience the message that there is life and hope beyond the farm. They assert that those people of faith who can continue to farm and those who cannot are part of one body in Christ.

History records the crises and dislocations of the past. The farm community crisis of the '80s has brought intense suffering and it is taking its toll. But out of this crisis can come hope for people of faith. With optimism that has characterized the American rural community for generations, Christians whose vocation is integral to their witness will remain stewards of the Lord's land.

For study and discussion

1. How do you measure the farm crisis and how does that view of it affect your response?

2. After reading the Kansas Mennonite Farm Crisis Committee's statement of concern, write your own statement to reflect your definition of the problem, the responses you believe are necessary, and who should be making those responses.

3. Think of individuals or groups that you know who are responding in helpful ways to people caught up in the farm crisis. Write a profile of at least one of these persons and share it with others in your church newsletter, local newspaper, or denominational magazine.

4. What do you believe is the most creative solution to the farm crisis? Is it consistent with the biblical views of dominion and covenant in chapters one and two? Does it meet the criteria used to measure sustainability?

It is no doubt impossible
to live without thought of
the future; hope and
vision can live nowhere
else. The only possible
guarantee of the future is
responsible behavior in
the present.
—Wendell Berry

13. A vision for Mennonite agriculture

Robert Hull

This chapter lifts out for further discussion two key concepts of the preceding chapters: *ecological sustainability* and *cultural sustainability*, as these apply to agriculture. These concepts interact to form a third, merging concept: *community*. In this chapter, we will explore ideas about Mennonite community, both in its past and its present.

For isn't sustainability a key concern—indeed, sometimes a near-ultimate concern—for a people with a heritage, a tradition, a way of knowing themselves in relation to the world? These essays on faith and farming present (with two exceptions) Mennonites writing out of their experience in agriculture. (The two exceptions, of course, are our peace church neighbors, Don Reeves, a Nebraska Quaker, and Leon Neher, a Kansas Brethren.)

The concepts of ecological and cultural sustainability will serve as our compass. They can mark clearly on the horizon, in the midst of all that has been said about contemporary American agriculture, the realities with which we must come to terms. The attention we give to these concepts will largely determine, I believe, the direction we will go. Are we headed for a desert or a garden?

I have developed an image which keeps the goal in focus for me: I am walking along a country road. The view ahead has a unique depth of field because I see it from two angles: ecological and cultural visions of sustainability. As a Mennonite interested in the future of agriculture, I am conscious that frequent glances over my shoulder may give me the best line-of-sight to where I want to go. Let's begin the journey.

The agri in agriculture

We're caught up in a natural human response. The closer we come to a crossroad, the more attention it demands from us. Especially is this true if some parts of the way ahead show signs of danger. Much has been said in the chapters that have gone before about the limits of production agriculture. Many researchers point with growing urgency to the dangers of exceeding these limits. They see the almost certain results of expanding farm size, declining number of farmers, depletion of nonrenewable resources such as petroleum, increasing soil erosion, and groundwater pollution. The rest of that litany has become all too familiar.

We do well to remember, however, that projections of the limits to production agriculture are based upon the continuation of current practices. Researchers emphasize alternative choices possible for North American agriculture. Much of their research centers on finding alternatives that are economically feasible in the short term—the productive lifetime of today's farmers.

The focus, then, is on the notion of sustainability. If production agriculture continues as at present, it will not be sustainable. But if other practices are adopted, a sustainable agriculture may already be in sight.

The alternative ways of farming advocated have two things in common: first, a shift from an industrial model of agricultural science—measuring physical and chemical inputs and outputs in isolation—to an ecological model: an agricultural science which seeks to understand farms as whole ecosystems which need to be kept in balance; second, a respect for the farmer's intuition and knowledge, born of years of trial-and-error experience. Agricultural science should seek to be a servant, rather than a supplanter, of this customary knowledge.[1]

Listen to Wendell Berry, who speaks as a reflective farmer. "The good farmer, like an artist, performs within a pattern; he must do one thing while remembering many others. He must be thoughtful of relationships and connections," he says. "We will not understand what we mean when we say that he works with his hands, if we do not understand that he works also with his mind."

Berry defines the good farmer as one who applies knowledge in a unique way, not to any farm but to "this farm, my farm, the only place exactly like itself in all the world." The farmer uses his knowledge in a

1. Wes Jackson, "A Search for the Unifying Concept for Sustainable Agriculture," *Meeting the Expectations of the Land: Essays in Sustainable Agriculture and Stewardship*, Wes Jackson, Wendell Berry and Bruce Colman, eds. (San Francisco: North Point Press, 1984), pp. 217-18.

way that will nurture the land and not in a way "to violate it, to do it damage, finally to destroy it."

The mind of a good farmer, says Berry, "is inseparable from his farm; or, to state it the opposite way, a farm as a human artifact is inseparable from the mind that makes and uses it. The two are one. To damage this union is to damage human culture at its root."[2]

Berry speaks elsewhere of this knowing of a farm by its farmer as "solving for pattern"—perhaps the best image yet devised to describe farm knowledge as an ecosystem. A farming problem is not just a problem about agriculture, as though it had to do only with yield, method, or money. "The whole problem must be solved," he says, "not just some handily identifiable and simplifiable aspect of it."

Farming deals with life and one form of life is linked with all other forms of life. "And so a good solution in one pattern preserves the integrity of the pattern that contains it," says Berry. "A good agricultural solution, for example, would not pollute or erode a watershed."[3]

What these researchers are proposing, then, is a search for solutions at the level of whole biological systems, in addition to the inputs and outputs of physical and chemical components (which have been the preoccupation of production agriculture).

This is the first of our compass guides: a science that enables North American farming to be ecologically sustainable.

The culture in agriculture

Except for Art Meyer's survey of the ecological themes we have been discussing (chapter 3), the other essays deal with the part that culture plays in sustainable agriculture. Many definitions of culture are possible, of course. For me, it includes not only those aspects of society treated by the social sciences, but value questions as well: the dos and don'ts and whys of a society.

Again, we are asked to solve for pattern: this time we are looking for patterns of sustainable cultural systems. Not every economic system that runs smoothly will prove sustainable, for example. For another, cooperative relationships often last longer than those which feature competition. Here we want to find out how religious ethics help us determine whether a given cultural system will be sustainable.

Roy Kaufman has done a good job of outlining for us (chapter 2) Israel's

2. Wendell Berry, "Whose Head Is the Farmer Using? Who Is Using the Farmer's Head?" in *Meeting the Expectations of the Land*, pp. 19-30.

3. Wendell Berry, "Solving for Pattern," *The Gift of Good Land: Further Essays Cultural and Agricultural* (San Francisco: North Point Press, 1981), pp. 134-48.

struggle with and for its land. He notes how the early Canaanites monopolized the land and its productive wealth. The Israelites resisted the Canaanite cultural system, seeing themselves as an alternative society. From the conflict that followed and the values that the Israelite community championed, we can understand the way people and their way of life can be sustained.

From the first, the Israelites were a rural people who for centuries had been oppressed economically, socially, and politically by the rich who lived in the city-states of Palestine. Conflict between the rural people and the agents of the urban wealthy (census-takers and those who follow them: tax collectors, recruiters for the military forces, forced-labor taskmasters) went on for many generations.

Into this conflict situation came a new factor: a refugee group out of Egypt with a charismatic leader (Moses), bearing a revolutionary message. They said that the divine right to rule which the city-state kings claimed was forfeited by their conduct. Their ways of oppression were not God's intention. Rather, God would rule his people directly; through the covenant given at Mount Sinai, they would find God's will for human life. That covenant with God called for people to relate to each other as equals. This religious ethic stood over against Canaanite oppression. It encompassed many convictions and commitments of the Israelites. Prominent among these was concern for the economically disadvantaged in their society: widows, orphans, the poor, sojourning foreign traders, and the Levites.

One key concern was the distribution of income and wealth. A strong effort was made in the original assignment of land (Num. 26, 33) to balance its productive capacity with the population of each tribe. The more productive land went to the larger, and therefore more needy, tribes. Where differences in incomes and savings occurred, the more affluent Israelite was expected to both pay the levitical and poor taxes (Num. 18 and Deut. 14) and to give to whoever was in need nearby (Deut. 15, 24).

It may come as a shock to many that an economist who has made a thorough analysis of Old Testament rules concludes that Israel was not a capitalist society![4] Neither was ancient Israel a communistic or communalistic society, in which wealth was accumulated by the state (in the modern sense of state-capitalism). Rather, ancient Israel is best described as a covenantal society: one in which each person's surplus is ethically mortgaged for the survival needs of his or her neighbor.

---

4. Neal Soss, "Old Testament Law and Economic Society," *Journal of the History of Ideas* (1973), Vol. 34, pp. 323-44.

Where other economic systems feature a capital market (that is, the money available for lending is borrowed by the people with the greatest capability and willingness to pay the highest rates of interest), Israel legislated a zero interest rate on loans (Exod. 22:25-27; Lev. 25:35-37; Deut. 23:19-20). Israel called all interest *usury*—a negative term.

This almost totally eliminated the incentive for people with some accumulated capital to loan it out at interest to increase their wealth. Rather, Israel wished to use loans to maintain the economic security of the poor. "If there is among you a poor man . . . you shall not harden your heart or shut your hand against your poor brother, but you shall open your hand to him, and lend him sufficient for his need, whatever it may be" (Deut. 15: 7-8).

A second feature of Israel's economic system interacted with this law of loans without usury. Every seventh year was to be a sabbatical year, and every fiftieth year was to be a Jubilee year. In both of these cycles, when the sabbatical or Jubilee years arrived, all loans were to be canceled, all debts were to be forgiven (Deut. 15:1-2). Nevertheless, the wealthier Israelite was commanded to loan to the poor, taking no heed for the approaching seventh year (Deut. 15:9-11).

Such laws placed severe restraints upon capital accumulation. It meant that inequalities in the distribution of wealth would lessen, rather than increase. "A Marxian impoverishment of the non-wealth-owning class becomes less possible over time in Old Testament society."[5]

This religious ethic of equality had another prominent feature: it exhorted against land accumulation as well as capital accumulation.

> Woe to those who join house to house, who add field to field, until there is no more room, and you are made to dwell alone in the midst of the land. The Lord of hosts has sworn in my hearing: "Surely many houses shall be desolate, large and beautiful houses, without inhabitant" (Isa. 5:8-9).

> The Lord enters into judgment with the elders and princes of his people: "It is you who have devoured the vineyard, the spoil of the poor is in your houses. What do you mean by crushing my people, by grinding the face of the poor?" says the Lord God of hosts (Isa. 3:14-15).

Gathering more and more land and its productive wealth for private gain greatly increased after the kingships of David and Solomon, just as Sa-

5. Soss, p. 336.

muel's prophetic vision had foreseen (1 Sam. 8:11-18). The outcries of Isaiah and the other prophets predicted judgment and ecological devastation (Isa. 5:5-7).

We can conclude that in its laws, Israel expressed its conviction that God intended Israel to be a nation of small landholders, with only a few administrative and religious personnel (the Levites) subsisting not far removed from the earnings of the land. The engine of modern economics—capital accumulation for investment—is placed under severe restrictions, giving overwhelming priority to the needs of the poor and the disadvantaged. One might say that Israel rejected a trickle-down economics for an artesian economics—capital could be accumulated only after the needs of those at the bottom of society were met.

Israel placed emphasis on people rather than production. With its one day in seven of sabbath rest, its one year in every seven a sabbatical year, and its Jubilee of seven cycles of sabbatical years (wherein debts were forgiven, the poor who had sold themselves as slaves released and land inheritances restored), Israel was a society that sustained a culture in which all people related to each other as free and as equal. These periodic adjustments sought to insure that the wealthy and powerful did not engulf the weak and the poor (1 Kings 21; Mic. 2:2).

This is the taproot of the Judeo-Christian religious ethic. Its fruits have ripened repeatedly in Christian history.

Jubilee and usury in the teachings of Jesus

Jesus Christ, growing into adulthood as a Jew in Galilee, began his public ministry by proclaiming the Jubilee in the synagogue in his hometown, Nazareth (Luke 4:18-19).

Mennonite theologian John Howard Yoder has illuminated Jesus' attitudes toward the issues of debt, usury, and sabbatical and Jubilee forgiveness. Jesus preaches against the wealthy and powerful religious leaders of his day, "Woe to you, scribes and Pharisees, hypocrites! for you devour widows' houses and for a pretense you make long prayers; therefore you will receive the greater condemnation" (Matt. 23:14 margin).

Jesus' parable of the merciless servant (Matt. 18:23-35) shows that the Israelite is to extend forgiveness because he or she has already experienced Jubilee forgiveness. Unlike the scribes' and Pharisees' long, pretentious prayers, the believer's prayer is to be short. Jesus models brevity in the Lord's Prayer (Matt. 6:9-14): "Forgive us our debts [when / inasmuch as / to the extent to which] we forgive our debtors" (v. 12). Conversely, as the merciless servant tragically discovered, "there is no divine jubilee for those who refuse to apply it on earth."[6]

The supposed difficulties of an economy that sought to operate without usury were exploited by leaders in Jesus' day as much as they would be attacked by economists and financiers today. "The frequent remission of debts," says Yoder, "had a serious inconvenience, already indicated in Deuteronomy 15:7-11: it froze credit. Because of this the rabbis, even the most orthodox like Hillel and Shammai, who had become the champions of the strict application of the law of Moses, hesitated to demand the strict application of the jubilee."

As the sabbatical year drew near, the wealthy refused to lend to the poor lest they lose their capital when the debts were canceled. This brought the economy of the country to a standstill. The rabbis found a way to get around the law. "Adroit commentators of the law, they knew how to make it say the opposite of what it ordered."

Their solution was a process called the *prosboul* in which the right to collect a debt that would be canceled by the sabbatical year was assigned to the court. "The very existence of the prosboul proves that, contrary to the statements of some authors, there was at the time of Jesus a strong current favoring the strict application of the provision of the jubilee for periodic remission of debts," says Yoder. "Otherwise the institution of this procedure of prosboul would have been unnecessary."[7]

Jesus had something to say to both the worried creditor and to the negligent debtor. To the worried creditor, Jesus asked about his or her faith in the goodness of God (Luke 6:34-38). To the negligent debtor, Jesus says, "Don't wait until you fall into the hands of the court to reimburse the debt. If your creditor wants to take you to court [by way of the prosboul] to take away your tunic [which he keeps as security for the debt which you have not been able to pay him], let him take your coat too" (Matt. 5:40, paraphrased).

Jesus urges those who are in debt to make a serious effort to meet the terms of their loans. "Hasten to make your peace with the adversary as long as you are on the road with him, for fear that your adversary [using the prosboul] might turn you over to the judge, and the judge to the guard, and you might be thrown in prison, from which you will not get out until you have paid the last penny" (Matt. 5:25-26 paraphrased).[8]

6. John Howard Yoder, "The Implications of the Jubilee," *The Politics of Jesus* (Grand Rapids: Eerdmans, 1972), pp. 64-77.

7. Yoder, pp. 69-72.

8. Yoder, pp. 69-72.

Reformers abandoned restrictions on usury

Jesus was as much a foe of usury as the law of Moses had been during Israel's early days. The message of Jesus—in parables and sermons—was a renewed call to abolish usury.

It was so understood, and in the main adhered to, by the entire Christian community—the Greek and Eastern Orthodox, Coptic and Syrian as well as Roman Catholic churches—for over 1,500 years, until the Protestant Reformation.[9] As Martin Luther and John Calvin sought to fortify their reforms by alliance with the rising mercantile class in the European cities, they found it expedient to relax the usury prohibitions.

In the Reformation, the key element of the biblical pattern of a sustainable culture—the prohibition of usury (which led to capital accumulation)—was set aside. In its place, the Reformers left room for the spirit of private enterprise (what John Wesley later described as, "Get all you can, save all you can, give all you can"). The Catholic Counter-Reformation was not long in following those Reformation practices.

During the Reformation, the radical Anabaptists upheld and practiced the ancient ethic of equality, contesting with both Protestants and Catholics. Arising from the peasantry and from traders and craftsmen unwilling to embrace the newly-relaxed Protestant business ethics, they were attacked in print, in public debates, and finally by legislative and judicial means by Luther and Calvin.

The Anabaptist leader Conrad Grebel encouraged his followers to reject income from estates and church trusts called benefices. In 1524, he wrote to a wavering Thomas Muntzer, who had apparently embraced Anabaptist convictions but was reported to be moving toward those of Luther. "If your benefices, like ours, are founded on tithes and interest, both of which are simply usury," said Grebel, "and you are not supported by the whole congregation, you ought to withdraw from the benefices. You know well enough how a shepherd ought to be supported."[10]

The vision of people living together as free and equal and committed to periodic renewals of their system of distributing their resources has great power and a driving energy. Among the Israelites, early Christians, and the Anabaptists, whole populations were willing to give their lives to make the vision live. Each of these historical explosions changed beyond recognition the old cultural system.

---

9. Benjamin Nelson, *The Idea of Usury: From Tribal Brotherhood to Universal Otherhood*, second edition (Chicago: The University of Chicago Press, 1969).

10. Conrad Grebel, *Conrad Grebel's Programmatic Letters of 1524* (Scottdale, Pa: Herald Press, 1970), p. 25.

Note further that in each instance, it was the farmers and craftspersons of ancient Israel, of Galilee and Judea, and of South Germany and the Swiss Confederation who caught, championed, and gave their lives for the vision of a society of free and equal people. In each case, the Canaanites of the city-state structures, the Pharisees and Herodians, and the Protestant merchants and magistrates bitterly resisted such a vision. What level of stress needs to be reached in the relationship between the urban wealthy and the rural disadvantaged before a new order can grow to engulf—and perhaps replace—a whole cultural system?

Anabaptist models for sustainable communities

The various branches of Anabaptism had great creativity. Many of their social and economic patterns have continued for over four and a half centuries into the present. Four main patterns can still be seen:

1. The mainstream Anabaptist model (Swiss, South German and Dutch Mennonites) combined the ideal of austerity (expressed within the fellowship as mutual aid with unlimited liability, following 2 Cor. 8:8-15) with a posture that confronted economic practices outside the fellowship.

2. The Church of God in Christ Mennonite, following an intense study of the writings of Menno Simons by their founder, John Holdeman (1832-1900), have maintained a testimony against interest (usury) and excessive consumption throughout their 125-year history.

3. The Hutterite model of community of goods combined an ideal of yieldedness and surrender of the individual to the will of the group. One might say that their communities follow the divestment and common purse examples of the early church (Acts 2:44-45; 4:32-37).

4. The Amish and the Old Order / Old Colony Mennonites rejected new technology while remaining as unentangled with outside economic relations as possible. Their separated community model intends to avoid confrontation.[11]

The mainstream Anabaptist model is represented today by the larger Mennonite denominations. Confronting economic practices outside the fellowship has almost entirely ended. Indeed, most forms of finance, organizational structure, and institution building prevalent in the larger economy have been adopted by these denominations. This was also true of the Mennonite commonwealth in the Ukraine of the Soviet Union from 1770-1940.

---

11. Donovan E. Smucker, "Gelassenheit, Entrepreneurs, and Remnants: Socioeconomic Models Among the Mennonites," *Kingdom, Cross and Community* (Scottdale, Pa: Herald Press, 1976), pp. 219-41.

In this economic pattern, the mainstream Mennonite denominations have become increasingly indistinguishable from other North American Protestant denominations. (And one might add, the Protestants have become less distinguishable from the Roman Catholics.)

Mainstream North American denominations "now demand an affluent, business-oriented church," says Donovan Smucker, a Mennonite sociologist. He finds that current "educational, mission, service, artistic, and communications programs are marks of vitality and vision. They are possible only because we no longer need to restrain ourselves with the [ideal of austerity] of the sixteenth and seventeenth centuries. Indeed, if we did enforce such restraint the dynamism of the church in its present stance would be destroyed."[12]

Smucker reports on the work of a Canadian sociologist, Harold Barclay, of the University of Alberta, who has studied the Church of God in Christ Mennonite (Holdeman). Barclay shows "how they place capitalistic drives under severe restraints," says Smucker. "At some point the Holdeman businessman must restrain his business or leave the church. A definite ceiling exists over the dynamics of the business enterprise." Since its members are limited in their earnings they cannot support the institutions which are part of the witness of other churches: they have "no schools and only modest beginnings in missions and hospitals." Says Smucker, "The dilemma is obvious: capitalistic restraint plus limited outreach or large outreach supported by business surpluses."[13]

The two other models, the Hutterites and the Amish, are examined by Burton Buller (chapter 8). He finds the Amish continuing to reject almost all technological innovation, but maintaining healthy communities.

The Hutterites are encountering a mixture of pressures, to which various of their communal colonies respond differently. The drive for the latest agricultural technology in some colonies suggests they may be succumbing, at least in part, to the North American pressure toward production agriculture.

In the case of the Amish, both Wendell Berry[14] and Wes Jackson[15] praise the virtues they see in Amish agricultural communities. They point to examples of both ecological common sense handed down from generation to generation living together on the family farm, and the cultural common sense of the Amish religious community, possessing a clear understanding of what agriculture is for.

12. Smucker, p. 228.
13. Smucker, p. 228.
14. Wendell Berry, *The Gift of Good Land*, pp. 249-66.
15. Wes Jackson, *Meeting the Expectations of the Land*, pp. 215-16, 226-27.

Berry lists three reasons why he thinks the Amish have survived as a "closely bound fellowship of many communities." They are religious, unburdened by the need to support large institutions, and have kept themselves free from entanglement with technology.

As a religious community, they are united "not just by various worldly necessities, but by spiritual authority." While many sects pay attention only to the spirit, "the Amish have not secularized their earthly life They have not hesitated to see communal and agricultural implications in their religious principles, and these implications directly influence their behavior," says Berry. "The goal of Amish culture is not just the welfare of the spirit, but a larger harmony among God, nature, family, and community."

The Amish have chosen not to build many institutions, "so they are not victimized, as we so frequently are, by organizations set up ostensibly to serve them." The only institutions they have allowed are their elementary schools. These they have built "to keep the responsibility for educating their children and so, in consequence, to keep their children." Even their church life is limited in its institutional form. They have a lay ministry chosen from the members of the congregation, "and so they do not have a professional, a paid, an economically dependent, or an ambitious clergy." They meet in barns or in homes and their charities are simple and direct. "And so they do not have a church building or a building fund or church functionaries or administrators," says Berry. "There is little distinction between the church and its members."

When it comes to their way of living and farming, Berry finds that "the Amish are the truest geniuses of technology, for they understand the necessity of limiting it, and they know how to limit it. They have refused to see technological innovation as an end in itself. And so their religiously enforced family and community values are safeguarded against the social costs of changes which in their estimation did more harm than good to the community as a whole."[16]

Time to turn to our kinfolk for help

What contribution can the Mennonite experience, taken as a whole, make to the search for an ecologically and culturally sustainable agriculture in North America? The most important contribution, it seems, is for people in agriculture to know themselves as a particular community, seeking beyond individual profit the health of the community. Several tasks would seem crucial in making progress toward this goal.

16. Wendell Berry, *The Unsettling of America: Culture and Agriculture* (San Francisco: Sierra Club, 1977), pp. 210-217.

Could the denominational Christian churches establish a dialogue with the Amish and the Old Order / Old Colony Mennonites on which technological innovations might be good for the health of agricultural communities? Could we talk with the Holdeman churches about the damaging entanglements they discern to be involved in the giving and taking of interest?

Could we begin discussion about Christian community which extends all the way to the common purse with both the urban intentional communities, such as Reba Place in Evanston, Illinois, and rural intentional communities, such as Plow Creek, Tiskilwa, Illinois, and especially the Hutterites?

This is the sense in which the search for a stereoscopic Mennonite vision of a sustainable agriculture for the future should perhaps begin: by casting a view over our shoulders at our kinfolk, the Amish, Old Order / Old Colony Mennonites, Holdemans, and Hutterites.

For study and discussion

1. If you look toward the future, as this chapter suggests, by considering the concepts of a way of farming that sustains the land and a way of farming that sustains people and a way of life, what would you hope to see in tomorrow's North American agriculture?

2. Explain how the principles of sustaining the land and sustaining its people builds community? What would you see as the nature of such a community?

3. What does "solving for pattern" mean? How do you solve for pattern (link life to life) in your farm or your community, or your church? What would you do differently as you use this method? What would you continue to do?

4. Robert Hull suggests how Mennonites, in ways unique to their past, might contribute toward an ecologically and culturally sustainable North American agriculture. Readers from other ethnic and religious heritages will have other ways of drawing from their past to shape their future. What might this process suggest to you?

Epilogue

Hope for the people and the land

LaVonne Godwin Platt

We are shaped by the past and we shape the future. The seeds we plant today determine what will grow tomorrow.

What are the seeds of promise and hope for rural America that we can plant and nourish to grow the future we want? What are the values from our past that need to be retained or recovered? Where do we need to change direction? What are the criteria by which we determine our way?

In the biblical story of creation, the first duty given to humankind was "to till and keep" God's garden. Almost from the beginning, however, we became alienated from creation and from each other because we failed to follow the laws of nature, God's laws.

To let these laws of nature be our standard is consistent with the dominion and covenant theology with which this book began. Indeed, such a standard is *inherent* in the Judeo-Christian view of stewardship. It is basic as well to the Native American view of living in harmony with the earth. It is what Aldo Leopold, a conservationist writing forty years ago about people and land in community, called a land ethic.[1]

Rural America has become estranged from the land because we ignored the laws of nature. Our alienation has caused many losses—loss of soil, loss of family farms, and loss of our sense of community. We have even lost an understanding of our role in the ongoing process of creation, a role defined for us by our Creator.

---

1. Aldo Leopold, *A Sand County Almanac* (New York: Oxford University Press, 1968), pp. 201-26.

Despite these problems, many farm families have retained useful values from the past and have changed ways that hindered them from farming in a sustainable manner and living in sustainable communities. Many of them would agree with the farmer who told me, "We are not interested in maintaining family farms only because of the rural values and way of life they represent, but because it is a kind of agriculture that leads toward a just society and because it is the best way to produce food efficiently. It can use resources in a sustainable manner, and it benefits society."

Another farmer, borrowing (though he may not have known it) from a World Council of Churches statement on the nature of a responsible society, said we should work for a future in rural America that is *just, participatory, and sustainable.*[2] The Interreligious Task Force on U.S. Food Policy (now Interfaith Action for Economic Justice) used the same terms:

> We seek a *just* society in which human dignity is recognized, human rights are respected, human needs are fulfilled. We seek a *participatory* society in which freedom is celebrated, power is shared, and all members have some say about the shape of their future. And we seek a *sustainable* society in which the integrity of the environment is respected, the biological and social systems that nurture and support life are neither depleted nor poisoned, and in which all decisions are made with due regard for the carrying capacity of our finite earth.[3]

These three concepts can help us shape a vision of agriculture[4] and rural communities for the future. For such a future, we must orient public policy decisions to protect the land and benefit people. Applying the concept of justice will cause us to consider global agriculture, human and nonhuman interdependencies, and the ongoing process of creation. For justice in these terms to occur, individuals must participate widely within their own societies and in the world community. We must see ourselves as partners with other forms of creation. Participation at its deepest level shows us clearly that we are partners with God and accountable to God.

For justice and participation to work, sustainability is necessary. Sustainability provides a standard that measures human activities by their

2. Consultation of the Commission of Church and Society, World Council of Churches, statement on the nature of a responsible society, 1979.

3. Interreligious Task Force on U.S. Food Policy (now, Interfaith Action for Economic Justice), *Identifying a Food Policy Agenda for the 1980s: a Working Paper,* Washington, D.C., 1980, p. 4.

4. For a fuller discussion, see C. Dean Freudenberger, *Food for Tomorrow?* (Minneapolis: Augsburg, 1984).

cost to the ecosystem, their impact upon quality of life at the global level, and their provision for the welfare of unborn generations. With this standard of sustainability, we can measure yields of agriculture and energy; we can judge waste and pollution in consumption of resources; we can evaluate material growth.

We who have shared our thoughts in this book look toward a future for rural America that will be just, participatory, and sustainable. It will be a future in which rural people live in covenant with the Creator as responsible stewards of the land and its life-supporting gifts. In this future, people will recognize their relationships to one another in everwidening circles of community that link them together across geographic boundaries and generations of time. In such a future, people will expand their sense of community to recognize their relatedness not only with one another but also with the other creatures with whom they share the gift of life.

Wendell Berry says that a sustainable society must be "predominantly cooperative rather than competitive. A people cannot live long at each other's expense or at the expense of their cultural birthright—just as an agriculture cannot live long at the expense of its soil or its work force, and just as in a natural system the competitions among species must be limited if all are to survive."[5]

Marty Strange, co-director of the Center for Rural Affairs, has a vision of a sustainable agriculture "filled with people who own the land they work, who employ technology with restraint, who farm small enough to farm well, small enough to remain humble. Their earnings stay in the communities where they live, supporting churches, schools, businesses. These people respect social values, and are proud to believe that farming is more than a business. It is a way of life—an honest way of life."[6]

Strange says that the agriculture he envisions would have three economic principles:

- you can pay for land by farming it well;
- you have to pay for the land by farming it, and you have to farm it well;
- there is no other reason to own farmland.[7]

To fulfill the vision that Strange describes means that we must orient our political values to adjust to greater regulation by society on our

5. Wendell Berry, *The Unsettling of America: Culture and Agriculture* (San Francisco: Sierra Club Books, 1977), p. 47.
6. Report of the Center for Rural Affairs, 1985-86, Walthill, Nebraska.
7. Center for Rural Affairs.

individual behavior. It means accepting limits of production and limits to the right to profit at the expense of others. It means taking back control over rural institutions such as the farmer-owned Farm Credit System whose lending policies have placed borrowers in jeopardy. It means "we need to reevaluate self interest" and to recognize that "individual interest is never greater than the social good."[8]

In practical terms, the future we envision would be one in which public policy encourages widespread ownership and use of land, recognizes the rights of workers on the land, and accepts the responsibility to use the earth's resources at a renewable rate. Public policy decisions would protect the land and benefit people, now and in the future. We would renew rural communities. We would develop agricultural research based on the laws of nature and an understanding of sustainable systems. We would accept our stewardship responsibility to the earth and to future generations. We would make soil conservation not an option but the ethic of the society. We would adopt a fairer food and nutrition policy so that the poorest and weakest are not the ones who pay for improving the farm economy.

Such a future fits the biblical concept of *shalom*: "the intended order and harmony of creation itself, *all* of nature as well as humanity."[9] In such a future we will experience more fully our relationship to one another, to our world community, to other created life, to the land on which we all depend, and to our Creator who gives meaning and sacredness to all creation.

8. Center for Rural Affairs.
9. Birch and Rasmussen, *The Predicament of the Prosperous* (Philadelphia: Westminster Press, 1978), p. 147.

Resources

The following resources are suggested for further study. Chapters in this book that correlate with each resource are listed in parentheses. For addresses of periodicals and audiovisual suppliers, see *Organizations* and *Addresses for resources*.

Books

Belden, Joseph N. *Dirt Rich, Dirt Poor.* Boston: Routledge & Kegan Paul, 1986. (3, 5, 9, 10, 12, Epilogue)

Berry, Wendell. *The Unsettling of America: Culture & Agriculture.* San Francisco: Sierra Club Books, 1977; New York: Avon Books, 1979. (3, 4, 5, 6, 8, 13, Epilogue)

_____ . *The Gift of Good Land: Further Essays Cultural and Agricultural.* San Francisco.: North Point Press, 1981. (2, 3, 6, 8)

Bhagat, Shantilal P. *The Family Farm: Can It Be Saved?* Elgin, Ill.: Brethren Press, 1985. (5, 7, 10, 12)

Brueggemann, Walter. *The Land: Place as Gift, Promise, and Challenge in Biblical Faith.* Philadelphia: Fortress Press, 1977. (1, 2)

Carmody, John. *Ecology and Religion.* Ramsey, N. J.: Paulist Press, 1983. (1, 2, 3)

Catholic Bishops of the Heartland. *Strangers and Guests: Toward Community in the Heartland.* A Regional Catholic Bishops' Statement on Land Issues. Heartland Project, 220 S. Prairie Ave., Sioux Falls, S.D., 1980. (1, 2, 3)

Church of the Brethren. *This Land: Ours for a Season.* Report of a Study Committee on The Church and Agriculture, Church of the Brethren, 1974. (1, 3, 7, 8, 9)

Dillman, Don A. and Daryl J. Hobbs. *Rural Society in the U.S.: Issues for the 1980s.* Boulder, Colo.: Westview Press, 1981. (7, 10)

Doyle, Jack. *Altered Harvest.* New York: Viking, 1985. (3, 7, 11)

Eckholm, Erik P. *Losing Ground: Environmental Stress and World Food Prospects.* New York: Norton, 1976. (3, 11)

Freudenberger, C. Dean. *Food for Tomorrow?* Minneapolis: Augsburg, 1984. (3, 6, 11, Epilogue)

Granberg-Michaelson, Wesley. *A Worldly Spirituality: The Call to Redeem Life on Earth.* San Francisco: Harper & Row, 1984. (1, 2)

Hart, John. *The Spirit of the Earth.* Ramsey, N.J.: Paulist Press, 1984. (1, 2, 6, 9)

Hunsberger, Gordon. *Land and Development.* Development Monograph Series 10, Akron, Pa.: Mennonite Central Committee, undated. (11)

Jackson, Wes. *New Roots for Agriculture.* San Francisco: Friends of the Earth, 1980; Lincoln: University of Nebraska Press, 1985. (3, 5, 7)

Jackson, Wes, Wendell Berry, and Bruce Colman, eds. *Meeting the Expectations of the Land: Essays in Sustainable Agriculture and Stewardship.* San Francisco: North Point Press, 1984. (3, 4, 6, 8, 9, 11, 13)

Jegen, Mary Evelyn, and Bruno V. Manno, eds. *The Earth Is the Lord's.* Ramsey, N.J.: Paulist Press, 1978. (1, 2, 3, 4, 5, 6, 7, 9, 10, 11)

Jubilee Foundation for Agricultural Research. *Economics and the Family Farm: A Study Guide.* Guelph, Ont.: Christian Farmers Federation of Ontario, revised 1986. (4, 10)

Lerza, Catherine. *Saving the Family Farm.* Women's Division, General Board of Global Ministries, The United Methodist Church, 1980. (3, 4, 9, 10, 11)

Lutz, Charles P. *Farming the Lord's Land: Christian Perspectives on American Agriculture.* Minneapolis: Augsburg, 1980. (3, 5, 6, 7, 9)

MacFadyen, J. Tevere. *Gaining Ground: The Renewal of America's Small Farms.* New York: Ballantine, 1985. (3, 7, 9)

Merrill, Richard, ed. *Radical Agriculture.* New York: Harper & Row, 1976. (3, 5, 9, 11)

Morgan, Dan. *Merchants of Grain.* New York: Viking, 1979; New York: Penguin Books, 1980. (5, 7, 10)

Nelson, Jack A. *Hunger for Justice: The Politics of Food and Faith.* Maryknoll, N.Y.: Orbis Books, 1980. (11)

Paddock, Joe, Nancy Paddock, and Carol Bly. *Soil and Survival: Land Stewardship and the Future of American Agriculture.* San Francisco: Sierra Club, 1986. (1, 2, 3, 6, Epilogue)

Perelman, Michael. *Farming for Profit in a Hungry World.* Montclair, N.J.: Allanheld, Osmun, & Co., 1977. (5, 7, 11)

Strange, Marty, ed. *It's Not All Fresh Air and Sunshine.* Center for Rural Affairs, 1984. (3)

Thompson, Nancy. *Farmers Home Administration Loan Handbook.* Walthill, Neb.: Center for Rural Affairs, 1987. (4, 10, 12)

Vogeler, Ingolf. *The Myth of the Family Farm: Agribusiness Dominance of U.S. Agriculture.* Boulder, Colo.: Westview Press, 1981. (5, 7, 9, 10,)

Wessel, James. *Trading the Future*. San Francisco: Institute for Food and Development Policy, 1983. (5, 10, 11)

Working Group on Farm and Food Policy. *Beyond Crisis: Farm and Food Policy for Tomorrow*. Washington, D.C.: Rural Coalition, 1985. (3, 4, 10)

Magazines and periodicals

Agriculture and Human Values. Quarterly journal from the Humanities and Agriculture office, University of Florida.

Alternative Agriculture News. Monthly newsletter published by the Institute for Alternative Agriculture.

American Farmland. Bi-monthly newsletter of the American Farmland Trust.

Catholic Rural Life. The magazine of the National Catholic Rural Life Conference; published five times yearly.

Earthkeeping. Quarterly magazine on faith and agriculture. Christian Farmers Federations of Alberta and Ontario.

Economic Justice Prepare. Monthly newsletter of current information and ecumenically developed recommendations on economic justice and other federal policy issues of concern to the religious community. Published by IMPACT.

Interfaith Action. Newsletter published ten times a year by Interfaith Action for Economic Justice. Looks at public policy affecting agriculture and other issues of economic justice.

The Land Report. Journal published three times a year by the Land Institute. Reports on research and stewardship issues.

Land Stewardship Letter. Quarterly newsletter of the Land Stewardship Project; brief articles, excerpts of speeches, current updates of concerns in issues of land stewardship and sustainable agriculture.

Small Farm Advocate. Quarterly publication of the Center for Rural Affairs. Articles on current public policy and research issues.

Films and videotapes

[Check your library resource centers for availability before arranging to rent from producers.]

Agriculture's Vanishing Heritage. VHS videotape or slide show. 25 min. Examines causes of the extinction of crop and livestock genetic resources throughout the world, along with some possible solutions. Available on loan from Church World Service, Media Resource Center. (3)

The Amish: A People of Preservation. Highly acclaimed documentary by Burton Buller, John Ruth, and John Hostetler. Available from Buller Films. Rental—16 mm. $60 for 58 min. version and $40 for 28 min. version. (8, 13)

Another Family Farm and *Responding to the Farmer in Crisis*. VHS videotape produced by American Lutheran Church, 1985. 26 min. and 19 min. (on one tape) Available on loan from Church World Service, Media Resource Center. (12)

Blacks in Farming. 30-min. videocassette (3/4" U-matic), presentation by president of the Emergency Land Fund to USDA, Feb. 1984. Available from National Council of Churches Domestic Hunger and Poverty Office. (9)

Down on the Farm. 60-min. NOVA television documentary, 1984. Examines the system of U.S. agriculture that causes farmers, agricultural scientists and policy makers to look at the short term need for profits rather than the long-term needs of the land. Can be borrowed for return postage cost from Center for Rural Affairs. (3, 6, 10)

The Farm Crisis: Its Origins and Implications. 30-min. VHS videotape presentation by Cornelia Flora, Kansas State University. Available on loan free from the Consultation of Cooperating Churches in Kansas. (10, 12)

How Much Land Does a Man Need? 14 min. film produced by Woodland Films, 1978. A Tolstoy short story demonstrating the effects of greed on a person who was promised all the land he could walk around in one day. (Available on loan from Ontario Mennonite Resource Centre.) (6)

The Hutterites: To Care and Not to Care. Award winning documentary by Burton Buller, John Ruth, and John A. Hostetler. Available from Buller Films. Rental—16 mm. $80 for 58 min. version and $55 for 25 min. version. Videotape rental $65 and $50. (8, 13)

Potatoes. 28-min. film. Produced by National Film Board of Canada. Explains the complex economic and social factors that have combined to force farm families off the land in North America. Shows urban/rural interrelationships. Available from Bullfrog Films. Rental $50 plus handling. (5, 7, 9, 10)

Seeds of Tomorrow. A NOVA program that presents varied views about seed patenting and related issues. May be borrowed from Rural Advancement Fund for postage and handling costs. (3)

A Sense of Humus. 28-min. film. Produced by National Film Board of Canada. Looks at alternative methods of farming that preserve topsoil and scarce resources for future generations in ways that make commercial sense. Available from Bullfrog Films. Rental $50 plus handling. (3, 6, Epilogue)

September Wheat. 96 min. film. Explores the technology of the production of wheat from farm to local elevator to the Chicago Board of Trade. Looks at U.S. food aid as it relates to wheat and the world. Relates the story of the biblical Joseph in Egypt to modern North American agriculture. A powerful film. Available from New Time Film. Rental $125 plus handling. (5, 7, 10, 11)

The Uncertain Harvest. A videotape produced by a Salt Lake City public television station. Excellent program that looks at basic assumptions of conventional agriculture and agricultural research and then looks to creative alternatives. Includes interviews with people in the forefront of the movement toward a sustainable future in North America. Available from the Land Institute for cost of postage. (3, 5, 6, Epilogue)

The Water of Life. 50 min. film produced by Mennonite Central Committee Canada as a television special. Directed by Burton Buller. Looks at water projects in international development and at water resource use in North America. Available in both film and videocassette from Mennonite Central Committee offices in Canada and U. S. (3, 11)

Other resources

Agriculture's Vanishing Heritage. 25 min. slide set produced by Rural Advancement Fund. Examines the causes of extinction of crop and livestock genetic resources throughout the world, along with some possible solutions. Available from Rural Advancement Fund or Church World Services, Media Resource Center (Also available on videotape from CWS.) (3, 11)

From This Valley: On Defending the Family Farm. 19 min. filmstrip with audiotape and discussion guide. Produced by Rural Crisis Issues Team of National Council of Churches. Gives a biblical perspective on saving small family farms. Available on loan for handling and postage from Rural Advancement Fund. (3, 6, 12)

The Gift of Land. Five filmstrip set, 15 min. each. A biblical study on the use of land. Especially for people of faith who reverence and cherish the earth. Highly recommended. Free on loan (borrower pays return postage) from Church World Service, Media Resource Center. Also available from Ontario Mennonite Resource Centre. (1, 2, 3, 6, Epilogue)

Land: The Threatened Resource. 13 min. slide set produced by United Church of Canada. The threat to Canadian agricultural land by pressures facing farming communities are explored here. Available from Ontario Mennonite Resource Centre. (3, 7)

Planting in the Dust. Written by Nancy Paddock. A one-woman drama that looks at issues of land stewardship in a historical context. Contact The Land Stewardship Project for information about performances in your area. (3, 5, 6)

Sharing Global Resources: Toward a New Economic Order. 35 min. filmstrip produced by NARMIC, 1977. Jamaica and Chile are examples to show that North Americans are using too much of the world's resources made from raw materials from poorer Third World countries. Available from Ontario Mennonite Resource Centre. (3, 11)

Theology of Land Conferences, 1985 and 1986. Five audio-tapes each year. Contact National Catholic Rural Life Conference for speakers and topics. (1, 2)

Organizations

American Farmland Trust. 1920 N St., NW, Suite 400, Washington, DC 20036. A private nonprofit organization committed to the conservation of agricultural resources through public education, policy development, and land conservancy.

Bread for the World. 802 Rhode Island Ave., NE, Washington DC 20018. A Christian citizens' movement working on food and hunger issues affected by U. S.

public policy. Publishes a monthly newsletter and background papers on current issues. Recently added an agricultural policy analyst to their staff.

Center for Rural Affairs. P.O. Box 405, Walthill, NE 68067. Marty Strange and Don Ralston, co-directors. Focuses research on public policy issues affecting rural people and works to achieve economic justice in agriculture. Their reports encourage people to evaluate trends in agriculture in terms of the beliefs and values that have characterized rural thought. Monthly newsletter. Quarterly paper.

Christian Farmers Federation. Ontario CFFO: 115 Woolwich St., Guelph, ON N1H 3V1; Alberta CFFO: 107666-97 St., Edmonton, AL T5H 2M1. Public policy and education organization of Christian farmers (mostly Canadian). Publishes newsletters, a quarterly magazine *Earthkeeping* and study guides (recently *Economics and the Family Farm*).

Institute for Alternative Agriculture. 9200 Edmonston Road, Suite 117, Greenbelt, MD 20770. Garth Youngberg, director. A nonprofit research and education organization that encourages low-cost, resource-conserving, and environmentally-sound farming methods to promote a sustainable agriculture system. It provides a national information clearinghouse, serves as a voice for sustainable agriculture in Washington, and develops research and educational outreach programs. Monthly newsletter, quarterly journal (*American Journal of Alternative Agriculture*), annual symposium.

Interfaith Action for Economic Justice. 110 Maryland Ave., NE, Washington, DC 20002. An ecumenical agency whose Food and Agricultural Policy Work Group works on public policy issues relating to structure of agriculture, stewardship of resources, and food self-reliance and security.

The Land Institute. 2440 E. Water Well Road, Salina, KS 67401. Wes and Dana Jackson, co-directors. A nonprofit educational/research organization devoted to sustainable agriculture and earth stewardship. Programs include an agricultural intern program in 43-week terms beginning each February, a postdoctoral plant genetic research program to develop perennial polycultures, and an annual two-day Prairie Festival that celebrates community, culture, and the land.

The Land Stewardship Project. 512 West Elm, Stillwater, MN 55082. Ron Kroese, director. A nonprofit education program that works for the development of a sound stewardship ethic toward our nation's farmland and for public policy changes that will lead to the development of a sustainable agricultural system.

Mennonite Central Committee. 134 Plaza Drive, Winnipeg, MB R3T 5K9; and 21 South 12 St., Akron, PA 17501. International relief and development agency working also on food and agricultural issues in North America.

National Catholic Rural Life Conference. 4625 NW Beaver Drive, Des Moines, IA 50310. A helpful resource for people of all faiths. Publishes a bimonthly magazine, sponsors an annual theology of land conference, and provides devotional material for both a spring and a fall period of prayer.

Rodale Research Center. Maxatawny, PA 19538. Richard Harwood, director. Does research in organic agriculture on a 305-acre experiment station. Also associated with the Cornucopia Project (33 East Minor Street, Emmaus, PA 18049) which has conducted studies, state by state, of the U.S. food system, documents where the food system is vulnerable, and suggests how it can be changed to sustain and conserve the nation's resources.

Rural Advancement Fund/National Sharecroppers Fund. 2124 Commonwealth Avenue, Charlotte, NC 28205. Kathryn J. Waller, executive director. For nearly a half century, has carried out projects that address problems of farmers and low-income rural people in the South. Does research, education and consulting work worldwide in the areas of genetic resources and biotechnology effects on family farmers and the environment.

Small Farms Resources Project, Hartington, NE 68739 was initiated by the Center for Rural Affairs to develop a more resourceful agriculture that uses renewable and sustainable practices, creates socially just and equitable policies, and provides economic opportunity for farm families with limited resources. Funds a research internship program and cooperates with twenty-four farm families in on-farm research.

Addresses for resources

Buller Films, Box 651, Henderson, NE 68371.

Bullfrog Films, Oley, PA 19547. Phone: 215-779-8226.

Catholic Bishops Heartland Project, 220 S. Prairie Ave., Sioux Falls, SD 57104

Church World Service, Media Resource Center, 28606 Phillips St., P.O. Box 968, Elkhart, IN 46515.

Consultation of Cooperating Churches in Kansas, 4125 Gage Center Dr., Room 209, Topeka, KS 66604.

Humanities and Agriculture, 243 Arts and Sciences Building, Department of Philosophy, University of Florida, Gainesville, FL 32611.

IMPACT, 110 Maryland Avenue, NE, Washington, D.C. 20002.

National Council of Churches, Domestic Hunger and Poverty Office, 475 Riverside Drive, Room 572, New York, NY 10115.

New Time Film, P.O. Box 502, Village Station, NY 10014. Phone: 212-206-8607.

Ontario Mennonite Resource Centre, 50 Kent Avenue, Kitchener, ON, Canada, N2G 3R1.

Acknowledgments

Many persons have had a part in making this book, and to them I owe a debt of gratitude.

During the year of research and writing *Hope for the Family Farm*, I talked with and received letters from farmers and other people who gave helpful suggestions after reading the book proposal or the outline, provided research materials, responded to my questions in specific areas of concern, and/or reviewed chapters. For that help, I want to acknowledge the following persons: Fred Bentley, Gordon Brockmueller, Burton Buller, Roger Claassen, Arnold Cressman, Gregory Cusack, Kathleen Dougherty, Robert Engbrecht, Charles Epp, Mark Epp, Robert Epp, Walter Epp, Lester Ewy, Winifred Ewy, Sarah Fast, Cornelia Flora, Jan Flora, Elvin D. Frantz, Delton Franz, J. Winfield Fretz, David Gerber, Don Gingerich, Steve Goering, Leon Good, Diana Graber, Jim Graber, Tom Graber, David Habegger, Nancy Halder, Leland Harder, Chuck Hassebrook, Wilmer Heisey, Arlin Hiebner, Margaret Hiebner, Leroy Hofer, Curtis Hoyt, Robert Hull, Gordon Hunsberger, Dana Jackson, Wes Jackson, Neil Janzen, Carol Jenkins, James Juhnke, Maynard Kaufman, S. Roy Kaufman, Bonnie Krehbiel, Dwight Krehbiel, Ron Kroese, Dale Linsenmeyer, Dean Linsenmeyer, Charles P. Lutz, Paul McKay, Art Meyer, Jocele Meyer, Joe Mierau, Bill Minter, Stan Ortman, Marvin Penner, Dwight Platt, Kamala Platt, Richard Platt, Lois Janzen Preheim, Lynn Preheim, John Quiring, Don Reeves, Daryl Regier, Gladys Regier, Raymond Regier, Randall Reichenbach, Ed Roberts, Joe Smucker, Howard Snider, J. Lloyd Spaulding, Fr. John Stitz, Gene Stolzfus, Dwight Stoltzfus, Marty Strange, Larry Thimm, Willard Unruh, Annette Voth, Bill Voth, Keith Waltner, Susan Waltner, Tim Waltner, Ilene Weinbrenner, Trudy Wischemann, Cathy Wismer, Conrad Wetzel, and Robert Yoder.

I appreciate the generous hospitality of Sue and Tim Schrag, Emelia and Robert Epp, and Shirley and Gordon Brockmueller, in whose homes I stayed when I visited Beatrice and Henderson, Nebraska, and Freeman, South Dakota. I also thank them for making arrangements for me to interview others in their communities. I appreciate Margaret Hiebner's contacts on my behalf in the Henderson community and the hospitality of Dean and Bek Linsenmeyer in Lincoln.

I value highly the opportunity I have had to work with each of the writers in this project. I have appreciated their willingness to commit themselves, their writing skills, and their concerns to shape this book. I am also grateful to David Gerber, Chuck Hassebrook, and Tim Waltner who prepared parts of chapters, though their names appear only as footnotes in the text.

To list the names of persons who contributed to the making of this book, as I have done, does not convey the extent to which I am indebted to some for their special guidance and inspiration. As I typed their names, thoughts of the unique ways in which many of these persons have given meaning to this project flooded my mind. Although there is not space to share all these thoughts here, I must give special recognition to a few persons whose voices blend and give balance to this work.

Even when *Hope for the Family Farm* was only the germ of an idea, Robert Hull, Peace and Justice secretary of the General Conference Mennonite Church, kept the concerns of faith and farming issues alive for Mennonites as he sponsored the publication of *From Swords to Plowshares* for several years and then initiated the planning for the 1984 Faith and Farming Conference at the Laurelville Church Center in Pennsylvania. He gave encouragement and assistance to me at all stages of the research, writing, and editing of this manuscript.

I am grateful to Don Reeves whose enthusiasm, growing out of a broad experience in agricultural public policy issues, prompted many ideas that helped give me a sense of direction; to David Gerber, who shared with me materials, ideas, and experiences from his background in agricultural research, international development, and teaching; and to Raymond Regier, whose experiences through many years of farming and working with people within his church denomination, ecumenical organizations, and the cooperative movement, shaped his perspective on issues of rural life.

Many persons' interest in this book reminded me that there are others whose concerns center on the spiritual dimensions of land and people in covenant with the Creator—Gregory Cusack gave particular encouragement to me in this regard.

I appreciate Mark Epp's help. His concern for land stewardship and Jubilee living, his perceptive thinking, and his articulate expression influenced my choice of words and ideas. I am grateful that he took the time and had the interest to assist so generously in this project.

Lastly, I want to thank the members of my family. They gave me continuous support and encouragement. My husband Dwight Platt read and critiqued each chapter at least twice. Our children Kamala and Richard also reviewed the manuscript and made helpful suggestions. When I was trying to meet specific deadlines, my family members took over household responsibilities that are ordinarily mine.

LaVonne Godwin Platt

The Writers

Burton Buller is an award-winning photographer, producer, and writer of more than thirty motion pictures, including several international relief and development films, and documentary films on the Amish and the Hutterites. He is president of Buller Films Inc. and executive director of Daystar Inc. in Henderson, Nebraska.

Roger Claassen was raised on a farm near Whitewater, Kansas. Now a congressional aide in Washington, D.C., from 1983 to 1986 he was a volunteer and then staff associate for food and agriculture policy with Interfaith Action for Economic Justice, a coalition of national Protestant, Catholic, Jewish, and ecumenical agencies.

Mark Epp studied international agriculture and rural development at Cornell University. In his farming, he tries to apply the values he learned at home and from working with struggling peasants in South America (in a Mennonite Central Committee project) and with poor farmers in the South (working with the Rural Advancement Fund).

Robert O. Epp is a member of the national interim steering committee of Clergy and Laity Concerned. He has been chair of the Peace and Social Concerns Committee of the Northern District of the General Conference Mennonite Church. A farmer for most of his life, he has served on the Soil and Water Conservation Board of Supervisors and on an advisory committee to the University of Nebraska Water Resources Research Institute.

Ronald Guengerich grew up on a farm in Iowa, graduated from Eastern Mennonite College and Goshen Biblical Seminary and has done doctoral studies in ancient and biblical Near Eastern studies at the University of Michigan. From 1983 to '86, he taught biblical studies at Hesston College. He is now pastor of the Whitestone Mennonite Church, Hesston, Kansas.

Wilmer Heisey milked cows as a teenager and as a young adult was a Dairy Herd Improvement Association tester. For thirty years he served in mission assignments for the Brethren in Christ. He and his wife, Velma, began Mennonite Central Committee service in the Philippines after World War II. In 1982, he became executive secretary of Mennonite Central Committee-U.S. He leads Mennonite Central Committee's Farm Crisis Task Force.

Margaret Epp Hiebner grew up on a farm in South Dakota and lives with her family in Nebraska, on the farm where her life-partner is employed. As a board member of Nebraskans for Peace, a director of programs in her congregation, and a member of county and areawide agencies on aging, she has been involved in concerns that build community. She is employed with the Retired Senior Volunteer Program in Henderson.

Robert Hull is secretary for peace and justice for the General Conference Mennonite Church and a graduate of Goshen Biblical Seminary. He helped organize faith and farming conferences in Pennsylvania, in central Kansas, and in Ames, Iowa, in 1984 and 1985. Previously he taught environmental ethics and was assistant to the director of the Institute for Man and Environment, State University of New York at Plattsburgh.

Gordon I. Hunsberger farmed in the Waterloo, Ontario, region until 1975. Since then he has been with Mennonite Central Committee in development work in Haiti and in development education in Ontario. Retiring in 1985, he now does volunteer work in the community. For twelve years, he has written a column, "farm filosofy," for a local weekly newspaper.

Kansas Mennonite Farm Crisis Committee was formed in 1985 at the initiation of the Kansas Hunger Concerns Committee of Mennonite Central Committee Central States Region to respond at a local level to the farm crisis. The group has sponsored seminars on stress, bankruptcy, and other topics of concern to rural people. Members have served as mediators between bankers and farmers.

Maynard Kaufman, raised in the Freeman, South Dakota, community, recently retired from Western Michigan University where he taught courses in religion as well as environmental studies and appropriate technology. He and his wife operate a dairy farm where they also teach homesteading skills. His many publications include articles on homesteading and sustainable agriculture and a forthcoming book, *Visions of a New Earth: Apocalypse and the Transformation of Utopia*.

S. Roy Kaufman is a native of Freeman, South Dakota. A graduate of Goshen College and Mennonite Biblical Seminary, he has served with Mennonite Central Committee in Greece. For fourteen years, he was pastor of a rural General Conference Mennonite Church in Pulaski, Iowa. He is now pastor of the Science Ridge Mennonite Church, Sterling, Illinois. He is a popular speaker and writer on faith and farming issues.

Art Meyer was born and raised on an Ohio dairy farm. For thirty years, he taught science in Ohio public schools and colleges. He also taught in Grenada under appointment with Mennonite Central Committee. Since 1982, he and his wife Jocele have worked with MCC as development-educators, writers, speakers, and resource leaders in workshops on food issues. The Meyers live on a small farm where they are reclaiming land that had been strip-mined.

Jocele Thut Meyer grew up on an Ohio farm and lived in both rural and urban areas of Ohio during most of her life. She has taught home economics and English and for five years was a 4H leader. She worked with Mennonite Central Committee in Grenada and in Akron, Pennsylvania. The Meyers grow much of their own food, heat with wood from their woodlot, and live in a self-designed energy efficient house.

Bill Minter graduated from Colorado State University with a degree in professional forestry. He works with Michigan State University's Cooperative Extension Service as a regional forest resource extension specialist in southwestern Michigan. He is a natural resources management consultant to several Mennonite agency-owned properties and has been active in agriculture and resource-related issues through Mennonite Central Committee Great Lakes Region.

Leon C. Neher of Quinter, Kansas, is a farmer and Church of the Brethren minister. He has taught sociology and anthropology at Manchester College in Indiana and Colby Community College in Kansas. He has been a pastor to churches in Kansas, Montana, Ohio, and Indiana. He is in demand as a speaker on agriculture and farm-related issues, as well as church-related activities.

LaVonne Godwin Platt became interested in working on farm issues as an outgrowth of her work in seminars and workshops on world hunger concerns. She was volunteer editor of an inter-Mennonite newsletter, *From Swords to Plowshares*, from 1979 to 1982. She has written several articles on farm issues for Mennonite publications.

Lois Janzen Preheim now lives on a farm near Freeman, South Dakota, but most of her life she has lived in urban areas. She is a graduate of Goshen Biblical Seminary and was pastor of a church in San Francisco for four years. She has been a teacher in Arizona, Virginia, California, and Paraguay, and most recently taught English at the Freeman Academy.

Don Reeves and his wife Barbara are partners with another couple in a grain and livestock farm near Central City, Nebraska. They are members of the Religious Society of Friends. Don has served on the staff of Friends Committee on National Legislation, has been family farm consultant for Interfaith Action for Economic Justice, and is now on the boards of Bread for the World and the American Friends Service Committee.

Conrad Wetzel grew up milking cows and baling hay on a Tennessee, Illinois, farm. Raised in the Church of the Brethren, he joined Reba Place Fellowship and later helped establish Plow Creek Fellowship, where he is a pastoring elder. A doctor of clinical psychology, he has worked in several mental health positions. He is a conference minister for the Mennonite Church and Central District of the General Conference Mennonite Church.

Index